The Good Old Cause

The Good Old Cause

British Communism 1920–1991

Willie Thompson

 Pluto Press

First published 1992 by Pluto Press
345 Archway Road, London N6 5AA

Copyright © Willie Thompson 1992

The right of Willie Thompson to be
identified as author of this work has been
asserted by him in accordance with the
Copyright, Designs and Patents Act 1988

British Library Cataloguing in Publication Data
A catalogue record for this book is available
from the British Library

ISBN 0 7453 0578 4 hb
ISBN 0 7453 0579 2 pb

Library of Congress Cataloging in Publication Data
Thompson, Willie, 1939–
    The good old cause : British communism, 1920–1991 / Willie
Thompson
    266pp. 22cm
    Includes bibliographical references and index.
    ISBN 0-7453-0578-4 (hb). – ISBN 0-7453-0579-2 (pbk.)
    1. Communism–Great Britain–History. 2. Communist Party of Great
Britain–History. I. Title.
HX243.T58 1992
324.241'075'09–dc20   92-5360
                                                                  CIP

Typeset by Stanford Desktop Publishing Services, Milton Keynes
Printed in Finland by WSOY

Contents

Acknowledgements

My principal debt is to members and former members of the Communist Party who in informal discussions, taped interviews and by allowing access to written materials not only added greatly to my knowledge of the party but also gave me an understanding of its culture and atmosphere during periods outside my own experience. Except in instances where interviews were given with publication specifically in mind, I have not quoted directly from them or identified particular individuals.

The Communist Party archives in London are open to researchers. I have, however, quite deliberately not used this resource. The reason for this self-denying limitation is that the official multi-volume history of the party remains an ongoing project, and I therefore wished to avoid creating any difficulty or embarrassment for the party librarians. I have, however, made use of the Marx Memorial Library, London, and the Gallacher Library in Scotland and record my thanks to the staff of both, especially for the incomparable helpfulness of Audrey Canning, librarian at the Gallacher Library.

I also owe a particular debt to the historians who have already pioneered the study of the CP's origins and first twenty years, whose detailed examinations have made the writing of this volume a much lighter task than it would otherwise have been. I am grateful to Glasgow Polytechnic for according me the study leave which enabled this project to be undertaken, and especially to Anne Beech, Editorial Director of Pluto Press, without whose interest and encouragement it would not have seen the light.

Abbreviations

AEU	Amalgamated Engineering Union
BRS	*The British Road to Socialism*
BSP	British Socialist Party
CC	Central Committee
CND	Campaign for Nuclear Disarmament
CP	Communist Party
CPB	Communist Party of Britain
CPC	Communist Party of China
CPGB	Communist Party of Great Britain
CPSU	Communist Party of the Soviet Union
CPUSA	Communist Party of the USA
EC	Executive Committee
ECCI	Executive Committee of the Communist International
ETU	Electrical Trades Union
FSL	Fife Socialist League
ILP	Independent Labour Party
IS	International Socialism
IWW	Industrial Workers of the World
KPD	Communist Party of Germany
LCDTU	Liaison Committee for the Defence of Trade Unions
MFGB	Miners' Federation of Great Britain
NCP	New Communist Party
NEP	New Economic Policy
NUM	National Union of Mineworkers
NUS	National Union of Students
NUWM	National Unemployed Workers' Movement
PC	Political Committee
PCE	Communist Party of Spain
PCF	French Communist Party
PCI	Communist Party of Italy
PCP	Portugese Communist Party
PPPS	People's Press Printing Society
SDF	Social Democratic Federation

SLP	Socialist Labour Party – UK/Socialist Labor Party – USA
SPD	Social Democratic Party of Germany
STUC	Scottish Trades Union Congress
SWMF	South Wales Miners' Federation
SWP	Socialist Workers' Party
TASS	Technical, Administration and Supervisory Section (of the Amalgamated Union of Engineering Workers)
TGWU	Transport and General Workers' Union
TUC	Trades Union Congress
UCS	Upper Clyde Shipbuilders
UMS	United Mineworkers of Scotland
WRP	Workers' Revolutionary Party
WSF	Workers' Socialist Federation
YCL	Young Communist League

Introduction

The Communist Party of Great Britain (CPGB) throughout the seven decades of its effective existence was never of more than marginal significance in British political life. Restricting comparisons only to Western Europe and leaving out of account the mass CPs of Italy, France and the Iberian states, as well as the special case of Germany, it always remained of less account in numbers or influence than its counterparts in even Scandinavia or the Low Countries. Yet for a minor party its longevity was astonishing, far exceeding that of any comparable political organisation,[1] and the tenacity of its hold upon the particular niche it chose to occupy continued up to the years of its terminal decline. It never failed to generate controversy and to provide headlines and the subject of analysis for serious commentators. Even at the end it remained newsworthy enough for its imminent demise to occupy many column inches in the press[2] and for its Secretary to receive constant invitations to broadcast. Marginal it may have been but it was never negligible.

However, the organisation whose delegates in December 1990 resolved on a last quixotic bid for survival by turning it into something else had virtually nothing in common with the one which was established in August 1920 except the name. Political philosophy, objectives, strategy and style as they had developed over seventy years would all have been unrecognisable – where not abhorrent – to the founders and their immediate successors. The retention of the name during the intervening decades[3] did in this case represent a continuity of sorts: the survival, through innumerable vicissitudes and traumatic modifications, of a particular universalist tradition of politics – but one which had in the course of that period been remodelled and reformulated time and again until scarcely a single element of principle or practice retained its original form or meaning. The party's adaptability, pragmatism and capacity for reversing hitherto entrenched attitudes were unquestionably the key to its survival as a living organism rather than a political fossil, but were insufficient to counterbalance the heavy disadvantages under which it laboured or to save it, until too late, from political and organisational sclerosis.

1

Paradoxically, although the CPGB moved so far away from its beginnings, it remained more closely and necessarily bound to them than would have been the case for any political organisation outside of the communist tradition. In however distorted a form, these beginnings never ceased to be rehearsed within the party's internal discourse and they formed the starting point of the tradition with which all its activists were inculcated. The tension between the perceived image of these origins and the realities of what the party was doing at any particular moment generated recurrent strains and at times explosive breaks within its membership. The evolution of the Communist Party cannot in fact be understood except in terms of its origins – though evidently not of these alone: what is relevant here is the interplay between its initial purposes and the actuality of the conditions to which it was forced to respond in trying to attain them.

The nature of the party's formation, therefore, is the first clue to its subsequent career. Its foundation in 1920 was not only the culmination of developments occurring in Britain over more than a decade, but also an episode in an international process which had been in train years before the Bolshevik Revolution of 1917. Deepening inter-state tensions throughout the first decade of the twentieth century, issuing in the outbreak of general European war in 1914, are best viewed as one aspect of a general crisis of the late nineteenth-century global order dominated economically, politically and culturally by the industrial states of Europe and the USA. Within these states and in the nations subject to their hegemony the internal governing structures were shaken and threatened. Industrial militancy and class confrontation exploded throughout the developed economies. In France governments assumed exceptional powers to break transport strikes. In Germany the ostensibly revolutionary Social Democrats became the largest party in the Reichstag. In the USA the American Socialist Party achieved the pinnacle of its influence and vote. Russia in 1905, China in 1911, Mexico from 1911, to name only the most significant, were swept by revolution. In 1908 and again in 1912 the Socialist International threatened the ruling classes of Europe with dire consequences should they dare to plunge the nations into mutual slaughter. The war itself, far from abrogating these conflicts, deepened and redefined them; at its conclusion there resumed yet another phase of escalating social conflict or full-scale revolutionary outbreaks around the world. The Bolshevik Revolution was no isolated event, contingent upon the peculiar circumstances of an economically retarded and militarily defeated Russian empire, but the watershed of a protracted international revolutionary upheaval which spanned the years preceding and following the war.

Nor were the Bolsheviks by any means the only socio-political oppositionists before 1917 of an intransigent and unrelenting revolutionary temper: the circumstances propagated such people on a much wider canvas than that of the esoteric theoretical quarrels and mutual excommunications of the Russian socialists. Setting aside the still flourishing anarchist culture of Mediterranean Europe and dissatisfied left-wing tendencies inside the formally or actually[4] constitutionalist socialist parties, the most widespread and formidable revolutionary tendency in the early years of the century was undoubtedly that of syndicalism. Syndicalism derived its name from the organisations of French industrial workers, but was most widely established in the Anglo-Saxon world. Repudiating the existing structures and leadership of trade unionism no less than all forms of currently understood politics, both being viewed as corrupting and fatal to class consciousness, this current of revolutionary industrial unionism envisaged, through the weapon of the general strike, the overthrow of the bourgeoisie and the supersession of capitalist society in favour of a stateless polity administered by workers' councils.[5] Moreover, in the US-based Industrial Workers of the World (IWW) syndicalism possessed an international framework, although the IWW did not embrace all syndicalists.

Close to syndicalism in basic attitude, although diverging from it on questions of the need for – revolutionary – political as well as industrial organisation, the Socialist Labor Party (SLP), created by Daniel De Leon in the United States foreshadowed, in several respects, the approaches and practices later to be regarded as characteristic of Bolshevism, such as obsessive fixation with the details of Marxist theory, rigorous discipline and intense commitment of time and energy from its militants.

Such global movements embraced the British Isles as well and between 1909 and 1914 the stability of the British state trembled as seldom before or since. Mass strike action of unprecedented ferocity erupted throughout the labour force both on the mainland and in Ireland. The Triple Alliance of miners, railwaymen and transport workers openly adopted the name of the enemy European military coalition. The suffragette movement challenged, by civil disobedience and destruction of property, the legitimacy of the electoral system. Constitutional crisis divided even the ruling elites. Armed paramilitary formations of the right and the left, one of them explicitly a working-class force, recruited openly in Ireland and prepared to contest the issue of Home Rule by means of civil war. Senior Conservative politicians conspired with Irish-based senior officers to incite mutiny against the legal government.

The British Labour Party of the time was unique among European labour movements in its frank disavowal of revolutionary or socialist purpose (which is perhaps only to say that it was more honest than most) and in strict and uncompromising attachment to constitutionalism and legality. As class and political tensions heightened so did the suspicion with which this party was held, along with the parliamentary system to which it adhered, among the minority of labour or suffragette militants with a vision of total social reconstruction beyond the immediate conflicts or objectives of the day.

Syndicalism established a presence in Britain, especially among the miners of South Wales. A British version of the SLP came into being, and in the person of James Connolly effected a link with the industrial and national struggles in Ireland. Numerically it was very weak, counting no more than a few hundred members at the outside, but it was not without influence among certain industrial communities in the Clyde valley. For the radical left the principal source of political attraction remained the British Socialist Party (BSP), successor to the Social Democratic Federation (SDF) of the 1880s and explicitly Marxist in its orientation, but not strongly connected to an industrial base and mainly geared to propagandist activities. Even so, it numbered no more than a few thousand members. For the masses engaged in the battles of those years, whether industrial, feminist or national, the impact of explicitly socialist, let alone Marxist, ideology was very limited.

The outbreak of war destroyed international socialism as it had existed up to that point. The consequent disarray, in which the leading contingents of the former International assisted their particular governments in prosecuting the carnage, provided the opportunity for Bolshevism to transcend its role as a localised Russian phenomenon and step on to the centre of the world stage.

For revolutionaries Lenin succeeded in defining the meaning of the war. The interpretation which he advanced at the Zimmerwald anti-war conference of 1915, and which became thereafter the canonical version, had two fateful aspects. In the first place, it publicised the total bankruptcy and class treason of official socialism, which had become integrated into the bourgeois apparatus of rule. Everything of which the syndicalists and the SLP had accused the trade union and political leaders – 'labour lieutenants of capital', 'professional misleaders of the working class', 'the agents of capital in the workers' movement' – was amply and completely confirmed.[6] Socialist leaders unwilling to follow

Lenin in the conclusion he drew from his analysis, even if they were none the less unenthusiastic about the war and favoured peace, were assailed with no less ferocity than the unashamed chauvinists, indeed with still greater vituperation, since the degree of credit they might win from their dissent made them all the more dangerous. Lenin's conclusion, the second key element of his standpoint, was that the war, a catastrophic conflict of rival imperialisms, signalled the final débâcle of world capitalism and that international socialist revolution was on the immediate agenda. The priority had become to 'turn the imperialist war into civil war', and to accelerate the process by working for the military defeat of the revolutionaries' own state.

As an anti-war European socialist network based in the neutral countries began to assemble from 1915 onwards, Lenin, by a combination of revolutionary persuasion, force of personality and unscrupulous manoeuvre, made his standpoint prevail within it. It was then a portentous coincidence that military collapse occurred first in the country to which Lenin himself belonged; his perspectives were international, not Russian.[7] He was delighted when in March 1917 mass insurrection brought down the imperial regime in Russia and began the revolution; he would have been even more delighted if it had taken place in Germany, France or Britain. Lenin's accomplishment during the eight months that followed in leading his party to revolutionary power on the same explicit basis as he had previously sketched, and then maintaining it against the odds, looked like the most perfect combination of revolutionary theory and practice in history and ensured that the Bolshevik prescriptions would become effectively unquestionable among those who sought to imitate their politics.

The seizure of power in November 1917 was premised not only upon Lenin and Trotsky's assessment of conditions in Russia but also on the expectation of similar outcomes throughout Europe in the very near future. 'The ripening and inevitability of the world socialist revolution can be under no doubt.' 'We stand on the threshold of the world proletarian revolution.' In the Bolshevik perception, they were doing much more than taking control of the Russian government; they were doing nothing less than giving the signal to ignite capitalism's funeral pyre.[8] The failure of the German soviets at the end of 1918 was not expected to be permanent, but it was (mistakenly) thought to have been due to the absence in Germany of a party formed on the Bolshevik model. Even as early as 1914 Lenin had been demanding the recreation of an authentically revolutionary International, and with the anticipated collapse of the bourgeois order as the Central European empires dissolved and the victorious Western states were gripped by social crisis, that intention was identified as an urgent priority. Consequently, in March 1919 the Third International, or Comintern, was hurried into existence at a not very representative congress in Moscow,[9] with the object of acting as 'the general staff of the world revolution' and of forming, as its subordinate national sections, reliably communist parties in all possible countries and especially the politically more important ones – of which Britain, as a major centre of world imperialism and dedicated enemy of the existing Soviet republic, was unquestionably in the top league.

At the time Britain itself was in turmoil. The experiences of the war and the industrial relations which accompanied it had radicalised further segments of the workforce, particularly the engineers and shipbuilders on Clydeside, and generated at times an implicitly revolutionary temper in their local communities as questions of rents, poor relief and dissatisfaction with government repression and the continuing war were linked to industrial issues. The prewar conflicts were revived with fiercer intensity. In 1919 the political atmosphere was pervaded with strike action and threatened action, which reached far enough to involve even the police force. British soldiers in France mutinied in protest at the slowness of their rate of discharge. Guerrilla warfare raged in Ireland. British communism, however, did not succeed in recruiting mass support on the basis of these developments. To some extent it emerged out of them, but was unable to produce the prescribed break in mass consciousness that would have brought tens of thousands under its leadership. The traditional political mechanisms successfully absorbed the crises and the discontent.

The fact that the formation of the British party was sponsored and directed by the International is almost certainly irrelevant in this context; had its origins been wholly native there is no reason to believe that it would have accomplished a great deal more than it did. On the other hand it is almost certain that without the constant pressure exercised by the Comintern with the full weight of the Russian Revolution's prestige behind it the CPGB would never have been formed. Fascination with the achievement of workers' power in Russia and conviction that it was the pointer for the future motivated the founders of the party above all other considerations. It is easy to mistake the part played by the International and Moscow for manipulative action which blighted a potentially healthy alternative course of development. This is what is suggested in Walter Kendall's valuable *The Revolutionary Movement in Britain 1900–1921*, but as Eric Hobsbawm has noted, 'If anything is clear about the period 1917–21 it is (a) that the ultra-left passionately identified itself with the bolsheviks, (b) that it consisted of squabbling small groups, (c) that most of them wanted nothing more than to become the Communist Party.'[10] The hopes aroused among the revolutionaries were truly messianic: 'It was the first proletarian revolution... It was the beginning of world revolution. It was the beginning of the new world.... Social democracy and anarcho-syndicalism had failed, while Lenin had succeeded. It seemed sensible to follow the recipe of success.'[11]

In the long term it was the second of Hobsbawm's points above which proved to be of real historical significance. For all of the mass turbulence of the prewar, wartime and postwar years only a minute segment of the British working class, namely that organised in the far left parties and groups, had been sufficiently affected by these experiences to reject the British social and constitutional structure root and branch and to think in terms of an alternative soviet democracy. Large segments of the masses still adhered in any case to the Conservative Party. For those who did not the existing constitutional framework still appeared to provide ample scope for basic reforms; the more so with the Labour Party's adoption in 1918 of a more explicitly interventionist posture. The syndicalist workers and the SLP had adhered to an anti-parliamentary outlook even before 1914 and for them 1917 did not so much seize them with a new vision as confirm for them that their existing one was realisable in practice. Even so, those bodies and persons in Britain aspiring to become the Communist Party found it exceptionally difficult to do so, for no matter how much they shared a common notion of the world transformed, their disagreements over the manner of reaching that destination were bitter and profound. Without the Russians' intervention these disputes could not have been resolved. Once they had been, and the new party was in existence, the unified organisation had no greater success than its individual predecessors had done in dissolving the rigidities of the British political culture to its own advantage.

For the remainder of its history the CPGB has had its course determined by the triple interlocking heritage of its small size, its national context and its international sources of origin. The third of these was enormously amplified in influence by the first (although among CPs size has been no guarantee of autonomy). Marginalisation was further emphasised by the *manner* of the party's birth. It began as a coalescence of already minuscule groups which then failed to grow rapidly. The preferred Comintern method was to encourage a split between revolutionaries and reformists of the dominant socialist party in each country.

In these cases the status of the communists as a fraction of the labour mainstream, even when in the minority, gave them a leverage in the labour movements and institutions of their countries which proved inaccessible to the British communists. The reasons why it proved impossible to effect this in Britain must be attributed to the long-term marginality of the revolutionary left in the country's political culture, exceptional by European standards, and, in the immediate term, to the apparent success of the constitutional left within the Labour Party.

Having failed to attain the revolutionary breakthrough which looked possible or even likely at the moment of its formation, the Communist Party devoted itself to engagement in the social and industrial struggle, to the defence, according to its capacity, of the Soviet state and to reviewing its own internal structure and functioning. Effectively, if unadmittedly, it had settled down for the long haul and began to develop an internal culture which centred upon the party itself – partaking of the sacramental character of the international revolution – as an object of veneration: and here there is a sharp divergence from the outlook of the pre-1920 groupings, which were viewed by their members in a very different light. For the predecessors, 'The role of the party in this process was necessarily limited and essentially propagandist.'[12] In this change of attitude, too, the lead given by the Comintern was paramount.

Thus the essential character that the CP, regardless of changes in policy, purposes, strategies or social composition, was to maintain ever afterwards was set by the early 1920s. It did succeed in establishing itself as a permanent part of the British labour movement and wider political reality, but never as more than a marginal fragment. In doing so it represented until the Second World War an outlook and perspective denied elswhere in British political society even on the visible left, namely a rejection in principle of constitutionalism and the form of state which prevailed in Britain. It embodied that hostility in the title of its 1935 programme, *For Soviet Britain*. When combined with the prestige of its international connection that stance was to give it for many years a virtual monopoly of revolutionary aspiration among the British left. Within these limits the party's internal regime provided a further asset, for it schooled its activists diligently in both political analysis and practical organisational and agitational skills. They were therefore able to become very effective practitioners, influential far beyond their numbers, in trade union and political struggles, whether on the shop-floor, pursuing Comintern objectives in the British colonies or engaged in anti-fascist activity during the 1930s.

During most of its lifetime, while the CPGB's marginality was a fact, it could never be assumed to be an unalterable destiny, and until its final days the party was never resigned to it. It assumed in the first years of its existence that it would soon be leading millions, and even when that expectation was disappointed a permanent possibility remained that the correct form of engagement with history could turn it into a central force in British politics. As late as the 1960s growth to the status of a mass party was its publicly announced priority, indeed its principal one. From the mid-1920s to the late 1970s a series of strategies was adopted in the endeavour to escape from the political ghetto into which it was locked. Most of these were devised with the intention of adapting the party's aims and practice more closely and effectively to the realities of British class stratifications, political structures, labour organisations and lobbying networks. If they all failed it was not for want of effort, persistence or determination.

It is impossible to judge with any precision to what degree this failure was dependent upon the fact that the CP embodied a form of domestic politics intrinsically alien to the British political culture and to what extent it resulted from the party's Soviet connection, for both aspects were undoubtedly substantial. What can be asserted with confidence, however, is that the Soviet link constituted the primary factor in the CPGB's line of development even after it had ceased to commit itself automatically to every posture and action of the Soviet regime. Being unable to escape from its past – and being unable for that matter to come to terms with anything but an edited and sanitised version of it – it could not overcome the perception among the public at large that its primary function was to act as an agent of the Soviet government. In its internal evolution, too, it was faced with the fact that the tradition of loyalty to their image of workers' states was the bedrock of political conviction for most of its members and thus its scope for development was severely conditioned by this circumstance.

In long-term perspective it can be recognised that the dominant theme in the internal history of the CPGB has been that of slow but inexorable assimilation to the norms of the accepted British political tradition and that the successive strategies into which its politics were shaped drew it implacably in that direction. During its first eight years it pursued, with greater or lesser success, a strategy of insertion into the activity and institutions of the mass labour movement, both official and unofficial. This was in conformity with the tactic of the 'united front' promoted at that point by the Comintern as the appropriate measure for a period during which world capitalism had succeeded in stabilising itself and revolutionary breakthrough was off the immediate agenda. Simultaneously the CP was moulded through various political and organisational modifications into a wholly loyal and docile instrument under Comintern direction. As such it entered in 1928–9 the first of its notorious swerves against the grain of British labour tradition by repudiating any common action with all political forces outside its own ranks and declaring itself and the organisations under its control to be the sole genuine representatives of the country's working class.

The 'class against class' phase of total and bitter isolation was modified following Hitler's accession, being finally buried and the instinct towards unity allowed to reassert itself from 1935 when the last Congress of the International proclaimed the People's Front of all democratic forces against fascism. There followed the party's most successful and creative decade, in combating fascism both at home and abroad and culminating in the summit of the party's popular credibility in 1945 – interrupted only by the violent lurch of opposition to the war, again on Soviet instructions, between October 1939 and June 1941; an episode temporarily forgiven but not forgotten.

Despite the official semi-persecution of the CP during the Cold War era, the broad trend of drawing closer to the accepted definition of politics continued to prevail. In adopting as its new programme in 1951 *The British Road to Socialism* (*BRS*), the party implicitly (though not explicitly of course) repudiated the revolutionary basis on which it had come into existence, namely soviet power in opposition to parliamentarianism. Under the new programme parliamentary representation was made central to its political strategy, ironically just after it had lost its two parliamentary representatives. The Soviet leadership endorsed the new departure and had played a substantial part in initiating it. With Stalin's death and the liquidation of the Cominform[13] any remnants of direct Soviet supervision of the CPGB's affairs came to an end. None the less, emotional attachment to the Soviet regime was sufficient in 1956 and 1957 to ensure that all the manifest gains to be had from dissociating the party from the Soviet invasion of Hungary in November 1956 were spurned in favour of complete identification and at the cost of the most damaging upheaval the organisation had experienced up to that point.

These events, however, combined with Khrushchev's denunciation of Stalin's methods of government, proved to be a watershed. The CP seldom afterwards gave unqualified approval to blatantly offensive Soviet actions.[14] Stage by stage it moved further away from the Soviet orbit though it never entirely left it and the tensions remained. Likewise, though it still retained a considerable industrial base, its independent strength in the trade unions weakened and in the 1960s and 1970s growing emphasis was placed upon the construction of a 'broad left' (the term itself dates from the late 1960s, but the conception was elaborated much earlier), both industrial and political, to which the party expected to contribute a major input but in which it disclaimed any exclusive leading role. Successive editions of the *BRS* increasingly recognised existing British state forms as an acceptable framework for socialist advance and discussed how they might be utilised rather than destroyed.

The logic of this evolution towards a strategic concept of alliances between subordinated elements of society in which the party would act as a facilitator rather than a dominant force was strengthened by the increasing attention accorded to the writings of Antonio Gramsci, translations of which began to be published during these years. It was reinforced during the 1970s when the CP embraced social issues such as feminism, sexuality and British minority nationalism which lay outside traditional left-wing concerns, seeking dialogue and sometimes co-operation with the organisations established to promote them. These departures gave the party localised successes but none of them was capable of stemming a constant process of numerical decline, an ageing membership profile and a steady further erosion of an already threadbare organisational fabric. From the mid-1960s there appeared on the party's left the unprecedented spectacle of groups effectively presenting themselves as competitors for its revolutionary credentials, while the political and organisational successes of the Labour Party left in the late 1970s and early 1980s owed little to the CP and certainly brought it no recognition from its putative allies and produced no communist gains of any consequence.

From the early 1980s the disruptive tensions and pressures arising from the crushing defeats inflicted upon the British labour movement, the party's lack of growth and its decaying internationalist tradition were exacerbated by the contrast of advance in one area alone – the commercial and media success of the CP journal, *Marxism Today*, an achievement which was based upon explicit repudiation of most of the party's most sacred traditions. The resulting tensions tore the organisation apart and by the end of the decade had reduced it to a pale shadow of the position which it had occupied even in the early 1960s, let alone in still happier times. To this the collapse of communist hopes (as distinct from the overthrow of neo-Stalinism) in Eastern Europe at the end of 1989 and the USSR in 1991 was received only as the culminating blow.

Gramsci once remarked that the histories of parties are the histories of classes and certainly this proposition has some bearing on the CPGB, regardless of the fact that the party has never even remotely mirrored the prevailing attitudes and perceptions of the British working class. None the less, beside the fact that its members have always been over-whelmingly drawn from that stratum of society, and its leaders pre-dominantly so, its fortunes have in a very rough fashion shadowed those of the industrial workforce, relatively flourishing when it was politically and culturally strong, declining when it was on the defensive or suffering defeat. It was born at a point of unusual militancy and combativeness and expired at the end of a decade during which the forces of organised labour had been routed as never since the 1840s. No less than the major British parties or its more successful counterparts abroad, the CP's course has been determined by its relationship to the classes and fractions of classes forming the social structure of the country in which it acted.

The CPGB's career has been voluminously documented, not least by virtue of the fact that for a body of its size it has a publishing output greater – probably absolutely and certainly relatively – than any other political organisation in the country. Journals, pamphlets and books have spilled from its presses ever since its foundation. A selective bibliography compiled by Alan S. Mackenzie in 1982, incorporating only texts mainly or substantially about the party and ignoring those published by it on any other matter, included 466 items occupying sixteen double-column closely printed pages.[15] Yet serious analytic studies of any length have been few and, with one exception, confined to its first twenty years.

Only twice in the past have attempts been made to produce a one volume history of the party covering its full career up to the time of their writing. The first of these was in 1937, by one of the founding leaders, Tom Bell, still a party member, but it was stigmatised as heterodox and quickly withdrawn from circulation, probably because, at a time when the party was trying to attract the widest possible sympathy, Bell had been unduly forthcoming about the sectarian attitudes of its early days.[16] A study of a very different sort appeared in 1958 by Henry Pelling, entitled *The British Communist Party: A Historical Profile*, which concluded with the party's 25th Congress of 1957 (a subsequent edition, published in 1975, summarised developments up to the early 1970s, pp. xi–xiii). Although not altogether without merit, the text is vitiated by the fact that its purpose is denunciation rather than understanding and by the author's inability, not to say unwillingness, to grasp the motivations which induced British communists to act as they did. Up to the present these remain the only examples of their kind and Pelling's the only one easily available to the general public, though, even so, out of print. In the mid-1960s the CP began to produce its own multi-volume history, of which three instalments have appeared so far, covering the years to 1941. The initial two volumes, by James Klugmann, are very informative in certain respects, especially about what the rank-and-file were doing, but badly flawed by the fact that all the difficult questions, above all the CP's relations with the Comintern, are avoided by simply ignoring them.[17] The third volume, by Noreen Branson, is an altogether more honest and revealing account but still shows the marks of an official institutional history in that the basic validity of the party's intentions are assumed rather than argued – though its shortcomings are readily acknowledged.

Since the 1960s, also, a number of high-calibre academic studies have appeared dealing with the background to the CPGB's foundation and the early years of its existence. The first was L.J. Macfarlane's *The British Communist Party: Its Origins and Development until 1929* (1966), followed by Walter Kendall's *The Revolutionary Movement in Britain 1900–1921* (1969) and Ray Challinor's *The Origins of British Bolshevism* (1977). Particular aspects have been explored in Stuart Macintyre's *Little Moscows* (1980) and *A Proletarian Science* (1980), James Hinton's *The First Shop Stewards' Movement* (1973) and in Roderick Martin's *Communism and the British Trade Unions 1924–1933* (1969). Thanks to these texts it is now possible to gain a tolerably accurate appreciation of the party's formation, situation and purposes in its early years. I have shamelessly used their data, with the utmost gratitude for their achievement in this field of knowledge even where I differ most profoundly from their conclusions: the interpretations in this volume and their shortcomings are of course my own responsibility. More recently the examination has begun to be extended into the 1930s, with *Against Fascism and War: Ruptures and Continuities in British Communist Politics 1935–1941* by Kevin Morgan (1989) and two volumes relating to the reversal of line in 1939 on the question of the war, *1939: The Communist Party and the War* (1984), edited by John Attfield and Stephen Williams, and *About Turn* (1990), the verbatim record of the crucial Central Committee meeting, edited by Francis King and George Matthews, the last two being produced at the party's own initiative.

Perhaps it suggests a commonly held perception of the CP's waning importance that there is no book-length historical account of the party or any aspect of its activity for the years since 1957, nearly half the period of its existence, although there is a balanced and informative chapter in John Callaghan's *The Far Left in British Politics* (1987). Kenneth Newton's

The Sociology of British Communism appeared in 1969, and though containing much interesting detail is in sum rather banal and disappointing, the author giving an impression of surprise at discovering that the communists he encountered were nearly all serious, hardworking and morally upright citizens instead of the monsters of legend. Articles in academic historical journals are also sparse and those which exist tend likewise to concentrate upon the pre-1957 era.[18] A number of autobiographies (and occasional biographies) of varying quality are extant of party leaders or publicly prominent members, as are polemical exposés, whether by academics or repentant ex-members.[19] Once again the emphasis leans heavily towards the 1920–57 period.

As will be apparent from the foregoing comments, this analysis of the CPGB's historical project is neither apologetic nor denunciatory, nor is it neutral in its approach. My endeavour has been to understand and evaluate, in the light of both circumstances as they appeared to the actors and of historical hindsight, the significance of the Communist Party in British political, social and cultural life. It has also been, so far as humanly possible, to empathise, though from a critical perspective, with the sentiments and aspirations of the people who constituted it – leaders and grass roots, orthodox and dissenters – in the different stages of its development. To assist readers in evaluating my analysis, therefore, I feel it is appropriate to indicate what my own political conceptions are and the background against which I have approached this examination. I joined the Communist Party in the early 1960s, knowing virtually nothing of its past other than occasional anecdotes – although I had just taken a degree in history – because it seemed to me at the time the only consistently revolutionary force in British society. Additionally, the world movement of which it was part appeared, on the demonstration of Soviet space technology and Khrushchev's report to the CPSU 22nd Congress, to be materially outstripping a brutal and imperialist Western Alliance and probably before long would be doing so morally and culturally as well. I had also been highly impressed by the communists with whom I had come into contact through Labour Party and CND organisations – although as my understanding of the world communist movement had been formed largely by the writings of Isaac Deutscher and the early New Left, I was not unaware of its often deplorable and dishonest career.

I have remained a member since that time, involved to a greater or lesser extent in the party's organisation and functioning, and if it is clear that it has now reached the end of the line I do not view the prospect with any delight. While deploring with horror the fact that its members in the past gave their consciences into the keeping of a bloodsoaked tyranny, I am able to appreciate the motivations which caused them to do so. So far as the world process of which they were a part was concerned, in historical perspective it is hard to avoid the verdict that the presumptions and expectations upon which the Bolshevik Revolution was set in motion were so fundamentally misjudged that the débâcle of the end seventy-odd years later was implicit in the beginning and that contingencies like Stalin or the unremitting hostility of the American colossus, though important, were secondary considerations. I view that conclusion, however, as a matter for regret rather than satisfaction, and wish that it had been otherwise.

I feel similarly about the Communist Party of Great Britain. Exceptional circumstances such as invasion, occupation or a fascist regime did not revolutionise its prospects as happened on the continent. So long as the British political culture within which it was founded preserved continuity, the party's perception of reality, deriving from its essential character as part of the international communist movement, was so flawed that all the energy, self-sacrifice and enthusiasm of its activists were bound to be rendered nugatory in the long run and all its strategies to run into the sand. What I am referring to here is not so much even its international links, at least after 1957, as its self-definition as a *party* with its own separate rules, programme, electoral endeavour, leadership and internal culture. So long as a much bigger party existed with hopes of real office and access to real authority nationally and locally, satisfying – however inadequately – the aspirations of the same constituency at which the CP aimed, it could never hope to avoid the abhorred fate of being no more than a ginger group (though it usually avoided turning into a sect).

However, Minerva's owl, as Hegel had it, flies in the dusk and it is much easier to be wise after the event. I am strongly conscious of this and I am therefore writing out of great respect, even when being most critical, for the women and men who, according to their lights, devoted everything they owned in energy and talent to what they conceived to be a project of human emancipation. This volume is intended not least as a contribution to ensuring that they do not suffer what E.P. Thompson once characterised as 'the enormous condescension of posterity'.[20] I have already referred to James Klugmann's official history and its inadequacies, but he seems to me to have been exactly right when, in dedicating the volume to the founder members of the party, he wrote that 'it is harder to make history than to write it'. These are salutary words and I subscribe to them.

1 Origins and Development to 1928

The United Kingdom of Great Britain and Ireland presented at the beginning of the twentieth century a paradoxical and contradictory appearance. In its most obvious manifestation it was a state of stupendous wealth and power, indeed the most formidable and successful upon the globe. It remained overall the world's leading industrial producer, despite challenge from overseas competitors in certain specific sectors. Its merchants dominated the shipping lanes of all the oceans and its shipyards supplied nine-tenths of the vessels which trafficked on them. Its financiers controlled even more decisively the circuits of global transaction, investment and capital flows and by 1914 from their interests overseas of £4 billion drew in an annual revenue of £200 million. Its currency was accepted as the universal standard. It had just finished assembling the most extensive and populous empire in world history, embracing a quarter of the earth's inhabitants, and its admirals commanded the most advanced and concentrated military machine then available to any government.[1]

Yet it laboured under a condition of chronic social and institutional malaise and was viewed in this light by some of its most sensitive and perceptive commentators. The character of the malaise is best symbolised perhaps by the fact that of the volunteers who presented themselves for service in the colonial war in South Africa at the turn of the century, two-thirds were revealed to be medically unfit even by the unexacting standards of the times. By then statistical surveys had for a decade underlined the depth of wretchedness and poverty in which the majority of the nation's citizens were locked, with a third of the manual working class condemned to total destitution at some point in their life cycle. Housing, health and educational provision at these levels were of a comparable quality. Even so this still constituted a measurable advance upon the state of affairs which had prevailed half a century earlier when Dickens, Engels, Mayhew and Doré recorded the features of existence in the lower depths. Political and social argument turned upon the dilemma of continuing and strengthening, with government encouragement, that modest trend towards improvement – or else cutting back on it by wage reductions and more stringent relief policies aimed at lowering prices and strengthening British competitiveness in less friendly world export markets. Within another ten years the political and economic repercussions of that issue were shaking the foundations of the constitution and the social order.[2]

The polarised abundance and pauperism evident in Britain or any contemporary state of equivalent size and economic development was magnified in the global context. An elite of less than a dozen states, or more accurately their ruling classes, ruled and dominated, either through undisguised coercion or the mechanisms of the world market, the lives and destinies of South Americans, Arabs, Africans, Central Asians, Turks, Indians, Chinese – to mention only some of the most numerous ethnic divisions. For the overwhelming majority of these the standards of the average British worker would have looked like affluence. Famine remained a constant visitor to what would later be known as the Third World and to parts of eastern Europe as well. Through countless mechanisms varying from forced labour to unequal trade, in mines, plantations, handicraft workshops or occasionally industrial enterprises, whatever these helot peoples could produce above bare subsistence (and often enough below it as well) was siphoned off to augment the riches of foreign capital or of their indigenous rulers manipulated by the foreigners.

It was the age of capital. It was the age of empire. None the less it was also the age of hope. It truly was at once the best of times and the worst of times. In a century there had been greater changes than in all the millenia since the dawn of civilization, and the foundations, at least, had been laid for the universal society of abundance. To thinking minds there seemed no reason to expect that the process would not continue to broaden and deepen until the spectres of want, ignorance, superstition and oppression were banished to the history books. Whether this happy outcome was seen as arriving through the triumph of market principles or through their suppression, European opinion held it to be inevitable and assured. Meanwhile, Malthus and the nightmare prophecies with which he had opened the nineteenth century were thoroughly discredited.

While sheer desperation inspired constant but as yet futile revolt among the 'lesser breeds' overseas, being wrenched from their age-old roots and ground in the mill of history, the contrast between the promise of the future and the iniquity of the present was nowhere sharper than in Europe to the eyes of the classes concentrated in immense urban locations, living on the edge of destitution, organised by machine industry and bureaucratic administration yet largely literate and conscious above all that the present was different from the past and the future could be different again. They were, except to some extent in Britain, a new class – a creation of the nineteenth century and mostly of its latter half.

Their common demand was to claim a more adequate and appropriate share of the prosperity which their labour engendered and to participate, at least by means of the ballot, in the processes of government and legislation. Circumstances differed from state to state and each working class used the institutional means that it found to hand in order to press its claims – and the availability or otherwise of these means worked also to determine the form which the claims would take. In Germany, though in truth a militarist autocracy, the state was constitutional in form with universal male suffrage. Politically ostracised by the German middle class, the workers of that country therefore had both the opportunity and the motivation to establish a wholly independent political party to represent them electorally and to buttress it with a multiplicity of closely associated organisations from trade unions to literary societies.[3] Their Russian counterparts, by contrast, facing a medieval autocracy with no pretensions to constitutionalism whatsoever, were compelled to operate deep underground and maintain as their central political objective the violent insurrectionary overthrow of the regime.

Britain had followed its own distinctive variation on this pattern, marked by its situation as the first industrial nation. Within this authentically liberal state, with an omnicompetent legislature to which governments were genuinely accountable, the franchise had been widened by slow stages until by the end of the century it included the majority of adult males. The legislature was dominated by two political groupings which by the late century had assumed the form of recognisably modern parties. For historically specific reasons both were descended from the rival landlord factions of an earlier era, and both had, in their different fashions, aimed to attract the widening electorate by adopting the banner of reform. The Liberals (the name was current from the 1850s) had proved the more successful in this contest. A diverse coalition stretching from sections of the landed elite to the radical petty bourgeoisie, their essential political direction came from needs of industrial capital, whose political representative the party had become in the reform struggles of the early century. It had also succeeded in recruiting under its flag the enfranchised sections of the working class, a dramatic difference from the German model, or indeed any other European country. This development can be attributed to the fact that, for reasons too complex to consider here, it had, unlike its equivalents elsewhere in Europe (but comparable with the USA or Canada), chosen to keep open its lines of political communication with workers' organisations.

Of the latter, the trade unions were incomparably the most important. Following the death of the Chartist movement in the early 1850s, what had been in effect if not in form an attempt to organise the working class as an independent political actor was abandoned. The term 'working class' was no less problematic then than at any subsequent time. It was no unified entity, either in situation or in outlook, but, even when following a common political programme during the Chartist days, was a diverse and tension-ridden coalition of skilled and relatively secure handicraft trades, intensely exploited out-workers, miners and factory proletariat, with its only cement the claim for full political citizenship for all males. With the Chartist movement defeated by the forces of the state and the uncompromising hostility of respectable society, the class it represented fell apart culturally and ideologically into its constituent elements.[4] From these emerged the trade unions, their social objectives limited to bargaining in the labour market and acting as benefit societies, their political ones to establishing the most satisfactory framework for that purpose and to promoting broader liberalisation in association with the Liberals. Although it would be an oversimplification to suggest that these organisations were confined in their membership to skilled and comparatively highly paid workers, that was undoubtedly the prevailing trend, and since for these strata the lower middle class provided cultural models of respectability and self-improvement it is not surprising that they drew their political inspiration from the same source.[5]

By the 1890s the association with the Liberals, for a variety of reasons, was suffering increasing strain. Intensifying international competition was evoking from capital strategies of wage reduction and speed-up at the same time as a long phase of falling prices was being succeeded by an inflationary period. Trade unions of unskilled labourers had emerged, less committed to traditional political forms. The principle of a separate political representation for working people, of a more structured demand for the satisfaction of labour's interests, was gaining ground in their political discourse. It was specifically articulated by Keir Hardie's organisation, whose intent is fully appreciated only when the stress is placed on the first two terms of its title: *Independent Labour* Party (ILP). The leaders of the campaign for separate labour parliamentary identity, however, had no conception of dissolving the political bloc with Liberalism; on the contrary, from the better vantage of their asserted independence they intended to strengthen it.

The British developments, however, if not unique, were certainly atypical of what was occurring in Europe during those years, where emergent labour movements had tended on the whole to adopt as their basis the comprehensive and articulated theoretical structure of Marxism, combining a philosophy of history, a revolutionary economic perspective and a political programme. Marxism, with its stress on the ultimate irreconcilability of labour and capital, the necessity for political authority to be concentrated in the proletariat so as to initiate revolutionary economic and social reconstruction – 'the expropriation of the expropriators' – and not least Marxism's stress on the inevitability of all this, when systematised by Marx's intellectual heirs, corresponded better to the life experiences and expectations of continental workers than to British ones.

Marxism, therefore, in a variety of inflections and rival interpretations, emerged as the predominant form of European labour politics, with the great Social Democratic Party of Germany as its flagship. In Britain, however, the process of constructing labour as an independent interest group with autonomous politics had superimposed upon it the still living tradition of sectionalist exclusivism inherited from the pre-industrial era, adhered to by skilled workers[6] and embodied in the older trade union organisations. These, by being first in the field and long experienced, decisively influenced the political tone of their late nineteenth-century counterparts, which started from a different social base. Marxism, therefore, in spite of some promising initial contacts with the new unions, failed to take effective root in the consciousness of British labour. Instead, during these crucial early years it remained confined to a propagandist sect.

The Social Democratic Federation, originally the Democratic Federation, was the creation in 1884 of H.M. Hyndman, a former Conservative stockbroker who changed his outlook as a result of reading *Capital* and subsequent conversations with Marx himself, even though their personal relations broke down drastically. The impact of the SDF on British labour was very limited[7] and it never grew in size beyond a few thousand members at any time, although it did succeed in establishing and reproducing itself as a viable organisation, attracting such individuals, better-educated (and frequently self-educated) workers in the main, as it managed to inspire with a Marxist vision of their future, and getting itself accepted as one of the minor components beside the trade unions and the ILP in the formation of the Labour Representation Committee in 1900.

The explanation for its restricted growth and influence is partly to be discovered in the personality and behaviour of its founder, who continued to control the organisation for thirty years. His autocratic and devious habits alienated many a potential collaborator and his earlier Toryism was not forgotten, but a good deal more significant was a presumption, common to most turn of the century Marxists, which the tiny SDF shared with its immensely stronger and infinitely more sophisticated international colleague, the SPD. This was the conviction of inevitability, the certainty that the collapse of capitalism and the proletarian triumph were as foreordained as had been the earlier bourgeois rise to dominance.[8] The SPD could concentrate on organising its mass following and preparing their consciousness for the (indefinitely postponed) day of reckoning; the SDF, having no mass following at its disposal, regarded the dissemination of Marxist propaganda as its only remit, and understood that to mean exhorting workers to think only in political terms. Trade unionism and industrial action were viewed as useless diversions.[9]

Partly as a result of internal shortcomings, more importantly on account of the political composition of British labour, the SDF remained in limbo. Moreover, not long into the new century it found itself challenged by a rival, in some respects even worse afflicted with sectarian dogmatism than itself, but effectively exploiting the SDF's indifference to industrial relations and conflict.

Syndicalism derived its name from the union organisations of French skilled workmen appearing in the last third of the nineteenth century. Their peculiarity was their rejection in principle of political involvement as a universe of bourgeois illusion, since the real conflict between capital and labour occurred in the workplace and it was there that the class war would be ultimately decided – though that did not stop most French industrial workers from both being members of the syndicalist organisations and voting for one or other of the rival socialist parties.[10] In the French case the syndicalist stance derived from the continuing vitality there of anarchist traditions, but in the Anglo-Saxon world it assumed a Marxist coloration, which did not – as a rule – exclude political action but viewed industrial struggle as very definitely the primary reality.

The inspirational source lay originally in the United States with the Socialist Labor Party and its energetic leader, Daniel De Leon. The badge of Anglo-Saxon syndicalism was the conception of industrial unionism in diametric opposition to divisive and sectional trade unionism, the aim being to unite workers ideologically as a class and eventually to assume the functions of government. Its strategy was dual unionism, the promotion of industrial unions in rivalry to the allegedly hopelessly corrupt and class collaborationist trade union bodies – 'a nest of crooks', according to De Leon. De Leon was instrumental with others in founding in 1906 the Industrial Workers of the World, an international industrial union which achieved considerable influence among militant workers both in the United States and elsewhere. Earlier, in 1903 with James Connolly as mediator, he had co-operated from afar with SDF dissidents to establish a breakaway Socialist Labour Party of Great Britain which embraced his central principles, though differing in some respects upon political tactics.[11]

The stirrings of labour discontent in Britain, which were beginning to rise by the middle of the decade and had grown to tempest proportions at its end, were an international phenomenon that stretched beyond the industrial working classes of Europe and America as an interlocking combination of economic and political pressures destabilised the global system of elite rule and exploitation. The British SLP, in spite of its theoretical principles, was unable to capitalise upon the growing frustration felt by rank-and-file British trade unionists at the inadequate response to the crisis by labour leaders in unions and parliament. In fact it enjoyed even less success than the SDF in recruiting members, but the SLP was wholly indifferent to that fact, valuing purity of doctrine far above mere numbers. It forbade members to hold even the most token office in their trade unions and expelled them for the slightest gesture of recognition towards the established authorities, such as attending a deputation. It was both dogmatic and inquisitorial. Its initial composition had been the Scottish branches of the SDF (Connolly came from Edinburgh), and it had failed to spread beyond the Glasgow–Edinburgh axis, but because of its possession of a printing press, industrial and social conditions on Clydeside which suited its style, and the zeal and application of its activists, it had acquired an influence there among workers disproportionate to its small numbers.

Nevertheless, for all its theoretical commitment to the industrial struggle, the SLP's orientation, like that of its parent body, was essentially propagandist. Its scope even in that field was restricted as its spokesmen (and they were all men) were inclined to parade their doctrinal superiority at every opportunity. Neither the SDF nor the SLP was in the forefront of the outbreak of bitterly fought mass strike action in 1910 and 1911 which involved armed troops confronting strikers, gunboats threatening Liverpool and death on the picket line. Syndicalist conceptions increased their penetration of militants' consciousnesses, but they came from other directions, directly from the IWW, and through the veteran and much-travelled trade union leader Tom Mann, lately converted to syndicalism and direct action. The influence of the new current produced concrete results in the trend to amalgamation of industrially related unions and, once again independently of the two parties, to the appearance of bodies dedicated to the education of the working class along Marxist or syndicalist lines. The course of events served to reinforce among activists their already deep suspicions of trade union leaderships, the Labour Party and the value of Parliament, especially when they were shortly followed by the Liberal government's tender indulgence towards the treasonable military activities of the Ulster Unionists and the mutinous generals in Ireland.[12]

Even leaving the SLP out of the picture, the endemic sectarianism of the main socialist groups was demonstrated in the failure of the attempt to combine their forces into a British socialist party in 1911–12 under the impact of dramatic industrial and political events. This putative unification of the SDF, rechristened since 1908 the Social Democratic Party, with the left-wing of the ILP, the Clarion Clubs and other miscellaneous socialist organisations was ruined by infighting among its sponsors, whose behaviour suggested greater concern with keeping the charismatic Victor Grayson[13] out of the leadership than with the importance of socialist unity. A British Socialist Party (BSP) was indeed born out of the manoeuvres but it proved only to be a retitled SDF, with Hyndman and his lieutenants still leading it, if somewhat less securely than before. The political choice of industrial militants was restricted to the alternatives of weak reformism or ineffective sectarianism and it is scarcely surprising that among them distrust of all forms of political action was reinforced strongly by the course of this mighty strike movement and the irrelevance of the socialists to it.[14]

Nor did the Marxists show any greater ability to recognise the radical potential contained in the suffragette movement. Such matters were of course wholly divorced from the concerns of the SLP, but the SDF had been if anything even less able in this respect. Kendall's remark that it proved quite unable to canalise public feeling behind a demand for universal suffrage is a considerable understatement. Not only did it denounce the agitation as a plot to enfranchise wealthy women at the expense of poor ones but also one of its leaders, Belford Bax, repeatedly expressed virulent anti-female sentiments in speech and writing, and though he was censured by the party he was not removed from its leadership.

Then, in 1914, the European state system was gripped by a paroxysm of self-destruction and these Marxist or revolutionary collectives, with their organisational weaknesses and disunity, their inability to elaborate a clear perspective or definition of their objectives, were flung into the furnace of the First World War. Given the essential basis of the organisations' world views, they contained a strong potential for intransigent opposition to the prosecution of the war and the state apparatus which conducted it, although it took time for this potential to be realised. It is worth noting, however, that in 1914 British anti-war tendencies were intrinsically no weaker than their equivalents in other belligerent countries, all of which were initially swamped by tides of patriotic fervour as soon as hostilities commenced. It was indeed an extraordinary phenomenon, among the most remarkable of modern British history, that consciously or implicitly mortal enemies of the British state rushed to the colours if male, or provided material support for it if female – something which applied no less to Irish nationalist paramilitaries or to suffragettes than to industrial militants. Among miners, who had lately fought a series of intensely bitter strikes and among whom syndicalism was especially well entrenched, a fifth of the workforce departed for the recruiting offices and the front, creating, as it transpired, a severe labour shortage in the pits. It certainly reflected at that point a dissociation, at odds with reality, in the consciousness of these volunteers between the authority which waged the war and the one against which they were in revolt. It was the same in France or in Germany. Lenin was inclined to assume that the explanation was to be found in the treachery of their political and trade union leaders, who had deserted to the bourgeois enemy out of lust for wealth, power and status. There is no evidence, however, to suggest that the rank and file were any less enthusiastic than the leaders in their warlike sentiments or went to the slaughter reluctantly at their behest.

In Britain, however, although the Labour Party supported the war effort and entered the government in 1915, none of the three socialist parties – neither the ILP, an affiliated component, the BSP, which renewed affiliation in 1916, nor of course the SLP – adopted such a standpoint. Undoubtedly the fact that they took seriously the decisions of the prewar International owed a great deal precisely to the fact that they were not mass parties and hence were comparatively isolated from the encompassing militarist hysteria of the war's early days. In the BSP Hyndman always had been an enthusiastic chauvinist and advocate of a big navy. It was entirely in keeping with his outlook that he aggressively backed the war, but in spite of his record, his initial majority on the executive and control of the party organ, *Justice*, he and his supporters were overthrown by a membership revolt resulting in the affirmation of an anti-war stance and the withdrawal of the Hyndmanites from the organisation.[15]

In mainland Britain – it was a different story in Ireland – the circumstances of the war's development did not enable any party to recruit a mass following on the basis of opposition to it and alienation from the state. But if there was until the last two years no concerted opposition to the war as such and what there was never assumed revolutionary dimensions, dissatisfaction and discontent at its particular consequences revealed themselves before long. Escalating prices, adverse changes in work practices and government encroachment on civil liberty emerged as the principal grievances. Inflation was linked to runaway war profiteering. To raise output in the munitions and engineering industries traditional work practices and demarcations were, with trade union agreement, abrogated. Implementation of these new conditions both generated antagonism and – since the details had to be negotiated in each particular case – brought to the forefront as the effective spokespersons and leaders not the distant union official but the rank-and-file shop-floor representatives, the shop stewards.

Naturally they began to combine their information and effort and to establish linking committees, both within factories and between them. Developments of this sort occurred particularly in Sheffield and above all in the area of the Clydeside conurbation. Prior to these changes skilled engineers, archetypes of nineteenth-century trade union exclusivism and middle-class aspiration, affected moreover in Clydeside with religious sectarianism linked to employment allocation, were among the least socially radical of workers. The miners had refused to be bound by the Treasury Agreements,[16] and continuing resistance to government endeavours to raise production at the expense of conditions, including major strike action in 1915, played the same role as dilution and speed-up did for the engineers in preserving an oppositional consciousness towards the powers-that-be.

As early as 1915 industrial and social action had coalesced in Glasgow when a turbulent rent strike, provoked by profiteering in the accommodation market and organised by Glasgow women, was supported by strike action and demonstrations from the factories. A Clyde Workers' Committee was in existence linking the militant shop stewards in factories and workshops, though its inclinations, and those of its leaders, were either parliamentary or syndicalist. The sole instance of an approach similar to Lenin's was confined to the Glasgow area and was the work

of a single individual assisted only by a few colleagues. John Maclean
was a schoolteacher, and even before 1914 a locally renowned socialist
propagandist and educator. Following the outbreak he consistently
urged large audiences of the working class to prepare for revolution as
the outcome of the conflict. Moreover, he independently developed
international and strategic conceptions not unlike those advanced by
Lenin in his 1916 *Imperialism: The Highest Stage of Capitalism*.[17]

Maclean, too, saw the war as the product of a rapacious inter-impe-
rialist competition capable of being resolved only by international proletarian revolution, and predicted a further round within fifteen years
if that failed to happen. He recognised the importance of the threat posed
to the Empire by Irish nationalist insurgency but viewed Scotland as
potentially the weakest link in the imperialist chain and appropriately
situated for commencing the upheaval. As Kendall expresses it, he was
the only socialist then in Britain possessing a revolutionary will to
power. Although Maclean was a member of the BSP, the leading
figure in its local branch and prominent in its conferences, his activity
was undertaken on his own initiative and not in any sense under the
direction of the BSP's leadership. As he made a very considerable
impact, the authorities recognised the danger he represented and had
him imprisoned on charges of sedition.

The first Russian revolution of 1917 in March, bringing into being
the soviets – still far from Bolshevik – evoked enthusiastic acclaim
among the British left, going so far as to result in a proposal – ultimately
abortive – for the creation of workers' and soldiers' councils throughout
Britain, endorsed even by such as Ramsay MacDonald and Philip
Snowden. A year later the Bolsheviks had triumphed and war weariness
in Britain was further advanced, although the government by a combination of concessions, arrests, censorship and officially sponsored
hooliganism had succeeded in curbing the industrial and political
militancy of the previous two years.[18]

By the summer of 1918 the Allies, now including the USA, had gone
over to the military offensive and victory was in prospect, so ending the
murderous stalemate that had always threatened to provoke a wholesale
withdrawal of public confidence from the state. Dynamic and strategic
revolutionary leadership which might have drawn together the diverse
currents of opposition was lacking, especially with Maclean in jail.
The Bolshevik Revolution, with its successful seizure of authority
under the slogan of 'All power to the soviets', appeared to confirm the
uselessness of conventional politics to revolutionaries, a perception
underlined by Lenin's forcible dissolution of the Russian Constituent

Assembly early in 1918. At the other end of the left spectrum the impact of the war and the Russian Revolution had brought about far-reaching alterations in the programme and organisation of the Labour Party, giving it a much more explicitly socialist aspect and making it capable of inspiring hopes of socialist action unimaginable in the prewar era. By contrast, Maclean's presence in Glasgow, following his release from prison at the end of the war after serving less than a year of his five-year sentence,[19] was inconsequential for national politics – though not for the birth of the Communist Party.

The crushing of communist revolution in Germany at the beginning of 1919 and elsewhere in Central Europe shortly afterwards proved decisive for the world movement. The Soviet regime, too, had its back to the wall as the civil war approached its climax. The German Communist Party (KPD), growing out of the German extreme left and proclaimed on New Year's Day, 1919, had evolved largely independently of Russian influence; indeed, Rosa Luxemburg, the major theoretician on the German left before her murder in January 1919, was a severe critic of many of Lenin's basic policies. The Russian communists identified the KPD's spontaneous development as its crucial weakness and the chief reason why the German revolution had failed – temporarily, as they believed. It had been Lenin's objective since 1914 to create a new revolutionary International, but the matter was now perceived as urgent so as to lose no time in establishing the general staff of world revolution, guided by the Russian example, to take advantage of what Lenin fully recognised might be a short-lived revolutionary opportunity. With Russia blockaded and torn by warfare, the initial meeting of the new International was scarcely representative – it included in fact very few delegates living in areas outside Soviet control. Nevertheless, in March 1919 the Comintern was inaugurated, just as the European revolutionary wave was breaking, although there was no way of foreseeing that at the time.

More accurately, it was the wave in Eastern and Central Europe, for the Western countries, including Italy, were out of phase with the empires of Germany, Austro-Hungary and Russia. In the former cases, though the climax arrived somewhat later in 1919–20, it was still before communist parties could be formed to lead the masses – even supposing that to have been the missing element in the revolutionary scenario. The end of the war in Britain restored the electoral credibility of the government that had fought it and it is indicative that Maclean, though he stood as a parliamentary candidate in a working-class Glasgow constituency, came nowhere near winning.[20] Overall, the governing Coalition achieved a sweeping victory everywhere outside Ireland and even the Labour parliamentary leader, Arthur Henderson, lost his seat, though he had been a Coalition minister before falling out with Lloyd George. At the same time the end of the war broke the dam restraining mass industrial conflict and social dissension once postwar expectations were exposed as illusory and while a transient economic boom gave labour a favourable wage bargaining position.

Although the socialist organisations had members who were prominent among the shop stewards, and propagandised in relation to the industrial upheavals, the army mutinies and police strikes which shook the country throughout the year, they were in no position to lead them. They remained even more isolated from any influence on the guerrilla war which broke out in Ireland as the Sinn Fein MPs, overwhelmingly victorious in the 1918 election, embarked upon the project of expelling British power by force and instituting an Irish Republic. As still the greatest of imperial powers and a leading promoter of the armed assault upon Soviet Russia, Britain, in the eyes of Lenin's government, urgently required an effective revolutionary challenge. Throughout 1919 and the early months of 1920 the Comintern worked energetically to bring together the revolutionary groupings into a unified communist party guided by Bolshevik conceptions, but was confronted by a number of intractable difficulties.[21]

In the first place there was only the most minimal overlap between the revolutionaries and the mass political expression of organised labour, the Labour Party. The BSP was an affiliated organisation but that did not mean a great deal in practice and all of the other potential components were fiercely antagonistic to the party of class traitors as well as still continuing to be syndicalist in outlook to a greater or lesser degree; some were adamantly opposed to parliamentary tactics as well. These were typified by Sylvia Pankhurst, who wrote:

> The Labour Party is very large numerically, though its membership is to a great extent quiescent and apathetic, consisting of many workers who have joined the trade unions because their workmates are trade unionists....
>
> But we recognise that the great size of the Labour Party is also due to the fact that it is the creation of a school of thought beyond which the majority of the British working class has not yet emerged, though great changes are at work in the mind of the people which will presently alter this state of affairs....

[It] is for the Communists to build up the forces which will overthrow the social-patriots, and in this country we must not delay or falter in this work.

We must not dissipate our energy in adding to the strength of the Labour Party... We must concentrate on making a communist movement that will vanquish it...

Lenin answered her in *Left-Wing Communism: An Infantile Disorder*, the pamphlet he wrote to win over the doubters in Britain and elsewhere, with the assertion that:

British Communists *should* participate in parliament, should from *within* parliament help the masses of the workers [realise the uselessness of a Labour government]... To act in a different way would mean to place difficulties in way of the cause of the revolution, because revolution is impossible without a change in the views of the majority of the working class and this change is brought about by the experience of the masses, never by propaganda alone.[22]

What the Comintern usually tried to do was to draw its sanctioned revolutionaries out of the mass socialist parties, split them off and form them into a communist party, thereby bringing the strongest possible forces into the new organisation and enabling it to claim to be the authentic heir to the prewar socialist tradition. The fact that this was not likely to happen in the British case was not, however, viewed as an insuperable problem, as the assumption was that, once formed and as mass consciousness developed, the new communist party would soon attract millions away from its increasingly discredited rival.

The second obstacle was in the immediate term far more frustrating, for bringing together the scattered limbs of a putative communist body was a nearly impossible undertaking. The organisations which the Comintern aspired to unite were agreed only in their commitment to revolutionary action as a requisite for attaining socialism; they were profoundly and bitterly divided upon virtually every other political principle as well as being affected with considerable personal suspicions and rivalries. In the course of 1919 John Maclean became estranged from the BSP, and when it was clear that this party would numerically dominate the proposed new organisation he fiercely opposed its establishment. Nothing other than Lenin's prestige and the gravitational pull of his revolutionary regime could have overridden those antagonisms. That, and a substantial input of Comintern persuasion and resources.

Walter Kendall has documented beyond any possible question the extent of the Comintern's intervention and the very considerable funds which it supplied to attain its objective. To Moscow and to the British participants there was nothing unethical in such behaviour; national particularism was not part of their outlook and the enmity of the ruling class and its labour lieutenants made secrecy essential. Concealment from the rank-and-file participants themselves of what was happening behind the scenes was a necessary by-product – and there is no reason to think that the rank-and-file would not have shared that view had they known what was going on. During the negotiations in the course of 1919 and the first half of 1920 it was expected that the ILP along with the BSP would form the core of the new Communist Party and shed its right-wingers in the process.

It was undoubtedly the attitude of the Comintern, intensely distrustful of the ILP, which edged that party out of the preliminary negotiations in 1919. There remained a chance that the ILP might still join the constituted CP on the latter's own terms, but the decisions of the Comintern's Second Congress in July–August 1920 destroyed any such possibility by asserting the twenty-one conditions to which all parties seeking membership of the International were obliged to adhere. They included the creation of an underground network parallel to the party's legal presence and agitational work among the armed forces. As Ralph Miliband has noted, the conditions make sense only on the presumption that the Comintern was an international army preparing itself for the decisive assault.[23] That, of course, was exactly how its leaders did see it. Such notions were anathema to the deep parliamentary reflexes of the ILP membership and the party resumed its own course. In the end only a very few of its members seceded to the CP.[24]

Initially, the majority of the SLP was left out as well. The sticking point for them was the acceptance, at Lenin's insistence, of the need to pursue affiliation to the Labour Party as a tactic for gaining mass support inside its ranks. However, four of its leaders, J.T. Murphy, Tom Bell, Arthur McManus and William Paul, insisted on proceeding, along with the minority they were able to convince. The Communist Unity Convention took place at last in London at the end of July 1920, including along with its two main elements members of the South Wales Socialist Society and the Shop Stewards' and Workers' Committees, though these organisations were not formally represented. The former had emerged from the prewar industrial conflicts and was a loose federation of socialist clubs with a small membership. During the later stages of the war they had been contacted by Sylvia Pankhurst's growing

Workers' Socialist Federation (WSF) and were distributing her newspaper, the *Workers' Dreadnaught,* but had all but faded away by the time of the merger. The latter had been formed, with the Clyde as its inspiration, as a body endeavouring to co-ordinate the industrial action of 1916 and 1917. By 1920, though far from extinct, it had declined to a shadow of its former significance and become largely a propagandist organisation. Also involved were a number of left-wing adherents of guild socialism, which James Klugmann has defined as a form of 'respectable syndicalism'. A number of even more peripheral organisations were represented, such as the Socialist Prohibition Fellowship and a scattering of independent socialist clubs, but not Sylvia Pankhurst's WSF, which had ostentatiously retitled itself to form a rival communist party.[25]

The Convention resolved to designate the new formation the Communist Party of Great Britain and commit it to the principle of soviet power as the necessary expression of proletarian dictatorship. After extensive debate it approved by majority vote the Comintern's wishes for the party's tactical orientation, namely to use the parliamentary system as a campaigning platform and to apply for Labour Party affiliation. The leadership which it elected was balanced between the constituent groups and included Albert Inkpin, the Secretary of the BSP, in the same capacity in the new CP. He was, however, in spite of the BSP preponderance in numbers, its only representative to emerge early on as major leader and even so at that time the Secretaryship was not the politically dominant office it later became. The principal figures were the former SLP quadrumvirate, Murphy (elected at the second Congress), Bell, Paul and McManus; it must be presumed on account of their greater political forcefulness and wartime industrial records. Arrangements were made to continue the pursuit of significant revolutionary elements still remaining outside.

It is an index of the undefined state of original communist politics in Britain that in 1921 there were no less than four organisations which contested the Communist Party title (though not all existed simultaneously). Few Scottish organisations were represented at the 1920 Convention. Willie Gallacher, leading Clydeside shop steward and BSP member, had not been present, having been in Moscow instead, attending, though not as a formal delegate, the Second Congress of the Comintern. Being persuaded by Lenin in person that his rejection of parliamentary action and Labour Party affiliation was mistaken, he succeeded upon his return, at the cost of total rupture in relations with Maclean, in bringing the bulk of the Clydeside revolutionaries behind the CPGB.[26] Sylvia Pankhurst, too, was induced to swallow her doubts and agree to merge, although she retained the ownership of the *Workers' Dreadnaught*. At a second Unity Convention held in January 1921 in Leeds the CPGB absorbed two rival communist parties and in the following two years mopped up most of the remnants of the SLP which still held out. Once again the decisive factor was Comintern encouragement, prestige and money.

The International had achieved its objective and its relationship to the new party ensured the long-term cohesion of an organisation which otherwise would surely have been disrupted by its internal tensions, both political and personal. Sylvia Pankhurst did indeed not remain long within its ranks, being expelled for refusing to place her newspaper at the party's disposal. The essential contradiction affecting the party ran much deeper, however, and related to the circumstance that the CP had come into being at a point when its basic purpose was no longer applicable, if indeed it ever had been. On the historical evidence the likelihood for a proclaimedly revolutionary party winning mass support among the British working class and going on to launch a revolutionary offensive was slight, but if it had ever existed it had been in 1917 or 1919. By 1921 the state had ridden out the worst phase of its crisis, the labour movement, having achieved no substantial gains, was being pushed back on the defensive by rising unemployment, the Irish war was about to be concluded. The drastic cleavages within ruling-class political structures manifest before 1914 had disappeared and constitutionalism had reasserted itself, gaining a new lease of life with the appearance of the Labour Party as a serious competitor for governmental office.[27]

The only long term hope for the Communist Party to exert substantial political influence was to succeed in affiliating to the Labour Party and to direct its energies through the structures of the bigger organisation. It was a perspective for which a high proportion of its membership had no enthusiasm and when its initial application, framed in terms almost designed to ensure rejection, was turned down, the prevailing reaction was one of relief. Only on the Comintern's insistence was the solicitation continued but the Labour Party itself then closed the door and over the years progressively locked it more firmly to stop even individual communists influencing Labour Party affairs in any capacity.[28]

Shut out of the Labour Party the communists were thereby also locked into an isolation from which they had no realistic hope of breaking out so long as British political traditions retained their viability. The remarkable aspect of the years between the end of the war and the beginning of the 1929 slump is just how tenacious these traditions were in a decade of unprecedented economic disruption, mass poverty and political flux. Conservative or Conservative-dominated administrations were regularly returned to office by a mass electorate, and except for a fleeting interval were continuously in power throughout the period. Universal male franchise and a partial female one, instituted in 1918, made no difference.[29] The phenomenon can be explained by the cushion of low and falling food and basic commodity prices, made even lower by the possession of a subordinate empire; the existence of indefinite unemployment benefit, however niggardly and hedged round with restrictions, the removal of the Irish issue (and Irish nationalist MPs) from the House of Commons; and the split vote between the anti-Conservative political forces. None the less, the capacity of traditional elites to continue a largely unquestioned political hegemony is still astonishing.[30] If the Communist Party was marginal to the labour movement, it was more marginal still to the political culture at large. Certainly since the foundation of the SDF an oppositional culture had taken shape and put down roots; it had been strengthened by the experience of the war and was potentially available for mobilisation and moulding into a more coherent form, which is what the CPGB attempted to do. None the less, it was peripheral and likely to remain so.

All this, of course, was far from the party's own assessment of its situation. It was inclined rather to attribute its initial difficulties in achieving a breakthrough into working-class consciousness to subjective errors, particularly the syndicalist or industrial unionist background of so many of its militants and the difficulty they had in adjusting to a perspective combining political with industrial action. There may have been a measure of sense in this, but it is unlikely to have been decisive; the cardinal problems went much deeper. The syndicalists and guild socialists, however naively, had at least tried to address a question about which Soviet communists were no better informed than their British counterparts: the nature of a socialist society once workers' power was in operation, what was to happen beyond the transfer of authority to the working class or its representatives. The Bolsheviks had been gambling on a world or at least a European revolution; they had never expected to have to confront the issue on a Russian plane alone, and when forced to do so they improvised in reaction to events, with the ultimate consequences apparent in 1991. British communists did not try to develop the speculations of their predecessors; their attention was fixed on more immediate and pressing concerns and they soon adopted the Soviet model, implicit from the time of the civil war and translated into reality from 1928, of a strong state owning and planning both economy and social provision down to its minimal units.

For six years following its formation the party's activity was dominated by major industrial confrontations, most of them centred upon the coal industry. It was to this sector of the economy that the weight of government and employers' attack was directed, as cheap energy was central to the strategic aims of strengthening sterling and competing effectively in world money markets, particularly against the dollar. With obsolete technology, multiple competing units, hopeless management and government refusal to take direct responsibility, the only practical method of lowering fuel costs was to make the miners endure longer hours for less pay. Their union, the Miners' Federation of Great Britain, found itself compelled to engage in repeated defensive battles to protect its members' basic standards, and for this relied heavily on sympathetic support from fellow trade unions, particularly the transport workers and railwaymen. A series of crises punctuated with negotiations culminated in the General Strike of 1926 and total victory for the government over the Trades Union Congress, after which the miners were ground into defeat during a lockout lasting six months.

In the understanding of the party at the time and in subsequent left-wing interpretation a strong position was thrown away in 1921 on 'Black Friday', 15 April, when the railway and transport workers' leaders of the Triple Alliance reneged on their commitment to assist the planned miners' strike against drastic wage reductions. The subsequent demoralisation created in the labour movement was starting to be overcome by 1924, according to this interpretation, and the wave of renewed militancy, strengthened by 'Red Friday' on 31 July the following year (when the government made a tactical retreat by agreeing to subsidise mining wages for nine months), was capable of carrying all before it in the General Strike, had that not been sabotaged by the incompetence and betrayal of the TUC leaders. In regard to Black Friday there may be some justice in this view, but there is no reason to think that the General Strike had any hope of succeeding against a government determined to beat it as a maximum priority and with the resources and public backing to do so. It represented not a unique missed opportunity to overthrow the state but rather the last kick of a labour militancy which had suffered its definitive reversal as far back as 1919. The CP, with the maximum engagement it could achieve in these conflicts, used the general tactic up to 1924 of emphasising the militancy of the rank-

and-file and the potential treachery of the union chiefs, summarised in the injunction to 'watch your leaders!'

Partly on account of the union retreat after Black Friday, partly due to internal inadequacies, the CP quickly lost a substantial proportion of its initial membership, but from 1924 it began to grow again and during 1926 recruited extensively. Party leaders and members acquitted themselves in exemplary fashion during all the struggles, displaying energy and dedication of the highest calibre. They were singled out for harassment, police raids and prosecutions. In late 1925 virtually the entire leadership was put behind bars and thereby kept out of action during the General Strike itself.

The Comintern and the Soviet regime were perplexed and exasperated by the CPGB's inability to achieve significant growth and the Comintern devoted an attention to its affairs quite disproportionate to the party's size.[31] It also supplied it with a great deal of money, without which the party could never have hoped to operate upon the scale it did in terms of publications and paid organisers.[32] The fault, as noted, was assumed to lie in bad organisation and bad habits. Basic policies were never called into question, initiating a trend, as Macfarlane observes, which was to persist right through the CP's history and indeed far beyond the time at which he was writing.[33] In 1922 it was decided to rectify the shortcomings and to 'bolshevise' the British party. Near the beginning of the year a three-member commission was appointed to overhaul its structures and functioning. Two of the commission, Rajani Palme Dutt and Harry Pollitt, were afterwards to assume roles of cardinal importance for the CP's future.

Dutt was not an agreeable personality. It could never have been said of him, as it was often enough with truth of Pollitt, that he was 'much loved'. He is best defined as an intellectual revolutionary bureaucrat, a man of theses, resolutions and the editorial office. He possessed a brilliant intelligence – his Oxford degree was one of the best ever – but he came to employ it, principally through the medium of the journal he founded in 1921, *Labour Monthly*, in the composition of dishonest justifications for discreditable or criminal acts committed by the Soviet regime. He was attached to principle – he began his career suffering persecution and imprisonment for his anti-war stance – but he came to identify principle with unqualified subservience to Soviet *raison d'état*. Pollitt was the complete contrast. An extremely able young working-class agitator, a boilermaker by profession, he was also a highly amiable and unpretentious individual capable of inspiring confidence and great affection among his colleagues and winning a reputation for dedicated sincerity well beyond the ranks of the party.[34] Macfarlane supposes, probably correctly, that, as relatively unknown individuals, they were elected to the commission thanks to lobbying by Gallacher, who saw in them people with the drive and initiative needed to reform the party's inadequate practices.[35]

The commission worked for over five months, making intensive and exhaustive enquiries into every level of the party's organisation and apparatus, investigating the functioning of the basic units as much as of the executive and intermediate committees. Its reports were written mostly by Dutt and accepted without significant dissent towards the end of 1922 at the 5th Congress. It was a most important development for it instituted an organisational model that was to persist with only a few substantial modifications down to 1990. The foundation stone of this edifice was the principle of democratic centralism. It gave the CP a quasi-military aspect to complement the quasi-religious one it had already acquired from its messianic expectations. Formally speaking, democratic centralism implied only that while a question was under discussion a free and open exchange of views was necessary, but that once a decision had been arrived at all members, even though they were in the minority, were bound by it and bound to fight for it. In addition, higher committees, once elected, had the authority to take decisions, within the bounds of National Congress resolutions, that were binding upon all the membership subject to those committees; in the case of the Central Executive Committee this meant every party member. The justificatory myth was that this was the manner in which the Bolsheviks had been organised, although before 1921 that was far from the truth.[36]

In practice it gave the party leadership, so long as it stayed united, a virtually unbreakable control over policy and strategy and made challenge to them virtually impossible, by outlawing horizontal communication between the basic units except by permission of the leadership. It also gave rise to a mystique of leadership which ensured that no individual could break into its circles by unauthorised channels, since no one without its approval could hope to gather sufficient voting strength to do so. In effect it imposed a principle of cabinet responsibility upon the entire party, but it went even beyond that, for members were supposed not to accept a decision solely out of discipline, but to instil in themselves the conviction that it was the right one. Organisationally speaking, the framework was simple, though in detail it was immensely complex, far more so than was justified by a party of the CP's size, and once again made possible only with Comintern resources. Above the basic units, whatever they might be called – the name was changed on more than one occasion – stood the District Committee, elected by a District Congress and above that the Central Executive Committee, elected by the National Congress and divided into an Organisation Bureau and a Political Bureau, its administration handled by a Secretariat, all composed of Central Committee members.

Complication enters when account is taken of communists' activities in organisations which contained non-party members, whether labour movement ones like trade union and Labour Party bodies where they were very much in a minority, or those which were under the party's control and which were also extremely significant. The importance of these relationships increased as it became clear on an international scale that revolution was off the immediate agenda and a more or less lengthy period of further preparatory work lay ahead. From 1921 the Comintern began to emphasise the tactic of the 'united front', under which communist parties should work to draw closer to the social democratic organisations and exercise influence upon their members without necessarily trying to win them immediately to a communist position.

In Britain this meant more strenuous endeavours to secure affiliation to the Labour Party and, affiliated or not, to work inside its structures. The first aim received a total rebuff, but from it there emerged at the beginning of 1926 a National Left-Wing Movement, controlled by the CP, of local Labour Party organisations attacking the Labour leadership and favouring the participation of communists.[37] Thanks to the earlier co-operation, CP candidates were able to win two parliamentary seats in the 1922 election and though losing both in the following year got one back in 1924. Also under the party's aegis was the Minority Movement of communist and left-wing trade unionists. This had originally been the British element of the Comintern's rival international trade union centre, the Red International of Labour Unions, but with the adoption of the united front the tentative start being made to establish alternative communist-led trade unions in Britain was abandoned and the less provocative tactic adopted of building a left alternative inside the official unions.[38] Harry Pollitt was the leader of the Minority Movement and it achieved significant successes in influencing union elections, especially with the election of the radical A.J. Cook to head the MFGB.

In the Labour Party and trade union movement the CP's pretensions and its efforts to secure influence and positions were of course bitterly contested, but in its drive to organise the million or so of long-term unemployed it had the field to itself, with each union claiming those who had belonged to it but seeing in them primarily a threat to the wages of its employed members, and the Labour Party showing little beyond a rhetorical interest. The CP was instrumental in the foundation of the National Unemployed Workers' Committee Movement and wholly directed it under the leadership of Wal Hannington, a charismatic figure and extremely able organiser.[39] Only a very small fragment of the unemployed, however, were organised in the NUWM (the 'Committee' in the title was later dropped).

The aftermath of the 1922 Battersea Congress also saw significant changes in the CP's propaganda style. Since its foundation its weekly organ had been *The Communist*, a twelve-page journal, in effect the BSP's *The Call* transmogrified. It retained the characteristics of the pre-1920 propagandist organs, with lengthy articles and reports of a frequently didactic nature (though it also possessed an excellent and effective cartoonist, 'Espoir'). At the beginning of 1923 it was replaced by the *Workers' Weekly*, the recognisable ancestor not only of the subsequent *Daily Worker* but also of the present-day journals of the British far left, like *Militant* and *Socialist Worker*. Its content was agitational, its headlines short and sloganeering, its content designed to achieve impact principally upon the factory floor.

It was not only in organisations operating upon a national scale that the party was able to establish an enduring presence. The phenomenon of the 'Little Moscows' demonstrated that it could also, given the right conditions, put down roots and exercise a long-running influence among well-defined local communities. Three widely separated localities constituted the Little Moscows – the mining valley of the Rhondda, the mining area of West Fife, particularly the village of Lumphinnans, and the Vale of Leven, a part of the Clydeside conurbation west of Glasgow but dominated by dyestuffs manufacture rather than the more usual forms of heavy industry or mining. Significantly, all were outside England.[40] The local Communist parties of these industrial villages were deeply integrated with every aspect of the community's social life and culture as well as exercising their strengths in the workplace.[41] In the context of the 1920s that meant above all the endless struggle to ensure that the maximum legal entitlement (or more) to poor relief was extracted from the local guardians, but the local party groups were active, too, on housing questions, in co-op societies, sports, recreations and even the establishment of flute bands.[42]

Communists secured election as councillors in these localities and electoral pacts were reached with Labour and the ILP, often through the medium of the trades council. These municipal councils were as a result controlled by Labour and Communist representatives collaborating as a governing coalition. What appear to have been crucial elements in the maintenance of CP strength were the compact nature of the communities, the result of local employment and services leading to frequent face to face contact in a defined area, and the early establishment in the crisis-ridden Britain of 1920 of a party organisation which combined proselytism and community spirit with devoted attention to immediate social problems. In Fife and the Rhondda that had emerged out of the miners' reform movements, in the Vale from an active SLP branch whose younger members set up the CP organisation and added social activism to the industrial and political dimensions of the SLP.

John Callaghan makes the pertinent observation that in pursuing the united front tactic communists were necessarily living a contradiction, for they were seeking co-operation with organisations and individuals which they were in due course pledged to destroy and replace with their own leadership.[43] As T.A. Jackson famously expressed it, he would happily take the Labour leaders by the hand as a preliminary to taking them by the throat. It made any honest or equal collaboration impossible, but then the communists were not interested in that. Their communist theoretical judgement was joined to the bitter prejudice against reformist organisations inherited from SLP or syndicalist tradition and from their point of view these bodies were important only as vehicles for the party to reach the mass membership they contained. The communists disdained to conceal that their intention was to gut them and then throw away the carcasses. Correspondingly, they felt no guilt or qualms over the fact that their activities in this field were bound to be often conspiratorial. Convinced that they had a monopoly of political virtue, they did not regard the agents of capital inside the working class as worthy of any consideration or reciprocal trust.

The General Strike of 1926 can be evaluated from a number of diverse angles. In one dimension it constitutes in British terms a heroic myth: the climactic confrontation between capital and labour in over a century of their mutual development; one in which the trusting rank-and-file were betrayed by their cowardly, treacherous leaders, with the miners betrayed worst of all. In spite of its storybook simplicity there is a lot of truth in this image; the question is what the event signified, for even an interpretation in the above stark terms can have very different possible meanings. In one version it can be viewed as the culmination of the industrial militancy building up since the war, an unrepeatable opportunity to win a revolutionary outcome in Britain, lost only because of the class treason of the TUC chiefs and the blameworthy feebleness of the alternative communist leadership. Or it may be regarded as the last hopeless stand of a labour movement which had been outmanoeuvred and defeated years earlier.

As indicated above, my own view is that the second interpretation is the one which best accords with the evidence, although it was not the contemporary opinion. The left took it for granted that betrayal was the issue and the explanation for what had happened, but disagreement existed on the left's own role. Trotsky blamed the British CP for investing, under Comintern guidance, too much confidence in the left-wing elements on the TUC General Council and false hopes in the Anglo-Russian Trade Union Committee, as well as for advancing the slogan 'All Power to the General Council'.[44] Subsequent Trotskyist accounts have repeated this analysis.[45] Again, it would appear unrealistic to have expected the party to have played an independent leadership role in the strike, to have taken command of its forces when the General Council abandoned it, and the fact is that the CP never tried to do so. 'It was noteworthy that in the British General Strike of 1926 the communists played practically no part at all.'[46] That comment, however, confuses leadership and activism, and communists certainly did not spare their efforts in the conduct of the strike at its local levels, where they frequently assumed the leadership.

During the six-month lockout of the miners which followed the collapse of the General Strike the party once again directed its energies towards sustaining the struggle. During this period, as the most determined and selfless of bodies supporting the miners, the party grew very rapidly, sometimes recruiting almost whole meetings of striking miners after they had been addressed by a CP speaker.[47] Following the union's defeat it quickly lost most of them again. For the Communist Party the events of 1926 had two main outcomes. On the one hand, for the official labour leaders both in industry and politics, castigated by the party for their treachery and about to embark upon a course of deeper collaboration with employers and state, it strengthened the determination to drive the communists, from whom they could expect nothing but exposure and merciless opposition, so far as possible out of the labour organisations. From 1927 the purge was seriously put in hand. For the communist activists themselves, these events redoubled their conviction that they alone understood and represented the genuine interests of the British workers and that even the most left-wing non-communist was a broken reed at best and most likely a renegade in the making. The ground was well prepared for a regime of sectarian exclusiveness.

In spite of the social and political earthquakes of the 1920s, the early CP was not able to break out of its isolation on the labour movement's margins and assume the leadership of significant numbers. That initial failure was probably decisive, although it was to be compounded in the subsequent decade. Capitalism was in the grip of an unprecedented crisis, but its economic and social reserves were more than adequate to beat off the assault upon it, for all the zeal and determination with which the attack was prosecuted. The depth of this commitment among the early communists is well conveyed in an article written by one of the party's founders, J.T. Murphy, thirty years later:

No-one can deny that the members, leaders and led, have worked and striven with fanatical devotion, performed feats of endurance and sacrifice, displayed such energy that membership in any other party appeared dull and pedestrian. Have what grievances one may against the leaders and damn them for their authoritarianism, and all the rest of it, there were no passengers, no parasites, among them. Damn it, a spell in Wandsworth was a 'rest cure'.[48]

2 Days of Faith: 1928–1938

The achievements of the CPGB during the first eight years of its existence, if very modest or even derisory relative to the hopes which had accompanied its formation, were nevertheless impressive in comparison to what its predecessors of the SDF/BSP and SLP managed to achieve in their respective thirty-six and seventeen years. As a political force on the left it still remained marginal, with fewer than ten thousand members and isolated by proscription as well as by internal culture from the central stage of British politics. At the same time its modest membership constituted a dedicated cadre of activists unlimited in their readiness for toil and self-sacrifice.[1] Although barred from the official bodies of the Labour Party, it had succeeded in building up and controlling a network of sympathisers in the National Left-Wing Movement, some inside the Labour Party, some in disaffiliated local parties, all of which represented a major source of embarrassment and nuisance to official Labour.[2] The CP's position in the union movement had inevitably suffered damage in the attack from the TUC hierarchy, yet the Minority Movement had not been destroyed and still retained the confidence of many trade unionists outside the party's own ranks.[3] Within the organisation of unemployed workers its leadership was unchallenged. In the communities of West Fife, the Vale of Leven and the Rhondda it had put down deep social roots and shared in the control of their local authorities. It had begun to spread communist influence among industrial workers in India, and the persecution of its missionaries there by the imperial authorities brought them and their party deserved credit. All in all these things constituted a significant presence in diverse fields of struggle, assets which had considerable potential for growth should the labour movement at large recover from the exhaustion of the late 1920s, or the political stability of British institutions be seriously disturbed.[4]

Yet the party, deliberately and with its eyes open, cast them all away, behaving in a manner which was probably even more damaging in the long term than its still more notorious behaviour in 1939, and made worse by the drastic internal self-mutilation which it inflicted upon

its own body. It acted in this fashion not on account of any development of affairs in Britain but because its leaders had discovered, along
with all their counterparts in the non-Soviet parties, that there really was
no alternative to doing what the International, i.e. Stalin, required.[5]

Until 1928 the British party had been in especially good standing with
the Comintern in spite of its inability to achieve a political breakthrough.
It had never presumed to try to interfere in the internal strife affecting
the Soviet party but had dutifully endorsed whichever faction had
come out on top. Not only had it refrained from giving any support
to Trotsky but it had also produced no dissenting minority and had
suffered no split over the issue.[6] By 1928, however, these virtues were
beginning to be stigmatised as weaknesses as the alliance between Stalin
and Bukharin crumbled and the USSR embarked upon a radically
changed course with implications for all foreign parties.

Between 1921 and 1928 the course of events in the Soviet Union had
been defined by the New Economic Policy (significantly, such a
peculiar hybrid in terms of Marxist orthodoxy that no better name could
be found for it). In essence a form of market socialism, it instituted a
regime of largely free enterprise in agriculture and consumer goods while
reserving the 'commanding heights' of foreign trade, currency and
heavy industry to state ownership, although even those had to operate
within a market framework. Its ideologue was Bukharin and it was an
approach which favoured agriculture at the expense of industry;
Bukharin's exhortation to the more prosperous peasants was 'enrich
yourselves'. Even the notion of 'Socialism in a single country', dating
from 1925, was originally conceived within these limits, the idea being
that a large agricultural surplus would resource a gradual industrialisation: 'socialism at a snail's pace', to quote Bukharin again.[7]

The NEP did restore the Soviet economy from the abyss of devastation to which the civil war had reduced it, but after seven years its contradictions were surfacing as the Soviet grain producers went on a
delivery strike to improve their bargaining position. The state responded
with forcible expropriations, at first of the grain surplus and then of
private agriculture, in a bloody collectivisation drive. Stealing and
retailoring the Trotskyists' clothes, it embarked simultaneously on a
programme of breakneck industrialisation in the first Five Year Plan.
A war scare accompanied and was used to justify the drive to give the
USSR a modernised industry capable of matching the Western
armaments capacity. Bukharin, the peasants' protector, fell from power
(though not from office as yet) and Stalin reached the unchallenged
pinnacle of his authority.[8] Soviet considerations therefore determined

the turn which occurred in 1928, but enormous shock waves were felt throughout the international communist movement.

A 'left turn' of this magnitude in the domestic sphere required justification in international as well as internal terms. Accordingly the Comintern posited the onset of a 'third period' in revolutionary development – the first being the era of insurgency between 1917 and 1923, the second the relative capitalist stabilisation which had prevailed since then. Now, as the world entered a period of renewed breakdown and turmoil, communist advance and socialist revolution once again headed the agenda and the appropriate response for communist parties was to adopt a stance of 'class against class', to assert their exclusive right to represent the proletariat and expose and combat the social democratic misleaders and their parties, which now because of their reformist and constitutionalist standpoints were defined as the most dangerous enemies of the working class and appropriately stigmatised as 'social fascists'.

Confronted with this requirement – which ran wholly against the grain of British realities – first at the the ECCI plenum in January 1928 and then more forcefully at the 6th Congress of the International in July of the same year, the British delegates objected and even dared to criticise the Comintern assessment of economic conditions in the colonies, but, being outvoted, were forced to submit and on their return from Moscow to begin to put the new line into operation as best they could. It was proclaimed at the 10th Congress in January 1929 but the leadership was subsequently indicted for the damnable heterodoxy of being motivated by discipline instead of conviction and the Comintern set about restructuring it.[9] Constitutionally the ECCI possessed the authority to appoint or remove leaders by fiat, but such was not its preferred option. The normal method of effecting leadership changes in a member party of the International when there was any resistance to Comintern prescriptions was to exploit divisions which were already present by giving the International's encouragement to the faction of which it approved, reinforcing this by the incitement of grass roots attacks against the leaders it wished to censure.

Among the old guard of the CPGB, Bell, Inkpin, Gallacher, J.R. Campbell and A. Rothstein were under suspicion, particularly the last two, and the same would have been true of MacManus had he not died in 1927. They were judged to represent the 'right danger'. The fervent advocates of the new line in the older and middle generations were Murphy, who was stationed in Moscow as the British party's representative with the Comintern, Pollitt and Dutt. Dutt, however, was permanently absent in Belgium owing to ill health, while Pollitt was fully engaged as Secretary of the Minority Movement and had certain reservations. Nevertheless, since he was basically a proponent and his ability was evidently enormous, he was transferred in the middle of 1929 to join the party Secretariat at King Street, displacing Inkpin, who thereafter declined into obscurity. The Comintern sought further partisans capable of assuming leading positions and found them among the London leaders of the Young Communist League.[10] Three in particular featured in this role, Bill Rust, Dave Springhall and Walter Tapsell. The young communists, with Comintern incitement, opened a vehement attack on the established leadership for its alleged rightism and this was picked up on and amplified throughout the Districts and basic units. District congresses one after the other passed resolutions condemning the politics of the incumbents and even Pollitt was not spared. Indeed, so comprehensive was the assault that Dutt and the Comintern had to counsel moderation and warn against a wholesale rejection of experienced talent in instances where the faults were remediable.[11]

The drive culminated in another Congress, the 11th, held before the year was out, at the end of November. This one achieved the results sought by the Comintern and the partisans of the new line. A Central Committee (CC) was elected containing twenty-three new faces and only twelve who had previously held office, few of those belonging to individuals regarded as seriously tainted. Two who did survive were Wal Hannington, because of his great popularity as a mass leader of the unemployed, and J.R. Campbell, who received Dutt's endorsement as capable of being saved. This congress also saw an innovation which was to become central to the CP's political culture and to haunt it to the end, namely the panel system of election. This derived its title from the 'panel' of names prepared by a committee of the Congress, which the delegates were invited to approve *en bloc* as the new CC. On future occasions the panel committee was to be the instrument of the retiring executive and the means of ensuring a self-perpetuating leadership, but, owing to the peculiar circumstances of this Congress, it was constituted for its hostility to the previous leaders, dominated by their antagonists from outside the CC and chaired by Rust. That the Congress was not completely dominated by the new-liners is shown by the fact that the panel was adopted on a divided vote and that Wal Hannington, who had publicly refused 'to stand on the penintent's bench', was subsequently added – though he had to argue that he had been following the new line all along.

The British party had therefore not only changed its political line but also overturned its leadership as, following the Comintern's prompting, it was bound to do. What followed has always been regarded by outsiders, but also, subsequently, by the party itself, as the most disastrous episode in the CP's career. It is therefore worth examining the collective motives which induced it to act in this fashion. At the most immediate level, of course, there was simply no alternative to obeying the Moscow dictate. If the CPGB wished to remain part of the international communist movement, it had to accept the decisions of that movement's accredited representative body. To have brought exclusion upon itself and endured separation from the International would have been unthinkable and cancelled the whole meaning of the party's existence. Had (unimaginably) the British CP broken with the Comintern, a rival organisation carrying the International's seal of approval would promptly have been created.

That this was not the only consideration, however, can be appreciated when it is remembered how insistent was the demand that the new line be accepted on the basis of conviction and not merely of discipline. Most if not all members succeeded in convincing themselves. This was the case not least because in the course of its initial application during 1928 and 1929 most of those in substantial disagreement left the party, which suffered a precipitate drop in its membership. Among those who, on the basis of their experience of the British labour movement, were inclined to doubt the applicability of the directive, reservations were stilled by the certainty that the International's analysis and assessment of the possibilities could not fail to be superior to their own paltry understanding – although the most prominent communist in the miners' union, Arthur Horner, only barely escaped expulsion on account of his reluctance to apply the line.[12] They were assured that the masses would stream towards the party if only the line were applied firmly and consistently enough; if the masses failed to do so that could never be the fault of the policy but only the inadequate way it was implemented. Macfarlane estimates the number of activists who were also unquestioning adherents and who set the tone of the denunciations against the leadership throughout 1929 as being no more than 500.[13] In this regard it is necessary to appreciate the grass roots frustration engendered by the labour movement's incorrigible reformism, the failure of the CP to break out of isolation by applying the united front policy or to find in that tactic protection from the witch hunt being conducted against it by the right wing of the trade unions and Labour Party. It was tempting to imagine that a stance of bold confrontation might encourage better prospects.

In consequence the Communist Party marched into battle against the 'third capitalist party', the 'social fascist' Labour Party, as its principal enemy. In opposition to that party and the organisations which provided its economic and social base the CP presented as militant alternatives, competing for the allegiance of workers, the networks which it had established over the years at considerable cost in patience and effort. The result was to destroy them all and effectively liquidate the CP's restricted but tenacious foothold inside the official labour movement. The new communist leadership was indifferent to the protestations of the non-communists with whom it had worked inside these organisations and whose presence there served as a most important bridge between the party and the wider masses. Indeed their objections and hesitation in jumping to the CP's new bidding were seen as only confirming the validity of the 'class against class' thesis.

James Maxton MP was the chairman of the Independent Labour Party and the most prominent spokesperson for the parliamentary left. He was also the chair of the CP-controlled League against Imperialism. A pretext was discovered for not only evicting him from this responsibility but also expelling him from the League, and the socialist manifesto he had composed along with A.J. Cook, hitherto the party's closest ally in the trade union movement, was stigmatised and derided.[14] After a certain amount of debate and hesitation the National Left-Wing Movement was judged to be operating more as an alternative to the party than as an auxiliary to it and was accordingly wound up and its highly regarded paper, the *Sunday Worker,* closed down, notwithstanding the unwillingness of its non-CP leaders.[15] Party voters and supporters were forbidden to cast their ballots, except on the most restrictive conditions, for Labour candidates, even when no communist was standing.

The Minority Movement took longer to expire, although its demise was foreshadowed as early as 1929 when the initial impact of 'class against class' provoked a sharp reduction in the organisations represented at its conference. It was invested with the impossible remit of emerging speedily as an alternative revolutionary rival to the official trade union leadership at a time very unpropitious for militant action. It endeavoured to fulfil this responsibility by intervening in industrial disputes to promote strike actions and to support them by encouraging the formation of rank-and-file strike committees incorporating both unionised and non-unionised workers and from which official union representatives were excluded. The party never went so far as to propose the destruction of the existing trade unions and their national machinery, but it certainly came close to it. It did call upon them to disaffiliate from the Labour

Party and withhold the political levy (even the Comintern thought this was excessive), though it stopped short of asking for the political levy to be transferred to the CP.[16]

Under the aegis of the Minority Movement and the Communist Party two breakaway unions were in fact formed to challenge right-wing control in the industries concerned. The United Mineworkers of Scotland (UMS), although guided and directed by the CP, was very much the result of a genuinely spontaneous revolt by Scottish miners against the right-wing caucus which controlled the union there and maintained its position by ignoring ballot results whenever it lost. The failure of the MFGB to call its Scottish leaders to order and its weak acceptance of their claim to continue representing the Scottish Miners' Union inspired the formation of the UMS early in 1929, although its influence was confined largely to Lanarkshire, where its strength was approximately equal to that of the older union, and Fife, where it was overwhelmingly stronger.[17] The action of instituting a breakaway, however, fatally compromised it in the eyes of the wider movement and it proved unable to displace its rival. This failure led to its uncontested re-amalgamation after the end of the 'class against class' line, but its career left behind a strong residue of communist sentiment in West Fife and at least gave Willie Gallacher the satisfaction of defeating Will Adamson, the chief right-wing manipulator, in the parliamentary election of 1935.

The United Clothing Workers, also formed in 1929, was a much more artificial creation, though not without a surge of rank-and-file indignation in London propelling its formation. A combination of internal strains, badly managed intervention from the CP leadership and failure to spread beyond London destroyed it in less than a year.[18] Overall, the Minority Movement's campaign from 1928 onwards, with scarcely any victory to its credit and a string of humiliating defeats, was a disaster and effectively wrecked it as a significant force while alienating potential sympathy among workers who might well have been attracted by a less sectarian approach in the turmoil of world slump and Labour government débâcle. Following catastrophic decline it was finally wound up in 1933.

'Class against class' also cost the party the position it had built up over nearly a decade in the local government and community acceptance of the 'Little Moscows'. Its standing in the Vale of Leven, Lumphinnans and the Rhondda was something it maintained not in isolation, never having a straight electoral majority, but in close association with left-wing Labour Party councillors who in the world of the council chamber and its committees were able quietly to ignore the Labour prohibitions on collaboration with communists. With the Labour Party declared to be an agent of the class enemy and individuals within it tolerated only so long as they followed the CP lead on everything, continued co-operation became impossible and the party lost its share in the control of local authority affairs. Its local electoral strength did not disappear overnight and unusual numbers of communist councillors continued to be elected, but they were now reduced to the position of an oppositional minority instead of partners in the administration.[19] It was a position which was never recovered in spite of Gallacher's parliamentary success in West Fife and the fact that the CP tradition lingered for a great many years among the communities there and in the Rhondda.

The NUWM was the area of party influence least affected, and indeed it continued to expand and develop, but despite that and the achievement of a certain measure of national publicity it was in two senses an isolated phenomenon. Its relative health compared to other party organisations was indeed an index of its weakness, for that was maintained only because it was no organic part of the wider labour movement and therefore less liable to suffer from the sectarianism of 'class against class' driving away potential allies. The Communist Party had succeeded in largely monopolising the leadership of unemployed activism, but there was little they could do to give a wider purchase to this achievement in conditions where the NUWM was shunned by the official unions and where, in spite of everything, including on occasion imposed cuts, real wages over the years expanded on average for those workers fortunate enough to retain their employment. The other sense in which the unemployed movement suffered isolation was of course that it comprised, even at the most minimal level, only a minute fraction of the unemployed workforce and was almost entirely male in its composition.[20]

Historical speculation is often a futile exercise, as is identification of missed opportunities, but it is hard to escape the conclusion that in the period of the new line the CP abandoned a position which it could never subsequently recover. The organic connection which it had managed to establish with working-class culture and its institutions was peripheral certainly, far removed from the centres of power and under persistent assault from its enemies, but had up to 1928 shown great endurance under the most unpromising of circumstances. To indulge in counterfactual reasoning for a moment: if from 1928 to 1931 the party had been seeking unity instead of division on the left, upon the shameful collapse of the MacDonald government in August of that year and the co-option of the Labour leaders by the Conservatives, the CP's warnings and jerimiads would have sounded in retrospect immensely convincing and made it that more difficult for its opponents to keep up the barriers designed to exclude it as far as possible from the movement. Supposing that to have been the case, and adding to that reputation the party's anti-fascist record during the 1930s, then supposing again that the Comintern had permitted it in 1939 to continue supporting the war while denouncing the Chamberlain government, then the accumulation of credit, considerable enough in any case between 1941 and 1945, would have been enormously enhanced and the party could hardly have been denied an honoured and considerable place in the framework of the labour movement. It would have been unlikely even then to have exercised real political power, but might well have secured the place in the British political spectrum for which it strove so vainly in the decades after 1945. None of these alternative possibilities is unimaginable in the way for instance that the notion of the CPGB defying the Comintern would be, and the point of envisaging them is to stress that possibilities were open in the late 1920s and early 1930s which were closed forever by the party's own actions. Their combined effect, by weakening the CP's organic links, was to ensure that any gains made in the future would be the more difficult to consolidate and hold on to. Additionally, they sowed a permanent crop of suspicion in respect of the unscrupulous and opportunist nature of the party. The taunts of 'social fascism' would not be forgotten.

All the same it has been a characteristic of British communist history that as one door has closed another has tended to open, and this proved to be the case in the 1930s. There was one outcome of the 'class against class' line which did turn out be be highly beneficial and result in the creation of a major asset. To sustain the CP's pretension to be the sole authentic political representative of the British proletariat a daily newspaper was regarded as being an immediate priority and with heroic effort and sacrifice the first number appeard on 1 January 1930, although the previous November Harry Pollitt had considered the projected date to be too ambitious.[21] The effort and sacrifice had to be continued to keep the *Daily Worker* viable in the face of refusal by wholesalers to handle it, so that the distribution had to be undertaken by party members collecting the bundles of papers off the early morning trains. It is significant that members of the new team who had come to the forefront in the November 1929 purge were put in charge of the paper. Bill Rust, in spite of having virtually no journalistic experience, was appointed as editor and Walter Tapsell as business manager. Without any doubt the existence of a daily paper, regardless of its limited circulation – which was around 20,000 as a rule and higher at weekends when party members were more generally available to sell it on the streets – did more to disseminate the communist viewpoint than any other form of available publicity could have done.

Although the adoption of 'class against class' resulted in a precipitate loss of membership, it did not stop recruitment, and it was in fact during this period, well before the reversal of the line, that the party began to establish a foothold among the traditional English middle-class intelligentsia and in the scientific community. It may be reasonably surmised that this had less to do with the indigenous work of the CPGB than with the proclaimed achievements of the USSR in the Five Year Plan as a spectacular example of directed social reconstruction and rational application of scientific technique. It would seem to be largely a matter of accident, at least initially, that the spread of communist commitment and sympathy among the academic community was centred upon the University of Cambridge, although the presence there of the economist Maurice Dobb, the only British communist academic up to that time, may have been a consideration. The appearance of an organised communist presence in the university is generally regarded as dating from 1931, when David Guest, who had lately been in touch with German communists during a continental visit, took the initiative in forming the group.[22] Once established it took the form of an extraordinarily cohesive intellectual community which endured for many decades as a personal network even after many of those involved in it had ceased to be party members. Several others went on to fill leading roles in the party apparatus, particularly James Klugmann and the philosopher Maurice Cornforth, a pupil of Wittgenstein who sacrificed a brilliant academic career to work as a full-time party organiser. Others, most notably John Cornford, died in the Spanish Civil War.[23]

The scientists included Richard Synge, a future Nobel laureate, but the outstanding personality and publicist in this field was J.D. Bernal, although he held formal party membership only very briefly. Bernal, as well as being an outstanding physicist in his own right, pioneered the study of the economic context and social function of science.[24] The poets who were at the time the best known representatives of the intellectual Marxist trend, however – Auden, Spender, MacNeice and Day-Lewis – sustained only a very distant relationship with the CP. Spender joined in 1937 but did not remain long and parted on bad terms.[25]

This is probably the appropriate stage at which to make some observations upon the Cambridge spies. That a number of the male students there who were attracted to communism in the thirties went on to a subsequent career of espionage in the Soviet interest is a matter of historical notoriety as well as of a limitless quantity of hot air from professional scavengers in these matters. Although definitive proof is lacking and likely to remain so, there is no evidence that the CP was in any way connected with their activities, indeed it would have been remarkably stupid for it to have been – from the standpoint of Soviet espionage no less than that of the party, since the party was a soft target for government penetration and would have provided easy leads for the secret services to follow had there been anything there to pursue. Party members like Percy Glading or David Springhall who *did* use their jobs as armament workers to indulge in espionage of a sort proved to be hopeless amateurs and were quickly apprehended. Loud and often repeated accusations that James Klugmann was a Soviet agent, even the much-sought 'fifth man',[26] are scarcely to be taken seriously in view of the fact that he was an extremely public communist leader, scarcely the most appropriate qualification for a spy.

As for the spies themselves, had the competing espionage systems of the West and the Soviet blocs never existed it is hard to imagine that it would have made much difference to the historical outcome of the conflict. But whatever may be thought of them, moral indignation certainly seems out of place. It may well be that they behaved stupidly and uselessly and wholly wasted their considerable talents, but if they saw in the USSR a society and a future worth committing themselves to, then to serve it in any manner they were asked made practical sense. It is only in the light of the mystique and sacramental rite with which the British state legitimises itself that their actions appear as monstrously reprehensible.

It is important to emphasise that while the recruitment of a distinctive middle-class component in place of the occasional isolated individual who had joined its earlier ranks marked a significant departure for the CP and was to affect its development substantially in the long run, it nevertheless remained an overwhelmingly working-class organisation in terms of its membership composition. The intellectuals who joined in the 1930s, or, like John Strachey, were closely associated, enjoyed a high publicity profile but made up no more than a tiny fraction of the overall membership and were largely concentrated in south-east England. In the Scottish District during the late 1930s, when expansion beyond the working-class base had become a policy, the party leadership was obliged to set up a special committee to promote 'middle-class work', so deficient had its performance been in this respect.[27]

The CP's advance upon a middle-class terrain showed its value from the middle of the decade when 'class against class' was buried and the party emerged as the most vocal partisan of unity upon the left in opposition to fascism and war.[28] Once again the driving force behind the change was the Soviet regime via the Comintern, but in this case it did not contradict the local necessities of British society and politics. Even as early as 1931 there had been some modulation of the dominant theme, in so far as it became permissible to emphasise the concept of 'united front from below', although this was still in the context of total abhorrence for social democratic leaderships. The shift was made with Germany principally in mind, where the confrontation with fascism was direct and physical, but it did not suffice to prevent the Nazis' accession to power at the beginning of 1933. When it had become clear that Hitler's power was stable and successful in extirpating the KPD,[29] and that the new German regime was a potential menace to the Soviet Union as well, the lesson of the disaster produced in Germany by the 'Third Period' line was appreciated if never publicly acknowledged. Moreover, the first Five Year Plan had been basically successful in attaining its objectives and the USSR was now an industrial giant. There is some evidence that Stalin's colleagues in the light of these realities had successfully pressured him to adopt a less confrontational line both in the Soviet Union and *vis-à-vis* the bourgeois democracies, and to seek allies among them.

The 7th (and last) Congress of the International, held in July–August 1935 and assuming more the character of a political rally than a debate with opposing viewpoints affirmed the intention 'to *establish a united front on a national as well as international scale*'[30] (original emphasis) and 'to overcome, in the shortest time possible, the survivals of sectarian traditions which have hindered them in finding a way of approach to the Social-Democratic workers...'[31]

The four years which followed were to enable the party to reach and present itself to a far wider public than it had ever previously had the opportunity to do. Partly it was the direct impact that the party was able to make in a generally more sympathetic climate; to a greater extent it was the ability to get its approach taken seriously through the medium of bodies of which it was a part and which it might or might not control. A few months after the 7th Congress Baldwin's government called a general election. In accordance with the united front policy – which was a wholly one-sided one, for the Labour Party ignored it – the CP presented only two parliamentary candidates in opposition to Labour. One of them won, giving Willie Gallacher the West Fife seat, which he held for fifteen years. It was a modest enough success for a party which in the same year had adopted a programme entitled *For Soviet Britain*, but it gave the CP its first parliamentary representation since Saklavalta lost his Battersea seat in 1929.

Paradoxically, and in this instance for the party it certainly was a case of 'the worse the better', the circumstance which engendered the improved climate was fascism both at home and abroad.[32] A great deal of the CP success during those years has to be attributed to the fact that it was the only political party in the country which adopted a militant and uncompromising stance towards the danger, along with the practical steps it took to translate that into reality. The Labour Party record by contrast was a sorry one. Its Executive and parliamentary leadership temporised and vacillated, followed in the trail of the Baldwin and Chamberlain governments on foreign policy and did nothing to mobilise physical opposition to the British Union of Fascists (BUF) marches and provocations in London and Lancashire.

In a period of modest but discernible economic improvement and stable constitutional right-wing government it is most unlikely that the BUF represented a serious challenge to the British political system, but it was the symbolic aspect which was important.[33] The East End of London contained a high proportion of Jewish residents, many first- or second-generation immigrants, along with much sweated labour employed in minuscule enterprises: an environment in which Mosley's followers had hopes of finding mass support and which they tried to mobilise by anti-semitic propagandising, harassment and intimidation. The Communist Party counterattacked fiercely and in 1936 organised the 'Battle of Cable Street', which ended with the fascists' humiliation and wrecked Mosley's hopes of asserting any control of the streets. Consequently the party recruited a numerous and devoted following in the East End, which it reinforced by its attention to employment and social issues.

The territorial expansionism of the Axis powers and their appeasement by the Western democracies was for all elements of the left or socially concerned persons the most terrifying political phenomenon of the 1930s. The 7th Congress had stressed the necessity for the constituent parties of the International to emphasise the link between anti-fascist struggle and 'the fight for peace and for the defence of the USSR'. The Spanish Civil War, breaking out in July 1936, crystallised all the choices and all the issues relating to those developments. A democratically elected, socially reforming republican government constituted as a Popular Front including communists was militarily attacked by the regressive forces of Spanish society – military traditionalists, landowners, capital, clergy – assisted by armed intervention from the fascist regimes of Italy and Germany. While the democracies, paranoid about social revolution or communist influence, procured, behind a screen of non-intervention, the destruction of the Republic by denying it access to armament purchases, the USSR was its sole supplier of military equipment. British communists applied their energies to aiding Spain by publicising the nature of the conflict, by making collections for food and medical supplies, and, especially, by their participation in the formation of the International Brigades.[34]

This volunteer force was organised by the Comintern and was a major military asset to the Republic, though insufficient to save it in the end. The party took the lead in recruitment in Britain and its own members supplied a high percentage of the volunteers; it likewise organised their transport to Spain, clandestinely once the British government prohibited its citizens from fighting there. The British units were deployed on a variety of fronts, saw frequent action and suffered many casualties. Upon the left all this gained the Communist Party enormous credit and its leaders would not have been human if they had not derived some satisfaction from that, although the accusation by Valentine Cunningham that the leadership, and especially Pollitt, cynically manipulated for the CP's benefit the reputations of the party's dead does not stand up.[35] As even Henry Pelling acknowledges, they could have scarcely been gratified by the loss of so many of the most promising of the future leadership cadre:[36] Guest, Ralph Fox, Cornford, Tapsell, to note only the most celebrated.

The fascist danger and the dispiriting reaction to it of the Labour Party can also be regarded as the major consideration behind the success of the Left Book Club, which the CP did not control but where it did exercise prime influence. The idea for such a network, which would commission titles of a left-wing slant and supply them at reduced prices to its members, was offered to several publishers but taken up in the end only by Victor Gollancz. The response exceeded all expectations and membership at its height reached 57,000. The extent of the dissemination of these texts is attested by their universal presence into the 1950s and 1960s on the shelves of second-hand booksellers in the most remote parts of the country. The monthly selection was made by a panel of three individuals: Gollancz himself, Harold Laski, a respectable Labour Party left-winger, and John Strachey, not a party member but at that time very closely allied to it. The titles were mainly commentary on current political and international affairs with particular emphasis upon the character and spread of fascism. About a third of them were written by communists. The quality varied widely:[37] a volume of statistical demonstration that Soviet workers in the mid-1930s were materially better off than their British counterparts was scarcely the happiest example of the panel's judgement, but the assertion that Orwell's *Road to Wigan Pier* was the only worthwhile text to appear under the Club's imprint is fatuous. The selections for 1938 included A.L. Morton's *People's History of England*, regarded as the starting point of the British tradition of 'history from below' and virtually the foundation charter of the CP Historians' Group, which came into existence following the war and which was ultimately to exert considerable influence on British historiography. The Labour Party viewed the Club with distrust and disdain, regarding it as a competitor for members' loyalty and income as well as a vehicle of communist propaganda, although it did not go so far as to proscribe it formally.

No such indulgence was extended to groups within the Labour Party who pressed their aspiration for a united front with the communists to the extent of an organised agitation. The Socialist League, an affiliated organisation of the Labour Party made up of former ILP members who had rejected the latter's disaffiliation option in 1932, dared to adopt such a perspective, inspired by its most prominent spokesperson, Sir Stafford Cripps. In collaboration with the CP and the ILP it launched a Unity Campaign early in 1937 calling for the establishment of a united front of the British left.[38] The foundation of the weekly *Tribune* occurred as part of this initiative. The response of the Labour Party Executive was immediately to disaffiliate the Socialist League and proscribe its members, whereupon the League (on CP advice) dissolved itself and the campaign collapsed. The revival of the proposal in a slightly different guise early in 1939 incurred the expulsion from the Labour Party of its most vocal dissidents, including Cripps and Aneurin Bevan.

The Labour leadership in its justifications made abundant use of the disreputable behaviour of the CP during the 'class against class' phase and of the fresh atrocities occurring in Moscow but it is clear that their principal motives were of a different order. The worst ravages of the 1931 election catastrophe had been retrieved at the General Election of 1935, trade unions were being increasingly taken into government confidence and individual membership rose steadily throughout the decade. Having staked the future of their party upon a strategy of electoral advance culminating in a parliamentary majority, its leaders were all too conscious that success required a far-reaching extension of Labour voting strength beyond its working-class base and were convinced that this perspective would be badly compromised if the party were tainted by anything so vulgar as the mass campaigning which was the CP's speciality, quite apart from the CP's bogey reputation.[39] Hence the Labour Party's passivity during those years and its failure to institute any mass actions of its own as alternatives to those undertaken by the communists and their allies.

It was that passivity which infuriated the most active and concerned Labour adherents, and in fact at local level many Labour organisations quietly ignored the bans and engaged in joint work with communists, most notably during 1935 in resistance to the attempted introduction of yet more rigorous criteria into the Means Test. The CPGB was still more spectacularly successful with the youth organisations of the ILP and the Labour Party. The former was a relatively minor operation, when in 1935, still following the 'Third Period' tactic, the CP split both the ILP and its Guild of Youth, taking away in each case a section of their membership.[40] In the popular front phase the CP succeeded in winning to its positions the bulk of the Labour League of Youth and the over-whelming majority of its national committee, who were exasperated by the attitudes and behaviour of their parent body. Labour officials suggested that the communist attraction had been possible only because the youth in question were not old enough to recall the earlier behaviour of the CP. In contrast to the Guild of Youth the CP leadership did everything in its power to persuade the League of Youth committee, of which Ted Willis was the chairman, to remain within the Labour ranks, but in early 1939, as the Labour Party Executive Committee prepared to disband its insubordinate junior, its leaders, including Willis, as well as the editors of its journal and many complete branches, transferred *en bloc* into the Young Communist League (YCL).[41] The Labour Party student organisation, the University Labour Federation, amalgamated early in 1936 with communist groups and expanded rapidly in size. It was the last Labour Party body openly to accept communist members.

Engaged though it was in its high-profile political offensives, the CP did not neglect the industrial struggle, which it regarded as its foundation. The fact that it was less tempestuous than in the first fifteen years of the CP's existence did not reflect a downgrading or lessening of attention so much as the fact that trade union activity in general was muted during these years and still within the constraints of the Mond–Turner agreements.[42] Also, with the turn again to a united front, the party adopted a less confrontational posture by the party. The CP, now fully committed to the development of the existing unions, worked through rank-and-file movements, some of them, like the London busmen's, set up during the earlier phase, and through the reviving shop stewards' committees in the engineering union, where a lot of progress was made in the aircraft industry. The UMS, largely confined to Fife and implacably isolated and harassed by the right-wing officials of the Scottish county unions, was dissolved so that after a period of severe hardship its blacklisted officials were able to re-enter the county unions and win election to official positions.[43] In the Welsh mining industry communists were already occupying leading positions, with Arthur Horner elected as South Wales Miners' Federation (SWMF) president.[44] Among electricians the position was being established which would give communist union leaders a comprehensive grip on the Electrical Trades Union (ETU) in the postwar years.

For the sake of the united front the CP was ready to make a variety of accommodations with potential allies, but in one respect it was wholly unrelenting. It would appear that by the mid-1930s direct Comintern subsidies had ceased and guidance and control had been much reduced. This did not mean that the identity and self-perception of communism in Britain as part of an international movement was lessened in any degree. It was part of a historic mission so far attained in only one part of the world, the USSR. The workers there had overthrown the power of landlords, bankers and bosses and the workers ruled. The longing for a different order of things, which underpinned the original socialist vision, grew all the more fervent when it was transformed into admiration for the state where that was thought to have been accomplished. Furthermore, the Soviet Union represented not only itself but also the guarantee that similar revolution was possible elsewhere and the source of practical assistance to achieve it, as well as, more immediately – as Spain showed – the most reliable barrier against any further extension of fascism. The 'defence of the Soviet Union' was therefore at the very top of the party's agenda, and that was translated in the conditions of the thirties into acceptance and applause for every pronouncement, decision and action on Stalin's part. No ally of the party during the late 1930s, actual or potential, would escape castigation should they express the slightest or most discreetly phrased reservation about what was going on in Moscow between 1936 and 1938.

The searing purges of those years, with victims, enslaved or dead, running into the millions, and the structures of Soviet society and state wrenched and twisted out of shape, are now extensively documented, but not even the collapse of the regime has fully resolved the question of their purpose and motivation.[45] What is clear, although no one was safe, is that the principal targets were party members and the educated strata of Soviet society. The most plausible scenario, although it is still highly speculative, is that in 1934 an unwilling Stalin was pressured by the other party leaders to accept a relaxation of the internal war being prosecuted in the shape of collectivisation and the industrialisation drive and to submit to restrictions on his own authority. The murder of the rising political star, Kirov, in December of that year, whether or not engineered by Stalin, removed the chief obstacle to a renewal of state terrorism and supplied the pretext for it. Stalin and his entourage now resolved to shatter every centre of opposition, past, present or potential, and to uproot every imaginable source of dissent. The overwhelmingly greater part of the purges was conducted out of public view, with the anonymous victims after conveyor-belt administrative trials dispatched to labour camps or else their graves. British communists at large had of course no way of knowing about these matters, although their leaders, who frequently visited the Soviet Union, could not be unaware of the atmosphere prevailing there and the disappearance of former colleagues and acquaintances.

What everyone was fully acquainted with was the series of trials in Moscow in which all of Lenin's close colleagues still prominent in public life perished or disappeared forever. Three of these were show trials in 1936, 1937 and 1938. A fourth was secret but its outcome was publicised: the execution of most of the top military command of the Soviet armed forces. The men who appeared in the dock were accused of the most bizarre and preposterous crimes, of plotting in collusion with the exiled Trotsky the assassination of the Soviet leadership, the restoration of capitalism and the cession of large tracts of Soviet territory to Germany and Japan. They were alleged further to have practised extensive sabotage and wrecking of the country's industrial potential and of poisoning its food supply. The sole evidence brought against them was their own confessions and those of the insignificant individuals accused of being their accomplices.

The CPGB expressed its collective approbation and enthusiasm for these proceedings. Readers of the *Daily Worker* and other publications issued in relation to the trials were invited to rejoice at the liquidation of nests of counter-revolutionaries.

The criminals have received their well-merited sentences.[46]

It is the enemies of socialism and peace who have perished. We should not mourn.[47]

No true friend of the Soviet Union... can feel other than a sense of satisfaction...[48]

When the *Daily Herald*, Liberal newspapers and ILP leaders ventured to doubt the perfect equity of Stalin's judicial procedures they were abused intemperately and told that they were out of touch with their rank-and-file who understood perfectly the need to dispose of traitors and renegades.[49]

It seemed clear to me on direct study on the spot that the case was genuine, the trial fair and the accused as guilty as they themselves said.[50]

This quote comes from D.N. Pritt, a King's Counsel, Labour member of Parliament and renowned defender of left-wingers undergoing prosecution in the capitalist courts, whose credentials therefore looked impeccable and were in fact of great value to the party, of which he remained a lifelong and devoted sympathiser.

Two Left Book Club titles were devoted to the trials. The first, appearing in 1937 under the title *Soviet Justice and the Trial of Radek and Others*, was written by a barrister, Dudley Collard, who was present at the trial and like Pritt not a Communist Party member. He wrote:

After attending every session of the court...listening with care to the whole of the evidence...my own considered opinion, formed and expressed as a lawyer, soberly and deliberately, is that the trial was conducted fairly and regularly according to the rules of procedure, that the defendants were fully guilty of the crimes charged against them and that in the circumstances the sentence was a proper one.[51]

He even went on to declare that had he been the judge he would have imposed fifteen death sentences whereas the court satisfied itself with only thirteen (out of seventeen defendants).[52]

The second volume, published at the beginning of 1939, was the work of J.R. Campbell, by then editor of the *Daily Worker*, and entitled *Soviet Policy and its Critics*. In its preface he wrote that: 'It is therefore fitting that a Communist, a responsible member of the party which bases its policy and activity on these theories, should describe the struggle for their application...'[53]

At a distance of more than fifty years it is impossible to read this material – and the Left Book Club examples were more restrained than the newspaper articles and pamphlets – without a feeling of shame that individuals who were in other aspects of their lives humane and upright could have lent their intelligence and energies to such abomination. The evident unlikelihood that most of the chief leaders of the Soviet state and party had tried ever since the Revolution to sabotage it at the behest of foreign powers was explained away in a variety of disingenuous phrases and historical references. Glaring incongruities in the testimonies were ignored, the translated scripts of the performances were distributed through party outlets and Collard reprinted as an appendix to his book a lengthy verbatim extract of Radek's court interrogation by Vyshinsky the prosecutor. During it Radek — doubtless by prearrangement — explicitly incriminated Bukharin, still at liberty when the trial took place but arrested directly afterwards, as part of the conspiracy. Collard made no comment.

In any assessment of the British party's record regarding the trials it is necessary to distinguish between the top members of the leadership, who were in a position to know something of what was happening behind the scenes, and all the others who were not. All of the former are now dead and they never revealed what they really thought, except sometimes in later years cautiously to acknowledge or claim — including even Dutt — that they had been unhappy about some aspects of the purges and the Stalin personality cult.[54] Well they might, for the notorious case of Rose Cohen brought these developments close to home. A close friend of Pollitt's, she had married the former Comintern liaison officer with the British CP, D. Petrovsky, accompanied her husband back to Moscow and disappeared with him in the Terror. The British leaders appear to have made strong representations in private but got nowhere and they were certainly not prepared to raise it as a public issue.[55] Perhaps, like many a Soviet victim, they convinced themselves that it was just one ghastly mistake in a basically sound operation to destroy the enemies of the people and avert the fascist threat. At any rate they were aware that if they spoke out their acquaintances inside the USSR would be victimised and they themselves, branded as Trotskyists and fascists, excluded irrevocably from the movement which was their identity and their life. Whether their apparent sincerity in vindicating the trials was real or assumed is impossible to say.

Conversations and discussions I have had with people who were at the time mostly grass roots members, but occasionally in responsible positions,[56] result in a nearly universal claim that the trials evoked in their thinking very little doubt or apprehension and that they accepted the then official version unquestioningly because they were not very concerned about the issue, had their attention fixed on British concerns or the anti-fascist struggle and in general did not give it a great deal of thought. The manner in which Trotskyists were successfully portrayed as sabotaging the republican military effort in Spain and the image which had been created of Trotsky's persistent enmity towards the Soviet regime strengthened their assumption that he must be in league with fascism if the Soviet authorities said so. I have every confidence that these correspondents were truthfully reporting what they thought they remembered, but I am equally certain that their recollections of relative unawareness were playing them false and that a form of collective amnesia was at work due to the evil repute into which the trials have subsequently fallen. The British CP did not try at the time to play them down or to take as little notice as possible – on the contrary it applauded what was happening and instantly and noisily berated anybody on the left, in particular the mass circulation *Daily Herald,* who dared to question the defendants' guilt. It is unimaginable that any party member at the time could not have been intensely aware of these cataclysmic happenings and the controversy going on around them.

In trying to arrive at any assessment of the party's career between 1928 and 1938 it has to be recognised that its overriding concern was to fulfil its duties towards the world movement of which it was a part, the Communist International. That this had become no more than a tool cynically manipulated by the Soviet leaders was not appreciated by the ordinary members of the party, who would always back the USSR against their leaders if there should be a difference, and probably not fully appreciated by the leaders either, who preferred to see the CPSU's dominance as the product of its revolutionary lustre rather than a crude power relationship. When the Comintern's demands corresponded to the grain of British political traditions the CP made progress; when it contradicted them the party ran aground and was forced into beleaguered isolation, as happened between 1928 and 1935.

To immediate appearances the recovery made between the latter year and 1938 was dramatic. In numerical terms the ground lost earlier had been recovered and in fact the party, with 15,500 members, was bigger than it had ever been previously and still growing. More than that, it had succeeded in breaking out socially from the industrial sphere and isolated community politics in which it had been confined during the 1920s and had established, thanks to its role in opposing fascism, support and acceptance on a far from narrow basis among the intelligentsia and the educated public, in the organisations of students and left-wing youth. It seemed, too, to be successfully reconstructing its influence within the wider labour movement, and on much sounder principles than it had employed in the past, accepting the reality of the existing trade union culture and working to modify it by promoting rank-and-file movements while pursuing elective responsibilities in the official trade union hierarchies. The year 1939 saw the election of a communist, John Horner, as Secretary of the Fire Brigades' Union.

Yet these achievements, while not illusory, concealed a more profound defeat, for the CP had abandoned or been driven from the positions which really mattered. Although party members had made and would make more progress in winning union office and would also exercise great influence upon the shop-floor, they were accepting responsibilities within organisations which did not belong – at least legitimately – to the party, and might be, as in the case of the Transport and General Workers' Union (TGWU), actively and profoundly hostile to it. At any moment their responsibilities as union officials could come into conflict with the CP's current line, and although the party did not hesitate to co-ordinate the work of its members in official union positions as well as at the grass roots, this was not something which could be done publicly and was always liable to provide a pretext for accusations of communist manipulation and interference. With the Minority Movement it had lost an organisation linking different union sectors, a quasi-trade union centre such as the French Confédération Générale du Travail, which was openly and officially part of a communist network. For all its continuing influence within Labour Party organisations, those who joined the party itself had to conceal, at least formally, their CP membership in order to stay within its ranks, which was no basis for winning acceptance in that quarter. Like the Minority Movement, the National Left-Wing Movement was irreplaceable as a body struggling openly for the CP to take its place under the Labour Party's political umbrella.

Perhaps equally important in the long run, the party's behaviour from 1928 to 1935 and then over the Moscow Trials left an abiding and unsavoury memory which could be called in evidence against it whenever it was on the defensive. Both episodes went a long way to debase the orthodox democratic credentials which it had disdained during its first fifteen years of Leninist sovietism but from then on became increasingly anxious to acquire. The lag between its political rhetoric and its developing practice was evident in the character of the long-range programme adopted in 1935, *For Soviet Britain,* which rehearsed the impossibility of meaningful advance towards socialism via parliamentary structures and reasserted the necessity both for proletarian dictatorship and for soviet rule as its political form.[57] It did so just at the point when the CP was in practice abandoning that foundation stone of its early identity – an indication without doubt that the programme was not very important and that ultimate objectives had taken on a largely rhetorical status ceasing, by contrast with the early days, to have anything but the most tenuous connection with its current activity.

Taken overall, the Communist Party during this decade had made a bigger impact than ever before on the public consciousness, largely as a result of the intensifying fascist threat. Yet it was still in essence a peripheral fragment of the labour movement which continued to derive its identity from its revolutionary traditions; it could never have transformed itself simply into a broad all-inclusive anti-fascist front without any particular class allegiance. That status as a fragment, even more than its international, or rather Soviet, connections, was its central source of vulnerability, all the more so as by 1938 it no longer had the organic link to the organised labour movement which it had so painfully built up in the years before 1928.

3   World War and Cold War: 1939–1951

At the beginning of 1939 the Communist Party was still continuing to grow and to strengthen its position in certain industrial sectors as well as among students and in the Labour Party youth organisation. The German invasion in March 1939 of the Czechoslovak remnant vindicated all too forcibly the stance it had adopted and the warnings it had issued six months earlier at the time of the Munich agreement. In spite of that, even in the early part of the year signs of deep future trouble were starting to show. The final defeat of the Spanish Republic in the spring was an occasion of severe demoralisation after the hopes which it had inspired. The Moscow Trials and the party's strident defence of them, even if not yet evoking a strong negative reaction among those it sought to influence, created none the less an atmosphere of unease and dismay.

Once again it was the party's response to international developments which provided the focus for the strains becoming apparent between itself and the middle-class opinion favourably influenced by it in the course of the decade, negatively mirroring the fact that it had been mainly its posture on foreign affairs which won it that approval in the first place. As the likelihood of war increased steadily, the CP was obliged to define its attitudes to the approaching storm and consider what it would do in the event of its outbreak. The deliberations of its leadership were determined, not unexpectedly, by their chief priority, namely the security and survival of the workers' state, the USSR, and its regime. Any other consideration, regardless of its importance, was secondary to that.

According to Palme Dutt, war was regarded as imminent at the time of the Munich crisis, when the party's 15th Congress also happened to be in session, and he later recorded that such was the feeling of desperation among the leadership that Pollitt, Gallacher and Rust wanted to issue an emergency manifesto, which, he was to claim, he successfully opposed.[1] There is some reason for distrusting Dutt's account,[2] but there is no doubt, in the published record of the Congress, that a military attack by fascism upon Britain was predicted as the likely ultimate outcome of Chamberlain's diplomatic manoeuvres. Throughout the first half of 1939 the party constantly urged on the military alliance that the USSR was seeking with the Western powers, and its sensitivity to Soviet wishes was made clear in the attitude it adopted to conscription. When the Chamberlain government announced its introduction at the beginning of April the immediate response of the CP was to denounce it as an additional form of enslavement and attack upon civil liberties, 'putting Britain into Fascist fetters', according to Dutt. In a minor-key overture to what was to happen later in the year the *Daily Worker* reversed this stance in May and endorsed the principle of compulsory military service. The arguments advanced then and in subsequent justifications were that a people's conscript army was capable of being a politically progressive force, but more significantly that Britain's potential military allies, France and the USSR, who both used conscription, could scarcely be expected to understand if the British refused to undertake it.[3]

The signature of the Nazi–Soviet Pact in August certainly had a devastating effect upon non-party sympathisers, but it was probably not all that profound, so far as it is possible to judge, upon party members themselves. It could be and was presented in terms of a manoeuvre forced upon Stalin by the foot-dragging of the Western powers over military collaboration, as a way of avoiding been left isolated in face of a German military attack. In view of the reputation and record of the Chamberlain government and its clear unwillingness to get involved in serious military conversations with the USSR, this did not seem too implausible,[4] and of course the agreement to partition Poland was not made public. Party speakers explained it to the membership in terms of shop stewards being forced in unfavourable conditions to make stand-off agreements with the boss and it was presented as a refusal by Stalin to pull the Western governments' chestnuts out of the fire for them. Some party leaders acknowledged being impressed by Stalin's diplomatic finesse.[5]

It would seem fairly likely from what is now known of the events of the following two months that the British party leaders failed to appreciate the direction in which the Soviet wind was shifting. They saw in the Pact the Soviet Union safeguarding its own position but did not realise that this had serious implications for the anti-fascist struggle and did not see why it should have any basic effect upon what foreign communists were doing. In their eyes a decade of resistance to fascism was about to culminate in armed conflict since Hitler had double-crossed his Western confederates. Having no confidence in the Chamberlain administration and convinced of its fascist disposition, the party leaders' stance was for its replacement by a people's government which would prosecute the fight to military victory, possibly then in alliance with the USSR. Unawareness of the soviet change of line was also due in some part to the fact that communication with Moscow at the time was tardy and irregular.

There was nothing unlikely therefore about the party's initial reaction to the declaration of war, namely to define the conflict as the beginning of the road leading to the overthrow of Nazism provided that its prosecution was taken out of the hands of conservative reactionaries and fascist sympathisers identified with the years of appeasement. A pamphlet by Pollitt under the title *How to Win the War* was rushed into print.

In essence what happened at the end of September and beginning of October is simple enough. Broadcasts from Radio Moscow supplied an initial though ambiguous signal that the party was on a basically wrong track and they were picked up by the sensitive ear of Dutt. The Politburo was divided on its response, with the result that at the end of the month a Central Committee meeting was summoned to discuss the matter, during which an emissary, Dave Springhall, arrived from the Comintern headquarters with written instructions that the line must be altered. Following lengthy and impassioned debate during which insulting personal epithets were freely exchanged the inevitable decision was reached to bring the British party's stance into accordance with Soviet requirements and pronounce the war to be an imperialist adventure undertaken at the expense of the working class on both sides. Dutt as usual insisted piously that acceptance of Comintern discipline was not enough and the switch must be made out of conviction, without any refuge in private reservations. Gallacher accused Dutt of advocating policies in line with what the BUF was saying. Pollitt, Gallacher and Campbell maintained their view up to the end and voted against accepting the change, but all the other members of the Central Committee capitulated to the pressure, declaring in some cases that though they had begun the debate committed to the original policy they could not believe that the Comintern was capable of making a fundamentally wrong assessment and had been persuaded in the course of the discussion that the change was not only expedient but also correct.[6]

The Communist Party being what it was, and given the temper of its leaders' convictions, the outcome is not surprising in the least. What is more difficult to explain is the fury of the resistance that the three objectors put up, and to imagine how, with their experience, they could have hoped or expected to contradict the specific demands of the Comintern or to persuade the CC to support their dissidence. It does make clear, though, that however they had compromised themselves in the past with Stalinist malpractice, they were certainly not political hacks or mere apparatchiks, but people who retained their own standards of integrity within the context of the Stalinist monolith. Gallacher, who had asked that his vote be recorded with the majority and was an MP and public figure, escaped formal sanctions. Pollitt and Campbell were naturally dismissed from their posts and made in addition to sign humiliating admissions of error. A committee of three with Dutt in the lead was appointed to exercise the powers of the General Secretaryship and Rust reassumed the editorship of the *Daily Worker*.

There was for a long time a tendency to assume that the effect of the change in line was to shatter the morale of the party membership at large, to produce large-scale defections and to isolate it wholly from public sentiment. This is an assessment which at the least must be seriously qualified and is to some extent influenced by reading back into the circumstances of 1939 aspects of the party's career during the following two decades – none of which is to deny that what it did then was to figure eventually among the worst blots on its historical reputation.

For a start, although there is no way of knowing what would have been the opinion of the membership overall, there was certainly at least a substantial minority who, although kept by discipline from voicing any open objection, were unhappy with the original line and more or less enthusiastically welcomed the turnaround. There was therefore, quite apart from the rigorous political discipline which prevailed inside the party, no question of the new line being applied in any indifferent or halfhearted fashion, for there were plenty of zealots anxious to apply it with real commitment.[7] Establishing the actual numbers in the party at this time is difficult, for figures are ambiguous and confused further by the conscription of a number of members into the forces. Probably there was some decline but not a dramatic one. Recruitment undoubtedly continued and the circumstances of the war's early days were not unfavourable to the party's industrial activism in the same manner as the impact of World War I on the munitions factories had generated discontent and militancy. The CP avoided speech or action that was explicitly designed to sabotage the war effort,[8] in order to minimise the opportunities for legal action against it, but, while arguing politically in its journals for a negotiated peace, pursued the multiplying grievances and frictions on the shop-floor with all the energy at its disposal and organised, for example, a successful apprentices' strike, inspired by YCL militants on Clydeside in March 1941, over pay and conditions.[9]

Current recollections of people who were party members at the time conflict as to the extent of public hostility, especially in working-class milieux, arising from the line adopted in October, although most accept that it increased as a result of the party's unqualified support for the Soviet side in the Russo-Finnish war which broke out in December when Stalin used armed power to enforce rectifications in the border near Leningrad over which the Finnish government had been uncooperative.[10] The Soviet government did have a case and the Finnish rulers could be plausibly presented as fascists, so the episode probably did not cause undue strains within the party's own ranks – there is no evidence that it did at any rate – but it certainly increased its isolation from general public feeling. During the Popular Front years, a time when unity was being sought not only between British anti-fascists but also between the USSR and the Western democracies, the CP had muted, though never entirely discontinued, its attacks upon British imperialism and its iniquities. Its anti-imperialist propaganda was now stepped up again and readers of its publications were reminded that Indians suffered more from British rule than they did from German Nazism.

Any impression therefore that the party between October 1939 and June 1941 recognised itself, underneath its rhetoric, to be morally bankrupt or that it was regarded with universal abhorrence by patriotic British citizens must be discarded. The position should rather be seen in Hobsbawm's terms:

> There is something heroic about the British and French CPs in September 1939. Nationalism, political calculation, even common sense, pulled one way, yet they unhesitatingly chose to put the interests of the international movement first. As it happens they were tragically and absurdly wrong. But their error...should not lead us to ridicule the spirit of their action. This is how the socialists of Europe should have acted in 1914 and did not: carrying out the decisions of their International. This is how the communists did act when another world war broke out. It was not their fault that the International should have told them to do something else.[11]

The Communist Party at this juncture had a fair number of concealed members within the Labour Party who had joined it since 1935 and been told to remain inside so as to strengthen the CP's hand in seeking affiliation. They were now instructed to reveal themselves, and with few repudiating the CP they did so, often taking their whole local Labour organisation with them. The communists were also successful in getting the University Labour Federation to endorse their line, though at the cost of it being disaffiliated at once from the Labour Party, and Pritt, who assumed its presidency, being expelled. None the less, a conference of the National Union of Students shortly afterwards voted against the war.[12]

The period of the 'imperialist war' was one of mixed fortunes for the CP, by no means in the immediate term one of unrelieved disaster. Some of its actions were beneficial by any standards, such as when it assumed the lead in the campaign and direct action to have the London Underground stations used a bomb shelters against the resistance of reluctant authorities.[13] From the fall of France in May 1940 the theme of combating Hitlerism began to be re-emphasised, with stress on a 'people's peace' rather than the acceptance of Nazi victories and even a hint that the war would be legitimate if conducted by a 'people's government'.[14] The climax of its anti-government effort was reached with the People's Convention in early 1941 at which two thousand delegates, claiming to represent over a million workers, accepted a six-point programme including 'A people's peace that gets rid of the causes of war'.[15]

Cabinet records make it plain that the government was considerably worried by the implications of CP activities and did not regard them as an irrelevant pinprick[16] but feared that they might well be striking chords in popular feeling. Their suppression was discussed with some frequency, but banning the party would have necessitated the arrest of numbers of its members and leading figures working in war industry and this was regarded as likely to be more trouble than it was worth – which incidentally reflects on the government's perception of the standing of communists in the workplace. The party was, however, disarmed of its chief propaganda and agitational weapon when the *Daily Worker* was banned from publication and its premises seized in January 1941.[17] Ministerial discussions followed on outlawing other party publications, especially the leaflets circulating in factories, but again the difficulties of classification and the expectation of shop-floor trouble induced a policy of restraint.[18]

The party set up an underground apparatus for printing illegal copies of the newspaper and other material – one duplicated issue was produced just to demonstrate that it could be done. However, an elaborate printing operation based in London but with extensions in Manchester and Scotland was held in reserve for use if the party itself should be outlawed and the extremely dangerous enterprise of publishing an illegal forces' newspaper be undertaken. In the immediate term the still legal CP publications and *Industrial and General Information*, a bulletin distributed both to party members and to the commercial press, were relied upon. Although the ban on the *Daily Worker* was not lifted until September 1942 (during which the unpublished daily had the opportunity of building up its financial reserves), the Soviet entry into the war on 22 June 1941 and its rapid acceptance as an ally ensured that the underground network would not be required.[19]

Prior to that date, rumours of an imminent German attack across the Soviet frontier had not only been discounted by Stalin but also sharply denounced by the CPGB press castigating speculation about the possibility of Soviet support becoming available to the British side in the 'imperialist war'. Indeed an explicit statement from 1934, when a CP pamphlet, *The Labour Party and the War*, with some percipience imagining a scenario very like what actually happened in 1941, declared that in the event of a Nazi attack on the USSR the British party would 'in no circumstances' then support an Anglo-French attack on Germany. This was reaffirmed, and Pritt was writing in the *Labour Monthly* of June 1941 that: 'It is clear that the only way out of this very serious situation is for the working class to end the policy of "Coalition".' All the same, after 22 June both contemporary statements and subsequent recollections suggest that party members were overwhelmingly relieved that they were no longer obliged to swim directly against the mainstream national current and delighted that British labour was now linked through the Coalition government to the USSR in an all-out anti-fascist crusade.[20]

The energies which the party had hitherto directed towards impeding commitment to the war were now devoted to promoting it, and the CP entered the era of its greatest success and public credibility. Experience has shown in regard to the world communist movement that its parties after 1920 have enjoyed their greatest successes on occasions when they have been able to appear as the embodiments of national resistance to foreign conquest and enslavement – China, Vietnam, Cuba, occupied Europe – standing for both independence and social transformation. In a more modest degree it applied in Britain as well. For a few years it was possible to combine patriotism with communism. As the public mood increasingly embraced a vision of radical postwar social reconstruction as well as military victory, as the Red Army inflicted irrecoverable defeats upon the German war machine and cast a heroic glow upon bodies and individuals closely associated with it, the CP began to recruit as never before. By late 1943 its membership had risen to a little over 55,000, a tripling, or possibly quintupling, in only thirty months. (Some estimates suggest that it reached over 60,000 in the course of 1943.) Its international connection had at last become a positive advantage. The dissolution of the Comintern in mid-1943, decreed for the sake of Stalin's relations with his British and American allies, probably made very little difference to this one way or the other. The perspective of world revolution, moribund in any case for a long time, was of little moment in the light of the kind of world conflict which was then being pursued.

Not that the party became an altogether docile lapdog for the wartime authorities. Had it not continued to seek redress for industrial grievances and wartime dislocations – albeit now in a conciliatory rather than antagonistic mode – it could scarcely have hoped to expand its base and become embedded in the way it did among substantial sectors of the workforce, especially the transport and miners' unions and among the engineering factories, above all in the London area. It reflected, too – though there is no reason to imagine that explicit instructions were passed – Soviet dissatisfactions and irritations with the character of Anglo-American military policy. The party's most vociferous criticism of the Coalition administration up to June 1944 was for its tardiness in launching a Second Front in Europe to take some of the military pressure off the Soviet armies, and it organised much agitation and large rallies to this effect. In that respect, though, it was largely in tune with the public mood. It failed, however, in its renewed search for affiliation to the Labour Party, although this had looked like a realisable prospect in 1943. Even Herbert Morrison, who was also Home Secretary in the Coalition government and who had banned the *Daily Worker*, warned his colleagues that the pressure might be irresistible. But for memory of the party's record during the 'class against class' and 'imperialist war' phases it probably would have been, but in the event Morrison was able to win a decisive rejection at the Labour Party Conference of that year and the moment passed.[21]

Communist Party Congresses, suspended since the outbreak of the war, were resumed in 1943, at which gathering various organisational changes intended at the aborted 1939 Congress and subsequently applied were formally endorsed. Their overall effect, ironic in view of the CP's great industrial advances, was to shift the party structure much more towards one based upon residential branches capable of conducting electoral activity and away from the emphasis on factory groups, although those did not disappear. A profound change was occurring in the way in which the party envisaged its place in the British society of the future. Instead of deadly class enmity culminating in insurrectionary overthrow under the party's tutelage, political transformation, at least in the direction of socialism, began to be conceived of as possible by continuing into peacetime the class and party coalition which was fighting in alliance with the Soviet Union for the destruction of the labour movement's worst enemy. Again, while not out of step with the mood of the times in Britain, the ultimate rationale lay in the Soviet anxiety to continue on good terms with its wartime allies for the sake of their later reconstruction aid and to ensure that Western communists did not cause complications by any excess of revolutionary enthusiasm.[22] However much this may have contradicted the intentions of the CPGB's foundation, it nevertheless fitted in with the aspects of its development which drew it steadily towards its national labour movement and the political culture which infused it. Finally, under the impact of the Second World War's unexpected character the CP reached a position which it would always adhere to subsequently: in principle it wanted to join the mainstream. The question was whether it would be permitted to.

Accordingly, as the certainty of Allied victory drew closer, the Communist Party defined its standpoint. It came out in favour of the Coalition, trimmed of its more reactionary elements, being continued beyond the end of the war, and doubtless it hoped that it might become part of it.[23] It proved to be a very bad misjudgement and yet another cause for historical recrimination – if less dramatic than the previous ones – but it could not be said to have been in any sense unprincipled, for it would, if enacted, have corresponded to the British version of the Popular Front governments which took office throughout liberated Europe and probably led to results not very unlike those instituted by the Attlee government. As matters turned out, the party was forced to test its electoral strength independently and against its will in opposition to the Labour Party in the July 1945 General Election.

The outcome underlined all the disadvantages under the British electoral system of being a marginal party, even a temporarily well regarded one, at a point when enormous popular expectations were pinned upon the large and governmentally effective representative of labour and radical aspirations. The CP had an additional problem in that its swift growth had outrun its organisational ability to absorb its new members and integrate them into the party's culture and practices. In fact it was never able to exceed the figure achieved in 1943 and thereafter a decline set in, with membership in 1945 down to a little over 45,000. Although in retrospect the election results of 1945 look like the party's high-water mark, at the time they were a severe disappointment.[24] It put twenty-one candidates into the contest, winning an average vote of 5,000. Only nine saved their deposits. Harry Pollitt came a close second in Rhondda East and Phil Piratin in Mile End joined the party's sitting MP, Willie Gallacher, who retained his West Fife seat. Additionally, there were up to a dozen Labour MPs sympathetic to a greater or lesser degree and willing to work along with the party either occasionally or consistently. In the local elections that autumn the party made advances, ending up with over two hundred councillors, including two on the London County Council, but winning control of no local authority.

Whatever their domestic disappointments, British communists did not doubt that the wider world, Europe and Britain were all set for an epoch of progressive social advance in which they would fully participate. Fascism was to be extirpated. Communist parties were dominating or sharing in governments throughout Europe and had taken the lead in liberation movements in eastern Asia. A world trade union centre, the World Federation of Trade Unions, incorporating unions both inside and outside the Soviet sphere, had been established. The Labour government was committed to Indian independence, which might be expected to lead on rapidly to social revolution in the sub-continent. And as for Britain, it would be enabled to 'turn to the Socialist path leading to economic security, peace and world co-operation'[25] for which the CP would 'do its utmost to develop this unity and strengthen the organisations of the Labour movement and their active work in support of the Labour Government'.[26]

It took two years to become clear that there was no prospect whatever of these hopes being realised. International affairs were to take a very different turn and the CPGB was to be carried along upon their stream. The reforming intentions of the Labour administration are not in doubt, but this government and the state which it administered – including the military and civil service chiefs – was as committed as one led by Churchill would have been to maintaining the status of the United Kingdom as a Great Power, keeping most of the Empire and retaining a military establishment in line with these pretensions. A corollary of that status aspiration, as well as a source of material gain, was its determination to rebuild the City's enormous foreign investments liquidated during the war and to preserve sterling as a reserve currency in spite of the loss of overseas markets and a national debt quadrupled since 1939.[27]

In combination with the government's welfare and industrial reconstruction programmes it amounted to a crushing economic burden made sustainable only by an intimate financial and military relationship with the United States, itself intent on sustaining its war-generated economic growth by establishing a world economic and politcal hegemony. This project was confronted with revolutionary upsurges throughout the world following in the wake of the war, movements with which the Soviet government, on account of its traditions and perceived character, was obliged to identify with greater or lesser – usually greater – reluctance.[28] The USSR also had its own concerns in terms of security needs in Eastern Europe, matters which took priority even over the Kremlin's strong inclination to conciliate Washington for the sake of getting access to the latter's resources.[29] The breakdown of the wartime alliance and its collapse into two confrontational power blocs was implicit from the start of the postwar era in the antagonistic purposes of the superpowers. As their working relationship unravelled and developed into endemic hostility, Great Britain was accepted and welcomed as a willing and convenient junior partner for the United States which in turn was prepared to flatter the Great Power susceptibilities of the British with meaningless chatter about a 'special relationship'. Initially the primary concern of the Americans appears to have been directed towards the Pacific and Asia – it was what they had fought the war for after all – but Ernest Bevin played a substantial part in persuading them to raise their profile to challenge Soviet interests in Europe and the Middle East.[30]

It took time, however, for all that to become apparent. In the immediate term the CP did not have much quarrel with the domestic policies of the Labour government, the social deficiencies of which were as yet unrecognised, given that these initiatives were so much of an advance over what had obtained before the war. A repetition of the postwar situation following 1918 was not expected and did not occur. Nine million working days were lost in strike action between 1945 and 1950 compared with 178 million in 1918–23.[31] One issue which the CP did take up with some vigour, however, was the matter of housing shortages existing side by side with vacant properties. Party members were active in giving direction to and acting as spokespeople for the squatters' movements of 1945 and 1946, particularly in London.[32] The maiden speech of the new MP, Phil Piratin, dealt with payment for temporarily unemployed war workers and housing. It 'met with a good reception in the House'.[33]

Foreign and colonial policy was a different matter. The party's sharpest difference with the new government through 1945 was over Bevin's continuation of Churchill's policy of militarily suppressing the communist-led resistance movement in Greece in favour of a semi-fascist monarchy aligned with British interests. Churchill and Stalin had agreed in 1944 that Greece, strategically placed close to the Middle East, should be allocated to the British sphere of interest. Divergence, too, became more marked over colonial issues.

In November 1944 the CP's Executive Committee had issued an extensive memorandum under the title *The Colonies: The Way Forward* (excluding India) which did not fail to make a close comparison between the British and Tsarist empires and so emphasise the superiority of Soviet policy. The document conceded small merit to the Labour Party policy adopted in 1943 and accused it of ignoring the wishes of the colonial peoples in determining their own destiny. In the following two years the CP expressed its opposition to the government's anti-Zionist standpoint on Palestine (Moscow at that point favoured the establishment of a Jewish state) but did so much more vehemently regarding the course of events in Malaya, as here a fraternal communist party was the victim. As in Greece, wartime resistance to the occupier, in this instance Japan, had been led by communists. Representatives of the Malayan partisans had marched in the London victory parade in 1945 and their leader, Ching Peng, was awarded the OBE by the British government. In the face of the British determination to restore colonial relations in Malaya and retain control of its invaluable rubber and tin production the struggle escalated into armed resistance and full-scale guerrilla warfare which the British military countered without restraint or mercy.

Communist strength within the trade unions had benefited during the war not only from the popular regard in which the Soviet Union was then held but likewise from the forms of decentralised wage bargaining and Joint Production Committees which had inevitably supplemented government control of wage policy and which, comparable to 1914–18, had elevated the influence and importance of shop stewards, among whom the party was well represented.[34] To claim, as Henry Pelling does, that the CP by 1945 was within sight of having British industry under its control is a fanciful exaggeration,[35] but without doubt its successes had been great. Members were exercising trade union office in a great variety of sectors, including the major unions of the Amalgamated Engineering Union (AEU) and the TGWU, from which Bert Papworth, who had led the rank-and-file busmen, was elected to the TUC General Council. Communists by then were in tight control of the ETU and leading the Trades Councils in London and Glasgow. The apparent strength in this regard concealed nevertheless an underlying weakness in that the party officials in particular trade unions and the party-controlled unions in relation to the labour movement generally represented not so much the penetration and consolidation of communist values in the unions but rather people elected primarily for their personal qualities and standing, outposts in potentially hostile social territory – and who in the event of shifts in the political climate could very readily become isolated ones.

If British communists could take consolation, despite their own limited gains, from the advance of socialism and expanding communist influence throughout Europe and Asia, their situation, during the upswing of the Labour government, did present them with something of an identity problem. What should be their own distinctive role? It could not be confined indefinitely to offering 'critical support' for the government. It was self-evident that the strategy outlined in *For Soviet Britain* was obsolete but a good deal less clear what might replace it. Outlines of an alternative conception began to emerge in 1947 when the party issued a pamphlet written by Pollitt under the title *Looking Ahead*.

In this the Labour government is not yet quite written off,[36] (Gallacher declared in November that he was 'one who wants to see the Labour movement and the Government prospering in the great cause of socialism') but, according to the pamphlet, 'even within the Labour movement, sections of the old reformist leadership, fearing and hating the mass movement of the people, turn to Wall Street, that democracy of millionaires and Negro lynchers, and prefer to tie their countries to the US trusts...'[37] It was therefore incumbent upon the British working class to repudiate its treasonous leaders, for only by doing so could current national and international crises be resolved in a fashion which strengthened democracy and progress towards socialism. The precondition for this is for the working class to unite around a socialist policy and the principal theme of the pamphlet is the manner in which such unity could be attained. The model referred to was that of the postwar Popular Front governments in both Eastern and Western Europe, but more especially the former, where the communist parties were dominant. None of that was particularly surprising, but what was significant was the implicit recognition that in British conditions the existing constitutional forms would serve the purpose if only they could be given the right political content, and in the *Communist Review* of August 1947, shortly before Pollitt's pamphlet went on sale, Piratin was advancing suggestions for making the legislative machinery more efficient and responsive to popular feeling, 'bringing Parliament closer to the people'. There was no suggestion of course that all this constituted an abandonment of Leninism, though in reality it did. Finally, with the definitive rejection by the Labour Party of CP affiliation hopes, the objective of exercising leverage by building up a mass Communist Party independently of it was affirmed all the more strenuously. It was an important departure. For over forty years the basic features of this conception were to remain at the heart of British communist strategy.

A party author might refer in October 1947 to 'the urgent necessity, *and the opportunity*, that exist for the rapid building and strengthening of the Communist Party itself' (original emphasis),[38] but the storm that was about to batter the party and lose it most of its recent gains was already beginning to rise. Membership had in fact declined from its wartime peak to under 40,000 by the middle of 1947, a circumstance which reflected both the deteriorating image of the USSR and the competing attraction of Labour Party politics. It is worth noting all the same that it had not by any means collapsed and was still well over double the prewar figure. The obvious faltering of the Labour government during 1947, commencing with the economic disruption of the great blizzard in January and continuing through to the débâcle of sterling convertibility in July, and its steadily more evident subordination to American hegemony might have been expected to favour the CP and its energetic attacks upon those failures. Larger considerations, however, were in operation.

In the course of the year relations between the Western and Soviet blocs had all but broken down. In March President Truman had proclaimed the principle of US assistance to regimes resisting communist aggression, 'direct or indirect', with Greece and Turkey especially in mind, giving his name to the latest American 'Doctrine'. The initiative was followed by the renewed turning on for Europe of the US aid tap, previously shut off at the time of the Japanese surrender, under the title of the European Recovery Programme or Marshall Plan. It was intended both to forestall the possibility of economic crisis leading to greater communist influence in Western Europe and to tie those states more firmly to the US chariot. The Popular Front governments collapsed in both East and West as the two superpowers consolidated their hegemony in their respective security zones. Communist ministers were dismissed from Western European governments and independent non-communist ones treated still more brutally in the East, with the mixed Czech administration as the solitary survivor. The Cold War was underway.

In October 1947 Stalin created the Communist Information Bureau (Cominform) as an agency for co-ordinating the intransigent propaganda offensive against the West now judged to be necessary. Its membership consisted of the communist parties in power (with the exception of Albania) and those of France and Italy. It published a journal whose

singular title was, in English, *For a Lasting Peace, For a People's Democracy!*
The Western European parties which were not members were kept in
liaison by the two which were; in the case of the CPGB the PCF was
responsible for maintaining the contact. The Cominform at its inaugural
meeting defined the thesis of the 'two camps', the democratic anti-imperialist versus the imperialist anti-democratic. The Soviet bloc's ultimate
response to the Truman Doctrine made it plain that parties and labour
organisations would have to choose between them and moreover that
their support for 'anti-imperialist democracy' would have to be expressed
in deeds as well as words.

The CPGB thus found itself pitched into the front line of the Cold
War conflict and confronted with the necessity for even further intensification of its attack upon US stooges in the British movement. The
Labour leadership was now denounced for craven subservience to the
dictates of Washington and Wall Street. 'There is nothing in common
with socialism in what the Labour Government is doing' declared
Pollitt,[39] and the party gave greater currency to terms such as 'class
enemy' but also placed growing emphasis on the sell-out of British
national interests, the acceptance of a burdensome rearmament
programme at US behest and the obnoxiousness of the American
takeover not only in the diplomatic, military and economic spheres but
in the social and cultural ones as well. The CP did its best to inflame
spontaneous anti-American resentment among the British population
and to focus upon the objectionable behaviour of US service personnel
whenever the opportunity offered. In accordance with this line it propagandised with all its might against the Marshall Plan and, more
concretely, used its industrial strength and trade union influence to
obstruct the implementation so far as possible. Since the Plan was
widely and popularly viewed as an economic lifeline, this was not
likely to evoke an enthusiastic response among the workforce or to
enhance the party's credibility, already suffering on account of the
USSR's international behaviour.[40]

Worse was to follow. In February 1948 the Czech communists,
acting almost certainly on Soviet instructions, used their state and trade
union power to throw out their government partners and liquidate the
last surviving Popular Front administration. A few months later war
between the two camps seemed imminent when the Soviet occupation
authorities in Eastern Germany blockaded the Western sector of Berlin,
deep inside the Soviet zone. The height of that crisis had scarcely
passed and the Allies' Berlin airlift stabilised the situation when total
rupture occurred between the Kremlin and the communist government

in Yugoslavia. The latter had been the outcome of the popular support the Yugoslav communists gained in partisan warfare against the Germans. In fact Tito had crossed Stalin in 1945 by insisting on the installation of his government and refusing to share power with non-communist elements as Stalin, still seeking Western co-operation, had wanted.[41] In the circumstances of newly liberated Europe, however, even he had been obliged perforce to contain his irritation and accept the presentation of the Yugoslav communists as his most loyal allies. The breach in 1948 was provoked exclusively by the Yugoslavs' unwillingness to subordinate themselves totally to Soviet requirements and permit the control of their state apparatus by Soviet personnel.

The CPGB unhesitatingly lent its energies to broadcasting the Cominform version of all of these developments, although some of its individual members were less enthusiastic in regard to Yugoslavia. It sacrificed allies in the left of the Labour Party as well, many of them attracted by the notion of a non-Stalinist communist regime. They included Konni Zilliacus, the most effective critic in the Parliamentary Labour Party of Bevin's conduct of foreign affairs. Past relationships and political closeness on other matters did not save these people from being stigmatised as class traitors and dupes of Trotskyist-fascists, which is how the Yugoslav leaders were portrayed. Further discredit fell upon the CP when Stalin's response to the Yugoslav defiance was to stage a re-run of the Moscow Trials. This time Eastern European communist leaders suspected of possible Titoite sympathies appeared in the dock, beginning with Hungary in late 1949 and ending with Czechoslovakia in late 1952. Once more British communists had to disgrace themselves with vituperation of former role models and add their venom to the death sentences inflicted by the People's Courts upon veteran communists with records as Spanish War heroes and Occupation resistance leaders.[42]

It is scarcely surprising that as the party's identification in political and media discourse as a major domestic enemy was compounded by its own grotesque and absurd behaviour, the overall effect was to alienate all the sympathy or tolerance which it had acquired since 1941, to strip away its less committed supporters and to drive it into deep isolation. Cases of espionage in the atomic weapons laboratories and later the diplomatic service, for which the party was not responsible, inevitably tarred it also in the public mind as the agent of the Soviet fiend, which had become the national enemy, the source of all political evil, and without whom the Second World War would have been succeeded by an era of harmonious and prosperous international felicity. No day went by without the exposure in one press organ or another of some fresh communist iniquity, mostly abroad, as would be expected, but not infrequently in Britain. Communist trade unionists acting on Kremlin orders were blamed for bringing the British economy to its knees, communist schoolteachers for indoctrinating their pupils. Two members formerly in high party offices, Douglas Hyde, the news editor of the *Daily Worker,* and Bob Darke, a trade union official and local councillor, left the CP and published sensational revelations about both its subversive character and its internal regime.[43]

The times were opportune for a counterattack by the party's enemies in the trade union movement to nullify as much as possible of the advances it had made since the mid-1930s, and in this they were assisted by the state so far as legal provisions and constitutional practice allowed. The attack upon the CP coming from government and trade union establishment quarters was the most severe it had encountered since its very early days, surpassing in fury what it had been subjected to even during 'class against class'. The TUC General Council, which had in 1948 persuaded its member unions to accept a wage freeze for the greater success of the Marshall Plan, encouraged them to take steps making communists ineligible for union office. Several hastened to respond, most importantly the TGWU, which had nine communists on its Executive Council of thirty-four. Arthur Deakin, who led the union, a forceful personality like his predecesor Bevin, was able to induce the union conference to accept the exclusion of communists from any official position, resulting in the removal of the nine on its executive, including Bert Papworth, who also thereby lost his TUC General Council seat. Clerical and civil service unions did likewise. Attempts were made to institute similar moves in the engineering union, the AEU, but although communists did not control this organisation they were well enough embedded within its machinery and with enough rank-and-file support, in spite of the Cold War, to be able to frustrate the intention. Unions in which communists were so strong as to be invulnerable and which were in fact controlled by them were the electricians, the foundry workers, the firemen and the Scottish and Welsh miners.[44]

Government lent its assistance by a constant anti-communist propaganda barrage and by purges of party members and sympathisers in the civil service regarded as having access to delicate information. Strike action in sensitive industries, even when the product of simple grievance over a wage freeze in an inflationary period, was attributed to communist subversion and conspiracy. To counter unofficial strikes in the docks, led by rank-and-file committees upon which communists were naturally active, and which government, trade union chiefs and the Dock Labour

Board accused them of inspiring, the Cabinet resorted to wartime anti-strike legislation, prime-ministerial broadcasts and the mobilisation of troops to unload the ships.[45]

Paradoxically, the virulent hostility directed against it and the persecution and harassment which its members endured brought the party gains as well as losses. In the first place the wartime access of members, the growth to nearly the dimensions of a mass party, did not fit well with the CP's structures and character. In the course of its evolution it had grown accustomed to its small size and its organisational apparatus and habits were adapted to this fact. It had been a party of activists if not zealots and this feature made it possible for it to employ a disproportionate number of full-time officials relative to its ordinary membership, since no greater honour existed than that of being a professional revolutionary and they did it for minimal wages. The CP had grown accustomed to working in this manner and it meant, certainly, that the membership was exceptionally well serviced, but the party could not expand its staffing *pari passu* with its new influx. Accordingly, its capacity to maintain contact with its recruits, to integrate them into the party culture and provide them with 'party training' was degraded, a state of affairs intensified in any case by the conditions of the war.[46]

While the growth was occurring Pollitt had warned against alienating the new members by subjecting them to excessive burdens of party work. The 'obligatory minimum' was the payment of dues and these were based upon the principle of a *weekly* subscription (though it was possible to pay in advance). The party therefore acquired a penumbra of inactive members whose membership consisted only in holding a party card and making payments for dues and publications on the occasions when they were visited, while the shifting emphasis from factory- to locality-based units further emphasised that problem. Correspondingly, a greater proportion of the energies of branch officials (and higher ones, who were expected to do their share) was consumed in the Sisyphean labour of keeping the dues payments at a satisfactory level, with regular checks conducted upon District percentages. The persecutions and ideological contortions of the Cold War years did not have serious effects upon the more committed membership – there were scarcely highly placed or celebrated defectors over Yugoslavia, for example – but the fall-out of weaker adherents, while not eliminating the inactive penumbra, reduced it and enabled the party to concentrate its resources.

Secondly, the party, as it was beset from all sides and turned into a pariah, tended to respond by closing ranks and asserting more determinedly its beleaguered political identity. The discrimination and attacks were serious enough to make its members feel their need for solidarity and mutual support, but, lacking the fury of the United States witch hunt, not savage enough to cripple it as an organisation as happened to the CPUSA. For all the international setbacks of 1947 and 1948, with communists being evicted from government office in Western Europe and robbed of an expected electoral victory in Italy, with the dramatic assertion of US military and economic power, with the schism in the socialist camp, British communists still had much with which to console themselves and maintain their morale. Socialism continued to advance, and here the success of the Chinese revolution in 1949 cannot be overstressed, with the most populous country in the world joining the Soviet bloc. The insurrections in Greece, Malaya, Indo-China, Indonesia and the Philippines remained unsubdued and it was at that point far from certain that Anglo-American strategies in Europe would actually work out. In *The Case for Communism* published in 1949 – by Penguin Books – Willie Gallacher could write:

> The capitalist world system is finished. A large part of the world has already been liberated and in what remains the grave-diggers of capitalism, tens of millions strong, are applying themselves to the mission of ending the rule of exploitation.[47]

Gallacher's book contains a chapter on the Communist Party and provides some insights, though they are not enormously revealing, into the party's internal culture as it then was. As it happens, the nature of the CP community at that time has attracted more written commentary than for any other stage of its history. The two contemporary exposés already mentioned reach a highly pejorative evaluation, not surprisingly, while Raphael Samuel, writing in the 1980s, treats it in a positive or even romanticised manner.[48]

Even though the International had by then been dissolved, communism remained an international movement *par excellence* and as yet directed (apart from the Yugoslav anomaly) from a single centre. A member of the CPGB was therefore instantly in tune with another communist from any part of the world and acquainted through party education at least in outline with the problems they would be facing. They would also be connected by a bond of comradeship motivating them to offer to the other any help or assistance that could be provided. Someone has remarked that the Comintern was a sociological phenomenon unique in history in terms of the degree of voluntary obedience that it was able to exact from its adherents, and in terms of common perceptions among communists matters had not changed at all following the organisation's formal dissolution.

Anyone who joined the Communist Party in the late 1940s was embracing a secular church and enlisting in a political army. Unmistakably religious language might be used – Pollitt was fond for example of invoking 'the vision splendid' – but military terminology also abounded in the party jargon – campaigns, battles, fortresses, camps, discipline, featured constantly in its rhetoric. For a communist, next to commitment to the party and the international movement, discipline was the supreme virtue, indeed it was inseparable from the commitment. The CP saw itself not so much as the representative of the class conscious and politically advanced workers as the instrument for fulfilling their revolutionary destiny. Communist organisations had no time for constitutional nit-picking and only the total absence of that practice enabled its over-elaborate structure of committees and communication channels to function with any efficacy. The committees and meetings, however unduly multiplied, existed to get things done, even if much of what went on in them was expressive rather than functional behaviour. 'Talking-shop' was a term of abuse in party discourse, and standing orders, let alone their manipulation, were virtually unheard of.

The Communist Party undoubtedly regarded itself as a community of the elect and its internal community links were exceptionally strong, comparable to those of fervent religious groupings. Its members, or at least the committed ones, were likely to conduct their social and cultural activities as well as their political ones in the company of other communists. Members were expected to recruit their partners if these were not already members and to induct their children into Socialist Sunday School, the Woodcraft Folk or the Young Communist League. Strong friendships across party lines were very rare. Party or front organisations were available for recreational activities such as hiking and branches organised weekend entertainments, usually termed 'socials', for their members. In cities where conferences or congresses took place party members as a matter of course provided accommodation in their own homes for the delegates. In London and Glasgow the Unity and Citizens' theatres were effectively controlled by the CP.

Communist publications were prodigious in quantity. It was of course the only political party in the country which ran a daily newspaper. Legally speaking, the party was no longer the paper's sole owner, for in 1945 ownership had been transferred to a co-operative body, the People's Press Printing Society (PPPS), in which shares, which carried only one vote regardless of quantity, were available to any individual or organisation. The double intention had been to broaden the CP's appeal in the postwar climate of unity and to raise capital for a much more ambitious quality of newspaper. There was no pretence, however, that the PPPS was not under rigid party control. Although the Management Committee which contained a few non-communists nominally appointed the editor, the appointment was made in fact by the Political Committee (as the Politburo was renamed), of which he was invariably a leading member. The first editor under the new dispensation was Bill Rust, who would almost certainly have been Pollitt's successor had he not died unexpectedly in 1949. Rust was an able editor, and although he saddled the undertaking with a press that was inevitably underused, the circulation shortfall was as much due to government newsprint restrictions as to any lack of quality in the product.

The *Daily Worker* was certainly in easier circumstances after 1945 than it had been at the time of its foundation, with the lifting during the war of wholesalers' and newsagents' bans. However, it shared the general daily newspaper problem that cover price came nowhere near to covering costs, and one of its own in that it could attract very little profitable advertising. The answer was a 'fighting fund' to which readers were constantly prodded to make donations, supplemented by Christmas bazaars and collections at party meetings and rallies.

Other literature, published directly by the party, which owned a printing business of its own, Farleigh Press, catered for all tastes and covered every level of complexity. Its weekly journal was entitled *World News and Views* and there was in addition a monthly, *Communist Review,* dealing mostly with political questions but occasionally covering scientific and cultural ones as well. *Labour Monthly,* the personal responsibility of Palme Dutt, who had founded it and continued to edit it until his death, occupied a unique position and authority. Although, given the person of its editor, it never deviated one iota from the party line (except later when the party line was becoming critical of aspects of Soviet policy), it aimed to be identified as more and other than a CP journal, so sympathetic non-party contributors were diligently sought in its columns. They were mostly but not exclusively drawn from the labour movement and included personalities like George Bernard Shaw, but its really significant feature was the editorial, called 'Notes of the Month', usually written by Dutt himself, on which party activists placed enormous reliance for summing up the trend of domestic and international affairs. The Labour Research Department, despite its name, was likewise a wholly-owned subsidiary of the CP and published a valuable statistical compilation, *Labour Research.*

In December 1945 the party commenced to publish a theoretical journal, *Modern Quarterly*,[49] which, given the paper restrictions of those years was a surprisingly expensive-looking production. Its contributors were drawn from both inside and outside the CP and it sometimes allowed disagreement and argument to be expressed in its pages, as during the 'Caudwell controversy' about the posthumous philosophic and literary writings of Christopher Caudwell, a party intellectual killed in Spain. Overall, despite the due proportion of Stalinist panegyric, much of what this journal printed still makes interesting reading. The same could scarcely be said, except in a pathological sense, for the English-language journals dealing with life in the Soviet Union or other members of the bloc, produced in those countries, for which the party was the main British outlet.

None of this includes the ad hoc or specialist publications which individual party organisations issued, such as those of the Historians' Group. Nor does it cover the innumerable pamphlets on themes from Dialectical Materialism or economic planning to *Women and the World Today*, not to speak of the translations of Marxist classics produced in the USSR in either pamphlet or book form. Every self-respecting branch appointed a literature organiser whose responsibility was to keep members supplied with the basic publications and as many others as they could be persuaded to buy, in addition to the fact that in the major cities the party also possessed its own bookshops. It owned a publishing house as well, Lawrence & Wishart, which at that time brought out not only works of political or social commentary but also novels, unhappily never very memorable, by party authors.[50]

It is hardly necessary to state that although it shared many features with sectarian religious groups the party was the very opposite of introverted. On the contrary it was a militantly proselytising organisation conducting frequent membership drives. Although in their social intimacy and deeper levels of communication party members might fully relate only to each other, they were expected and required by the purposes of their party to engage all the time with outsiders and try to win them for particular CP objectives and campaigns, even when not potential recruits. This was to be done on an individual basis, certainly, 'on the knocker' or street or through social contacts in workplace or community, but more importantly in a collective manner, through all the organi-sations in which the party sought to entrench itself. This was what was known as 'mass work' and at trade union branch or tenants' committee the party member would 'give a lead' or if necessary 'take a principled stand' – something required more frequently as the Cold War deepened and hostility mounted. In the endeavour to extend mass appeal there was substantial pressure upon party members, especially prominent ones, to present a sober and reticent personal style, be models of family and communal propriety and avoid eccentric habits.

It was the inescapable fate of any party activist to spend a high percentage of his or her time in attendance at committees. In the party itself these extended from the branch through Areas, Boroughs and Districts to various specialist committees connected with particular interests or party groupings within wider bodies. The party committees at least, for the reasons explained above, were expeditiously conducted and not too much given to time wasting. Also requiring to be staffed were the committees of bodies which the party did not formally control but were effectively part of its apparatus, such as the various friendship societies linked to the USSR and the Eastern European states. With the onset of the Cold War the party began to devote itself to campaigning for peace and international concord, with the USSR presented as the champion of peace, sanity and national independence, and the United States as aggressively bent on world conquest. From 1948 a plethora of committees were established around this activity for which party members again had to take principal responsibility as well as conduct the petitioning drives among the public, such as the Stockholm Peace Appeal of 1950 which collected a million and a half signatures and considerably disturbed the government.

Beyond all that, party trade unionists, unless prevented by bans and proscriptions, could hardly avoid getting elected to positions of unpaid responsibility within their union organisations, which meant more committees in addition to the ordinary union membership meetings, at which of course they were the most conscientious attenders – not to speak of party caucuses inside the union bodies. It is not surprising that willing members found their non-working time totally consumed in CP-related (including union) duties. Aside from branch, committee and educational meetings, party rallies and public meetings, union and peace meetings, 'showing the face of the party' on door-to-door canvasses, street newspaper sales, possibly even street-corner meetings, demonstrations, poster parades, the loyal activist would have organising and paperwork duties arising from all of the foregoing.

It added up to a regimen that was possible only to sustain by a quasi-religious faith, which like other faiths achieved some of its purposes by the inculcation of personal guilt – for no matter how much you did you always felt guilty for not doing still more; nobody was able to be quite the perfect militant. Those who got nearest to it were the people occupying the highest party offices, and above all its full-time organisers. The CPGB was part of a national culture which was in its deepest nature hierarchial, authoritarian and sexist, and on top of this inherited the ultra-authoritarian and centralist traditions of the Comintern. Party leaders expected deference and received it, their experience and position were assumed to guarantee the correctness of their political judgements. Their mystique ensured that there was never any problem in achieving acceptance of the line or the tactical prescriptions for implementing it. They were figures of awesome, almost mythic, authority, the masters of the science of Marxism-Leninism; not merely the interpreters of the past, present and future but the engineers of history as well.[51] The hail of rank-and-file criticism orchestrated by the Comintern against the British leadership in 1929 would have been unimaginable twenty years later. However, the nature of the communist ideology and community meant that they were deferred to not in respect of their own persons but as embodiments of the party's collective will. It would have been unspeakable bad form and ultimately a matter of political censure if they had displayed arrogance, hauteur or prima donna tendencies. On the contrary, except in political leadership, they were the most modest and self-effacing of women and men.

Between 1947 and 1950 matters for the CP were bad enough. In the General Election of February 1950, with the party fighting 100 seats, the vote collapsed and both Gallacher and Piratin were defeated, ending for good the CP representation in Parliament which had been sustained for twenty-one out of its first thirty years. Upon the outbreak of the Korean War in June things got much worse. The party had no hesitation in taking up the Soviet position that the South Korean forces had begun the fighting and provoked the North's invasion – and it must be said that the argument is not quite so absurd as it was made to appear at the time. The party openly supported the North Korean side and the *Daily Worker* correspondent Alan Winnington reported from behind their lines.[52] British soldiers were now involved in a shooting war against a communist state – a more serious matter than the guerrilla struggle against the Malayan communists – and the party was driven into further isolation and membership loss, even more of a public enemy than it had been up to that point.

But even as the party was being more and more stigmatised as the domestic agent of an enemy power, the saboteur of national prosperity and apologist for totalitarian dictatorship, other currents were drawing it more closely towards the political mainstream or at least stimulating its own endeavours to get there. From the point of view of the USSR the first phase of the Cold War, though not without its setbacks, had worked out successfully in general. The bloc, with the exception of the Yugoslav escapee, had been consolidated and Western attempts to break it up or intimidate it frustrated. Although Stalin had disapproved of Mao's drive to power, the Chinese revolution had brought a temporary access of prestige to the Soviet Union as its protector. Wartime devastation had been repaired without having to rely upon Western assistance, and atomic weaponry acquired in spite of the Americans. Overall, the Soviet Union was in a considerably stronger position *vis-à-vis* the West in 1951 than it had been in 1945. Consequently Stalin had less need of what in 1945 had been a more significant asset to him, namely the Western parties, and for them the conception of differing national roads to socialism, one of the chief crimes in the indictment against the Yugoslav party, could be quietly instituted.[53]

It has long been appreciated that the Soviet leadership was closely involved in encouraging the British party to become constitutionalist in its aspirations. George Matthews has recently made clear the extent of the involvement and the fact that some of the new programme's key points were virtually formulated by Stalin.[54] However, in prompting the British party in this direction the CPSU was recognising and the CPGB giving way to the underlying logic of the latter's development since the first adoption of the united front tactic in 1921, for all the wrenching traumas of the two great reversals in 1928 and 1939.

Later on the party was to discover, truthfully enough, that these conceptions were implicit in Harry Pollitt's *Looking Ahead*, though mistaken in claiming that they represented a novel redirection of the party's oulook. One chapter of the pamphlet had been called 'The British Road to Socialism', and this was the title adopted for the new programme whose draft the Executive issued in 1951. A certain irony attached to the commitment to achieve the socialist revolution by using parliamentary tactics in view of the party having just lost its parliamentary representation. Naturally it did not renounce extra-parliamentary methods and industrial struggle as contributing to the process, but these were now accepted as secondary rather than primary elements of communist politics. Soviet Britain, a dead letter in any case for many years, was quietly laid to rest. John Callaghan notes[55] that no far-reaching prior discussion took place to reorientate the party before the draft appeared, rather implying that the rank-and-file once again accepted whatever they were told by their superiors, no matter how drastically it contradicted what they had been told before. It seems more reasonable, however, to suggest that the new line was adopted without any great furore because it fitted in with what had increasingly become the common sense of the party since 1941 if not 1935.

In a few isolated quarters there was opposition to the redirection and resistance to the fact that the last programmatic shreds of Bolshevism were being discarded, but the new programme was endorsed without much trouble or hesitation at the party Congress of 1952. The irony was perhaps underlined by the fact that between the draft and the Congress the party had once again fought in a general election and this time, concentrating on only ten candidates, done proportionately worse even than in 1950, losing every deposit. Though disagreeing with almost every judgement expressed in Henry Pelling's account, it is hard to resist his verdict in this case that: 'It was a miserable outcome for a party which only seven years before had been expecting to play a prominent role in post-war Britain.'[56]

4 Watershed : 1951–1957

The Communist Party might have drastically revised its outlook in 1952, or, rather endorsed, without really recognising or acknowledging, what had been a molecular process continuing ever since its formation, but this fact had few or no implications for its internal forms of organisation or the internal culture in which its members participated. Once more the character of the party as an institution lagged behind its policy perspectives, a pattern which had been evident in its previous history and which was to continue to the end.

It was indeed these practices and ways of living politics, far more than formal objectives and programmes, which gave the CP its distinctive character and made it at that time unique among political organisations in Britain. The hope of ever realising its original objectives might have grown so remote as to have become merely nominal, but it still continued to attract recruits by means of the concrete activities which it carried on and, once they were socialised to the party's norms, to serve for them as the alternative universe of political understanding, social behaviour and personal relationships which was the party's real strength and the basis for its reproduction as an organisation.

Following the various shifts in organisational practice and administrative terminology during the previous twenty years, a regular style had evolved which was to prove relatively permanent thereafter. The basic unit was the branch, consisting of two sorts, industrial and residential.[1] The move towards an electoral and parliamentary orientation had led to a growing emphasis and attention being given to the residential branches, and these were far more numerous, but the industrial ones were nevertheless regarded as very important and, though constitutionally equal, probably attracted in the mind of the ordinary communist greater respect and prestige. Branches, residential or industrial, could start at any size, but for residential ones twenty members would have been regarded as small and a hundred as very large. The average was around fifty.

The Secretary, who had to combine the functions of a political leader and all-round administrator, was the central figure in the branch, as was the case through all the levels of the hierarchy. The branches were

91

grouped into Districts, which could be large geographically, for example Scotland or Wales, and numerous in membership, with a figure of 8,000 or more in Scotland or London. By contrast they might be very small, such as Middlesex, or minuscule, like Devon and Cornwall. The larger ones employed a full-time staff, starting always with the Secretary and sometimes half a dozen or more in their central offices. Like the branches, the Districts were a constitutional component of the party and entitled to send delegates to the National Congress. In 1952 the latter adopted a standard cycle of meeting biennially, with District Congresses in the intervening years. District Committees, like the Executive Committee elected at National Congresses, counted as 'higher committees', i.e. their decisions were constitutionally binding upon party members and organisations within the District. They had of course to operate within EC policy and guidelines.

There were plenty of other committees, some with greater authority than the ones mentioned, but none had the status of higher committees and in a constitutional sense all were advisory committees. The crucial ones were the Political Committee, formally a sub-committee of the EC, but in fact the directing organ of the party. The same relationship was imitated in the Districts, where the equivalent of the Political Committee was termed the Secretariat. The likelihood of the larger committee rejecting the advice it got from the supposedly subordinate one was virtually nil, and only in the event of a split within the inner grouping would the latter exercise any real authority.

Larger Districts were likely to be divided up into Borough or Area groupings of branches. The directing committees of these groupings, too, were technically advisory, but, especially where they covered a numerous membership (say 500 upwards), had a great deal of practical responsibility. In the larger ones, too, such as Manchester or Glasgow, the structure of congress (in this case termed conferences), committee and inner group (here known as Executive Committees) was reproduced. Even the YCL operated a mini-version of the same procedure right down to Area level, though party officials sometimes expressed the view that this was going a little too far and that the YCL ought not to be a miniature CP. Big areas, Glasgow and Manchester again are examples, but sometimes medium-sized ones as well, even employed their own full-time staff. A rough estimate suggests that the ratio of members to full-timers was about 500 to 1, not counting *Daily Worker* employees, or those working in CP-linked enterprises.

Committees also existed which were specifically termed advisory committees. They varied greatly in importance and might merely exercise co-ordinating functions and supply outline guidance for work by members in the fields of culture, science or history. On the other hand, those for particular industries or for students were the party's eyes and ears in those fields and essential for the formulation of publicity and strategy – or caucus activity in the trade union sphere.

In 1952, after experimenting with a more open style the party had reverted to the panel system of electing its leading and Area committees. Congresses were stopped by the outbreak of war, that intended for September 1939 having to be cancelled. Upon their resumption in 1943 the panel method was not used and open voting was employed.[2] The result was somewhat embarrassing, for it was the best-known and high-profile figures from the party centre or in the news who got elected, and the resulting committee lacked representation from some geographical or occupational areas, which obliged the new Executive to resort to co-option to secure a more representative committee. After a couple of years, therefore, a modified panel form was reinstituted; a recommended list was presented to the delegates but was followed by a ballot upon all the candidates. In 1952 the ballot was discontinued and the Congress simply voted once again by show of hands for or against the complete panel, but in 1954 the ballot was brought back again.[3] Perhaps the thing most worth noting about all these changes is that the discipline of the party and control of its congresses was such that it did not make one iota of political difference which method was being used and probably not a lot of organisational difference either.

The binding element which tied together all the political and organisational strands was less the party's vision of a socialist Britain – though that was not unimportant – than its relation to the existing homelands of socialism and most importantly the USSR – developments in relation to which ultimately determined its policies, its practice and its standing among the British public. So long as Stalin lived, that relationship was one of unqualified subordination in everything, not only political questions. During the late 1940s he had decreed within the Soviet sphere an offensive against any influences which might be suspected of undermining Russian (not just Soviet) cultural hegemony. It was the era of claims to Russian precedence in all forms of scientific and technological discovery. It resulted not merely in political show trials but the intense persecution of Jewish culture and lifestyle under the stigma of 'cosmopolitanism'. It culminated with Stalin appointing himself supreme judge upon not only political, historical and cultural matters but scientific ones as well. The agronomist Trofim Lysenko used his political connections to advance his own eccentric notions of genetics and get them decreed as scientific gospel in the USSR. His critics and upholders of orthodox Mendelian genetic science were purged.

Whether because they received instructions or because they themselves felt that a display of solidarity was required, the British party leaders, despite their lack of scientific competence, publicly endorsed Lysenko (persuading George Bernard Shaw to join them in this)[4] and tried to make geneticists who were also party members put their names to the pronouncement. The upshot was the scientists' general alienation and the withdrawal from all participation of one of the CP's major scientific luminaries, Professor J.B.S. Haldane. In a novel departure, however, he was at least allowed to express his dissent in the party press.[5]

The party's response to the Tito break and the show trials of the late 1940s has already been noted. The Trials did not, however, cease with the stabilisation of the blocs in the early 1950s, and the last began in late 1952 with the leaders of the Czechoslovak CP in the dock. The British party once again applauded revolutionary justice, although the main defendant, the Czech General Secretary, Rudolf Slansky, had been a personal friend of John Gollan,[6] who after the death of Rust was emerging as Pollitt's most likely successor. James Klugmann, under the heading 'Lessons of the Prague Trial', wrote that,

> The use of labour spies and agents provocateurs against the Labour movement is as old as the battle of capital against labour...Slansky was able to place his men – Trotskyists, bourgeois nationalists, Zionists, agents of foreign intelligence – into hundreds and hundreds of key positions in the Communist Party and in the machinery of State. ...once again their efforts to turn history backwards will only allow it to move forwards with even greater speed.[7]

That issue of the *Communist Review* appeared in the month of Stalin's death, a grimly appropriate coincidence. The expressions of sorrow throughout the party were unquestionably sincere and many spontaneous tears were spilt at memorial meetings, although the printed tributes can now be read only with embarrassment. *Labour Monthly* was probably the most florid:

> The architect of the rising world of free humanity... the soaring triumphs of socialist and communist construction; the invincible array of states and peoples....
> After nearly six decades of tireless theoretical and practical activity and political leadership, rising from height to height of achievement and from triumph to triumph...

. If millions and scores of millions in every country of the world mourned the death of Lenin, hundreds and hundreds of millions have mourned the death of Stalin.[8]

The level of illusion in which the party leadership was capable of indulging comes across if anything more clearly in an article by John Mahon – 'New Perspectives for Unity in the British Labour Movement' – in the *Modern Quarterly* of autumn 1953:

Thousands of workers are also becoming aware of the quite different experience of the People's Democracies... such a society can solve problems which our Labour Movement has been unable to solve... the new policy and programme being put forward by the British Communists [is] winning increasing support among wider and wider sections.

Or in the following:

The challenge of the day is the deep desire of the labour movement to move forward to socialism.[9]

In fact the party was striving to convince its audience at this point that the basic material position of British workers was deteriorating thanks to the demands and policies of the American overlords, though masked, it was conceded, by a full employment which was not expected to last very long. In terms of factual judgement rather than moral stance it proved to be the most wildly mistaken assessment that the party ever made.

In actuality, once the initial shock occasioned by the Korean War and rearmament had been surmounted the British economy entered into the most sustained and untroubled four years of growth that it has experienced in the course of the twentieth century. In the main it was carried upwards upon the tide of a postwar boom but its own temporary relative strength – there were no balance of payments crises between early 1952 and late 1955 – owed something also to Marshall Aid and the austerities which the postwar Labour governments had enforced. With conditions such as these promoting expansion in most industrial and all service sectors labour shortages became manifest, leading to exceptionally favourable shop-floor bargaining opportunities – as well as the official encouragement of labour immigration from the Commonwealth. The coercive anti-strike legislation inherited by Labour from the war and used by it during its period of office had been repealed. There now set in a long era of rising wages, only partially sustained by

official union negotiation and equally dependent on the wage drift
brought about by unofficial bargaining or action in individual enterprises
and for which unofficial strikes were the cutting edge.

In its policies of economic management the Conservative government
elected in 1951 acted, after only the briefest hesitation, according to a
thoroughly labourist philosophy,[10] giving ear much more readily to TUC
lobbies than to Federation of British Industries ones. The same was true
of its handling of the welfare system. Contrary to widespread expectations upon the left, this government did not set about dismantling the
welfare state; instead it maintained what was already in existence and
had found it a worthwhile election pledge to undertake the building of
even more houses than the Labour government had, most of them
council ones. Significantly, the term 'Butskellism' was coined at this time
to describe the general consensus prevailing between the two front
benches on economic and social policy.[11]

In one respect, certainly, the party could not fail to benefit from these
developments. Its shop stewards and rank-and-file militants were in the
forefront of the wages advance, especially in the industries like engineering where it was traditionally strong. The media paid its tribute by
persisting in blaming communists for being the root cause of industrial
militancy and responsible for the deterioration in international com-
petitive edge which was observable even in that heyday. The workers
who ended up with bigger pay packets as a result of the activity of their
communist representatives naturally saw it differently, though that did
not make them any more inclined to vote for communists in *political*
elections. The CP's function as a wages bargaining force and a communication network for industrial militants was correspondingly
strengthened during these years and the unions where elective offices
were open to its members saw a strengthening of their position.

In spite of this asset and despite the programme elaborated in the *British
Road*, the party was theoretically and politically adrift. Its failure to grasp
the reality of what was happening to the British economy and society
permitted it to develop only the most abstract notion of what a socialist
Britain might actually involve, modelled upon the existing socialist states,
and an even more schematic one of how to get there. Along with rising
material prosperity, the consolidation of the blocs and the growing integration of Britain and Western Europe into American dominated
structures were a sign that the era of revolutionary upheaval in Europe
was at an end.

All the same, in view of its history and conditioning the perspectives
which the party advanced in the early 1950s were, however unrealistic,

the only feasible ones available to it. No form of a leftist course would have been credible in the face of improving economic and social circumstances, and, given the incapacity of the party to embark upon any imaginative exploration of contemporary reality, the idea of uniting the labour movement to escape from American clutches and then extending the postwar government's nationalisation and welfare measures as the first stage towards overthrowing the power of capital was probably the best it could have done. So long as Bevan was a member of the Labour cabinet the CP had attacked him with as much vituperation as it had his colleagues, if not more, because his left-wing poses were perceived as hypocritical.[12] After his resignation and assumption of the leadership of an organised Labour left in opposition to the Labour Party establishment the tone grew much more friendly and communist-influenced trade union votes were aligned with those of the Bevanite left at Labour Party conferences. The party had begun to try to reopen the bridges to the Labour Party which had been drastically narrowed after 1947–8, but it imagined no left-wing realignment in which it would not play the dominant role.

With domestic politics comparatively free of crisis, the CP concentrated much of its energies and propaganda upon foreign and colonial affairs. There was plenty to keep it occupied. The Korean War did not end until 1953 and the delay to its conclusion by the retention of Chinese POWs in the hands of the Americans made a significant cause for agitation. The Malayan guerrilla war was prolonged into the 1950s before the communist forces were overwhelmed, and the *Daily Worker* attracted especial hostility for its exposure of the atrocities committed by British troops, above all when it published in 1950 a photograph of a soldier holding the severed heads of two Malayans, one of them a woman. A similar colonial conflict with an opposite outcome was going on at the same time in Indo-China where the communist-led Vietminh were fighting the French. Elsewhere, in the outposts of the British Empire military force was employed to repress popular dissidence or insurgency of a Marxist or more commonly nationalist sort: 1952 in Kenya, 1953 in British Guiana, 1954 in Cyprus.

The CP did whatever it was able to in its campaigning around those issues and frequently co-operated with colonial liberation committees and groupings in Britain which were not simply party fronts. The main publishing event for the party in this period was Dutt's large volume *The Crisis of Britain and the British Empire,* and the CP's own specific contribution was to trace all these developments ultimately to the aggressive intentions of US imperialism and its command of the lesser imperialist satellites such as Britain or France. The party was in no doubt that the USA still intended war and was preparing the ground for an attack, an expectation which the development of the hydrogen bomb and insistence on rearming the emergent West German state seemed all too likely to confirm. 'Peace' therefore remained a high priority for the party by linking together all its international concerns in terms of both security for the Soviet bloc and objection to what Western military forces were doing to Third World peoples. According to Palme Dutt, 'Ban the Bomb' was being used as a slogan as early as 1950; certainly he was quoting it in 1954.[13] The party did its best to connect the theme of peace with that of national independence, focusing upon the presence of US military bases in Britain, drawing attention to American capitalism's displacement of its British rival and casting US hegemony as a surrogate for the role fascism had occupied in the days of the Popular Front.

It has to be acknowledged that most of what the party said about US ambitions, NATO and the practices of colonial warfare was actually well founded, but, as Callaghan observes, it was hard to take seriously rhetoric about national independence from a party which so evidently subordinated itself to an outside source of authority. But even in this respect some of the traditional pillars of its temple were beginning to shake if not yet to topple. An anti-Soviet revolt in East Berlin in June 1953 might be dismissed as CIA incitement and the execution of the Soviet security chief and Stalin acolyte L. Beria on charges of treason might be wholly within normal Soviet practice. None the less it did not need a particularly acute observer to realise that the growing emphasis on collective leadership, rapid reduction in the prominence of Stalin's name and the abandonment of the purge he had been preparing, together with the admission that its intended victims had been framed, all implied a tacit scaling down of cardinal aspects of the late regime. Finally in 1955 Khrushchev and Bulganin journeyed to Belgrade and repudiated publicly all the Cominform charges against Tito, the Cominform itself being wound up in the same year. A hint can perhaps be seen in Willie Gallacher's review of the ninth volume of Stalin's collected works in which he treats the author with relative sobriety; the furthest limit of his praise is to call it a 'truly great volume'.[14] James Klugmann reviewing the twelfth volume at the end of the year was almost equally subdued.[15]

The CP leadership was only too conscious of the party's isolation and political insignificance, re-emphasised at the 1955 General Election and every round of local elections, and plainly evident in Dutt's strained efforts to assert the contrary.[16] The 24th Congress, which met in April 1956, was designed to launch a drive for labour unity and reconnect the CP to the Labour rank-and-file, with the avowed intention of shifting that party leftwards. Accordingly, although Labour leaders were denounced as fiercely as ever, left-wingers like Zilliacus, even when sharply critical of the CP, were addressed with relative courtesy. Pollitt called upon the labour movement to rally round it a broadly based popular opposition to the government, and although there was felt to be no point in pursuing yet again the quest for Labour Party affiliation – 'We cannot go back to the past,' said Dutt – the Congress, calling attention to the need for 'mass united action of all the forces in the Labour movement to defeat the Tory offensive now',[17] demanded the removal of bans and proscriptions preventing members of the two parties from working together.

How realistic the party leaders actually thought this to be is a matter for speculation. As a political tactic it represented probably the best available of a very limited range of options. Possibly they anticipated that improvement in the public image of the USSR and the strength of communists in industry – which, it was hoped, was increasing – combined with a drive to advance the party membership, at last beginning again to show a slight upward turn, to 50,000, could exert a meaningful pressure. Dutt pointed out with relish that the Labour Party leaders had lately been approaching union general secretaries, some of whom were communists, for additional funding. He went on to ask, 'Recognising that the inheritance of the past will not be overcome in a day....Why not try to co-operate?' Although it would be 'idle phantasy' to imagine that conditions were ripe for settling the long-term future relations of the two parties, it was essential to advance the initial steps 'to the final aim of a united political party of the working class', and Dutt expressed his confidence that the good sense of the working class and profound desire for unity would prevail in the end over forces of division.[18]

Dutt mentioned, although only to dismiss it, the incongruity of the suggestion of unity between the 'fly and the elephant', given the respective strengths and standing of the two organisations. All the same it is possible that if the CP had stayed united and if the Khrushchev reform process in Eastern Europe had proceeded smoothly, the 24th Congress might have been the beginning of something important. As it was, it became irrelevant almost before the delegates had reported back.

The 20th Congress of the CPSU had been held in February, with Pollitt, Dutt and George Matthews attending as the CPGB fraternal delegates. On the final day, 25 February, with the foreign visitors excluded, Khrushchev delivered the sensational secret speech, revealing for the first time in an official Soviet context some of the criminal activities of the Stalin regime. The three British delegates may or may not have been provided with a summary version, but immediately rumours of its content began to filter out even before the publication of the full text by the US intelligence services in June. The code term, 'cult of personality', which had been used in the open sessions of the 20th Congress, was in public use at once, and the effect of the speeches there was to provoke a stream of questioning letters to the *Daily Worker*. Some of these were published, but as early as 12 March J.R. Campbell, the editor, declared the discussion to be closed. Five days later the official rehabilitation was announced of Laszlo Rajk, the chief victim of the 1949 purge trial in Hungary.

The commercial press certainly expected ructions at the party congress in late March but in the event the growing concern and alarm was confined to a private session during which sharp argument occurred. To the outside world the CP presented a united front, with a unanimous vote on the main political resolution and no publication of the critical speeches which had been made in the closed session. The party leadership was beginning to display the reaction which in one sense or another was to characterise its proceedings in subsequent crises involving the malpractices of the Soviet regime or scandals within its own organisation. Instead of the previous blank refusal to admit any fault, and pretence that the new turn was implicit in the previous direction, there was now the presumption that the party should formally acknowledge error and pass on to next business as though nothing much had happened. In addition, when the development or relevation was to the discredit of the USSR, there was strong suggestion that to discuss it overmuch would be an unfortunate distraction from urgent tasks needing to be addressed upon the British scene.

By that point, however, the cascade of discontent had become unstoppable. In April Pollitt tried to defuse it by publishing an article which, without acknowledging its source and without particular details, summarised the Khrushchev report and shortly afterwards, 'within the context of [Pollitt's] own narrow, unimaginative and basically sectarian assumptions', tried to analyse how Stalinism had come to dominate the USSR.[19] The following month Palme Dutt added fuel to the controversy, in the same article on labour unity as quoted above, by smugly declaring: 'That there should be spots on any sun would only startle an inveterate Mithra-worshipper.' The remark was not merely grossly insensitive but impudent as well, for that was exactly what Dutt and his colleagues had been for a quarter of a century. It provoked such outrage that in the following number of *Labour Monthly* he was compelled to apologise, so far as Dutt ever did so, and piously deny that he wanted to foreclose such discussion: but then, attempting a balance sheet of Stalinism, he tied himself only into even tighter knots of contradictions and incompatibilities.

In the same month Pollitt resigned as General Secretary on genuine grounds of ill-health and was succeeded in his office by John Gollan. Meanwhile, in one of the party's major working-class strongholds dissidence had turned into outright revolt. Lawrence Daly was one of the party's most promising cadres (leading activists) in Scotland. Not only was he a young miner of exceptional energy and abilities but he was based in Ballingray, Fife, close to the former 'Little Moscow' where a communist MP was a recent memory and, in spite of the collapse of its parliamentary vote, the party remained a living institution in the community, absolutely dominated the miners' union and still elected several local councillors.

Daly, a member of the Scottish District Committee as well as secretary of his trade union branch and former chairman of the Scottish NUM youth committee, announced in the press his break with the party, but he did not move into the Labour Party, dominated in West Fife by an extremely corrupt establishment. Instead in March 1957 he formed his own organisation, the Fife Socialist League (FSL), insisting that it *was* a political party. Daly, in explaining his action, denounced the CPGB for its subservience to the CPSU, displayed in the fact that it was now blackguarding Stalin as readily as it had formerly worshipped him, without any squaring of accounts regarding its previous behaviour. He emphasised in addition the CPGB's political impotence, noting that it did not control so much as a single parish council and had no hope of ever receiving the confidence of the British electorate. He proved that he was not an isolated voice when the FSL won seats against sitting communist councillors and Daly and his supporters defeated them in union elections.[20]

The developments in West Fife occurred independently of the better known upheaval involving academics and literary figures within the party. In this case the original centre of dissent was located in Yorkshire. John Saville, a lecturer at Hull University, and Edward Thompson, an extramural tutor in Leeds, exasperated by what they saw as blockages on discussion being maintained by the party leadership, began putting out their own publication in July as a means of ventilating the issues that were being smothered in the party press. 'If the British CP was to recover its self-respect, let alone the respect of the labour movement in general, it must encourage an honesty of discussion that would, undoubtedly, be painful to many.'[21]

They called their publication *The Reasoner*, after an early nineteenth-century radical periodical, and subtitled it 'A Journal of Discussion'; on the masthead was the phrase from Marx, 'To leave error unrefuted is to encourage intellectual immorality.' The editorial declared that:

> These discussions have revealed deep disagreements on the very meaning of 'Marxism': the presence of grossly irrational and authoritarian attitudes intermingled with claims to a 'scientific analysis': the hardening of theory into dogma, of socialist education into indoctrination: the absence of a clear common understanding, indeed at times of any common terminology, on fundamental questions of democracy, political morality and party organisation.

Two main articles appeared in the initial number, the first a critical examination by Ken Alexander of the CP's basic organisational principle of democratic centralism, from which he concluded that 'the linking of the ideas of authority and leadership has to be replaced in our theory by the concept of democratic control and initiative'. In the other, E.P. Thompson derided the pontifical reply George Matthews had made to a discussion piece by Thompson which had earlier appeared in *World News* and he confessed himself 'frankly appalled' at what Matthews had written on the question of morality. The number also printed material from the United States CP, including an acknowledgement of the extent of anti-semitic persecutions in the USSR.

By publishing independently the two had stepped outside the acceptable limits of dissent, although they had tried to avoid this, being committed party members, by setting up their own journal, 'addressed to members of the Communist Party', instead of taking their arguments into the non-party press. From the leadership's point of view, however, their action constituted a flagrant breach of democratic centralism. Publications outside the framework of the party hierarchy were totally unacceptable, although the culprits argued that there was no specific rule to this effect and professed themselves willing to discontinue publication if adequate official channels were provided for the necessary discussion, or alternatively to bring *The Reasoner* into the official framework if it were allowed to continue to fulfil its function. From the Executive's standpoint unofficial publications, apart from disrupting party unity, violated democratic rights because only members with access to the necessary resources would be able to initiate them and others would be disenfranchised.[22] There could therefore be no possibility of

securing consent for *The Reasoner*'s publication and no agreement on
the alternative proposal as that would constitute an admission by the
Executive that it had previously curbed discussion – something scarcely
to be expected. John Saville notes, however, that while the dispute was
in progress relations between the party leadership and themselves
remained courteous and civil.

There could be no meeting of minds. The dissidents stood their
ground on the moral and political crisis; the leadership used constitutional or legalistic argument. All the same, by the standards of past practice
the leadership showed extraordinary patience and indulgence. Instead
of the instant expulsion that would have once been their penalty,
Saville and Thompson were merely instructed at the September meeting
of the EC to desist from publishing the journal. The previous day they
had brought out a second number, which reflected in its content the
enormous correspondence, most of it sympathetic, which the first had
provoked and which made clear that the unease and need to reassess
communist politics felt by the editors and their immediate collabora-
tors was being experienced throughout wide sections of the party
membership. Meanwhile the leadership, regretting 'serious mistakes and
grave abuses' under Stalin,[23] had at last decided to bow to the storm to
the extent of announcing a special conference of the party – though
without decision-making powers – to debate all the controversial
matters at issue, and had appointed a commission, including known
dissenters on its membership, to examine the operation of internal
party democracy.

Saville and Thompson were still thinking of their project in terms of
reshaping the Communist Party. They had decided to produce a third
issue of *The Reasoner*, for which they must expect to be disciplined, but
to cease publication after that since they felt that the argument over their
right to publish was coming to overshadow the substantial matters at
issue. Still within the party context, they proposed to contest their anticipated expulsion or suspension and Saville, although with growing dis-
illusion about the nature of party structures and the character of its leaders,
was writing to sympathisers urging them to stay inside and work for
reforming principles: 'one should be prepared to accept defeat for the
time being and continue to fight in perhaps less spectacular ways,
always taking the long view...with Poland, Yugoslavia and the Italian
party, our party here is going to find it increasingly difficult to remain
unaffected'.[24]

The armed uprising against Stalinist rule in Hungary at the end of
October and its suppression by Soviet military force at the beginning

of November transformed this situation. The final issue of *The Reasoner* appeared with an article by E.P. Thompson under the title 'Through the Smoke of Budapest' which began: 'Stalinism has sown the wind and now the whirlwind centres on Hungary.' The editorial, dated 4 November and composed even as the fighting was raging in Budapest, demanded that the EC publicly dissociate itself from the Soviet action and called on CP members to condemn the leadership if it failed to do so. It also indicated that the appearance of a new journal was in prospect. For this the editors were suspended from party membership for three months, again in terms of precedent an astonishingly mild sanction, but, concluding by now that the CP was unreformable, they resigned.

The crisis which had been accumulating in Eastern Europe since the Poznań riots (during which 'We want bread!' had been the dominant slogan) had evoked all the ancient reflexes of the leadership and the party majority. During October Soviet intervention in Poland was averted only at the eleventh hour and when it occurred in Hungary instinctive identification with the Soviet regime prevailed. While it looked as if an accommodation might be reached between the Soviets and the reform communist government of Imre Nagy which the revolution had put into power, the *Daily Worker* hesitated and acknowledged that the revolt had a popular basis. When after a temporary withdrawal the Soviet forces moved back in and in the course of a ferocious bloodbath crushed the emergent new regime, the *Daily Worker* stopped printing the dispatches from its own correspondent which exposed the realities and instead discovered that the popular movement had been taken over by US-inspired elements and fascists emerging from the woodwork. As the Soviet attack was beginning the British party's EC met in emergency session and after an impassioned debate declared its support for the intervention, considering that 'the new Hungarian government and the action of the Soviet Forces in Hungary should be supported by Communists and Socialists everywhere'.[25] There was a subsequent claim that the Political Committee (PC) was divided and that opponents of the intervention even had a majority, but this has never been substantiated and George Matthews, who was a member of the PC, strongly denies it. Certainly, according to a witness, the outcome of the EC debate was never in any doubt.[26]

The first effect of the Hungarian tragedy upon the CPGB was to polarise intensely the differences which had been evolving over the previous eight months. Saville and Thompson were only two of very many who now resigned; the stream was expanding into a flood, among them some of the party's most eminent trade union luminaries.

They included John Horner, of the Fire Brigades' Union (his namesake, the veteran miner Arthur Horner, stayed), Jack Grahl and Leo Keely from the same union, Les Cannon of the ETU and Alex Moffat of the Scottish NUM (though he soon returned). In all some 7,000 members departed in the course of 1956. No less serious for the party's long-term prospects, a comparable haemorrhage occurred in the Young Communist League. The offices of the *Daily Worker* saw the resignation of between a third and a half of the editorial staff; these included some of its key personnel, the features editor and the cartoonist among them.[27] There appears however to have been only one resignation of a full-time *party* employee, Donald Renton, an Area official in Edinburgh. An unknown but not inconsiderable number accepted the leadership line with the gravest misgivings, believing on balance that the preservation of the CP as an organisation and what it stood for took precedence over their own reservations and that since the leadership was unbudgeable there was no alternative to submission.

The second effect was to combine the polarisation with a reactive self-defensive instinct among the majority of members. The response to a threat, and to what was coming to be perceived as the uninhibited onslaught of enemy class forces, was to close ranks around the leadership. John Saville has cited as one of the secondary reasons for closing down *The Reasoner* the increasingly bitter personal hostility being directed against its editors. When early in December a group of dissidents published in *Tribune* and the *New Statesman* a letter, refused by the *Daily Worker*, criticising the position taken on Hungary they received from Gollan an uncompromising rebuke and threat:

> At its last meeting the Executive Committee considered your action in publishing, in company with other members of the Party, a letter in the non-Party press attacking the Party.
>
> It instructed me to write to you and inform you that such an action is unpermissible and will not be tolerated in future...the Party cannot and will not give you the right to go outside the Party and make public attacks upon it.[28]

Responses from discussions in the party organisations suggest that the Executive had a clear majority, whether out of sentiments of loyalty or agreement with its line. Out of 332 branches making a report, 240 supported the EC, 69 opposed and 23 were undecided. Voting figures were available from 188 of these and showed overall figures of 2,095 for, 745 against and 301 abstentions, figures giving an average attendance at the branch meetings in question of 17 members. Area aggregate meetings returned voting figures of 1,029 for, 295 against and 89 abstentions. On committees, not surprisingly, support for the leadership was more unqualified, with overall numbers of 167 in support on Area committees as against 8 opposed and 7 abstaining, while in the District committees it was 291 for, 32 against and 17 abstentions.[29]

In one significant respect, however, the Executive had given way by December, in elevating the status of the intended National Conference into a Special Congress with decision-making powers and scheduled to meet at Easter 1957. It was to deliberate upon a fresh draft of *The British Road to Socialism* which had been prepared by early December and the reports produced by the commission on inner party democracy and finalised around the same time. The former represented an updating of the existing party programme but, beyond a mention of peaceful co-existence, made no reference at all to the Soviet bloc, let alone suggesting that there were any implications or lessons to be drawn from the revelations and events of 1956 which could be applied to the advance to socialism in Britain or the role of the CP. The inner party democracy report was an altogether much more explosive document. The composition of the commission which was to prepare it had marked a startling departure from all previous practice for, in order to obtain a spread of views, it included people who were appointed on the basis of their known discontent with the prevailing regime.

This estimable concession to democracy, however, was more than counterbalanced by the fact that the commission was overwhelmingly made up of full-time party officials, both central and District, no less than ten out of fifteen.[30] In a party with its biggest membership component composed of industrial workers and which emphasised its working-class credentials on every possible occasion, only one was an industrial worker. The commission had to do its work between September and mid-December, had no time for any detailed investigation and took no verbal evidence, not even from party leaders or officials. It therefore tended to concentrate upon general principles rather than the realities of how they had been concretely applied. It was also certain that the views of the established leadership would prevail. The agenda and discussions were structured by the commission's secretary, Betty Reid, of the Central Organisation Department, and it was chaired by John Mahon, the Secretary of the London District and member of the Political Committee. Malcolm MacEwen, who had been appointed as a critic and resigned as *Daily Worker* Features Editor as noted above, has written that Mahon 'did not see his role as leading an investigation:

he saw it as securing the defeat of the "revisionists" who were critical of democratic centralism'.[31]

The other two entrenched dissidents were Christopher Hill and Peter Cadogan. Together with Kevin Halpin, the sole industrial worker, they demanded a specific investigation of the manner by which the British party had been induced to follow the Cominform line on Yugoslavia; the control of the party press since the CPSU 20th Congress; and, on the question of the recommended lists for EC elections since the reinstitution of the panels system, what changes had ever been made between the original suggestions of the retiring PC and the final slate of candidates. These proposals were rejected by the majority. In the eyes of the three irreconcilables the full-time members of the commission acted throughout as a caucus whose objective was to secure the perpetuation of the existing tightly centralised system with minimal changes, to present it as basically sound and requiring only fractional adjustment. The three intransigents also concerted their efforts as a caucus. Caught in the middle were the two remaining members, Kevin Halpin and Joe Cheek, a teacher. They were brought around to signing the report prepared by the full-timers in the end, although both attached reservations, as did Harry Bourne, one of the District full-timers. Cadogan, Hill and MacEwen, having failed to get any accommodation with their viewpoint, wrote an alternative minority report.

The EC not surprisingly accepted the majority report and recommended it to the forthcoming congress, although in a further gesture to democratic norms they also attached the minority report and circulated it 'for information'. The majority document reaffirmed the need for a disciplined centralised structure not departing in essentials from what was already in use and with no more than cosmetic alterations. It denied, in the teeth of manifest reality, that the party leadership was self-perpetuating, disingenuously pointing out that every Congress delegate had the right to a secret ballot vote for whomever they wanted to elect. It was disingenuous, too, in asserting that democratic centralism simply replicated the principle of minority subordination to the majority and lower committee to higher, universal throughout the labour and democratic movement, but then became intellectually incoherent in trying to show that the forms of democracy operating elsewhere in labour organisations were unfitted for the CP. The majority did concede that the system's practice had been overcentralised in the past but confined themselves to exhortations to leaders and leading bodies to behave better in the future. The system was perfectly satisfactory, it was argued, so long as members participated actively in making it work.

The minority report was written principally by MacEwen. It opened by expressing the belief that 'the Commission has failed to discharge the task given to it' and controverted every one of the principal arguments used by the majority, concluding that whatever democratic centralism might be it certainly was not democracy. Although accepting that a degree of centralism was unavoidable it demanded 'a proper balance' between the two and insisted that the principle of compelling members to 'fight for' policies in which they had no confidence was counter-productive and self-defeating.

It is probable that the leadership would have had a safe majority at the Special Congress even if it had taken no special steps to ensure that one was obtained. But of course it did and the machinery of the party as much as the force of argument and persuasion was employed to ensure as far as possible that oppositionists were not elected as delegates. Members normally inactive whose loyalty could be relied on would be canvassed intensively to attend the relevant meetings. Beyond this, the leadership's task was assisted by the fact that not all branches were sufficiently large to be eligible to send a delegate: delegates were allocated by ratio to branch size. Consequently branches were frequently joined together for the purposes of electing delegates, and since it was the District committees who decided which branch should be yoked with which, there were extensive possibilities for juggling the distribution so as to ensure the return of loyalists.

The commercial media, as in 1956, predicted a catfight at the 25th Congress and this time they were not to be disappointed. It convened between 19 and 22 April in Hammersmith Town Hall amid burning antagonisms and recrimination. Harry Pollitt, who had been elected party Chairman upon his retiral as General Secretary, was sufficiently recovered from his illness to chair it, and did so with exemplary fairness. He showed no partiality: he did not have to, the party structures saw to that.

As was customary, the major proceedings opened with the General Secretary's political report. In spite of the fact that the Congress had been summoned on account of a nearly unprecedented crisis in the party, Gollan discoursed at length on the problems of international peace and the arms race, the condition of the British economy, the iniquity of the Tories and the inadequacies of the Parliamentary Labour Party. Even when he proceeded to the CP he spoke at length in general terms upon its role in British politics and relations with the Labour Party. Finally reaching, two-thirds of the way through his address, the questions which were currently agitating it, he declared of Hungary: 'It was a tragedy these events could take place. It would have been a bigger tragedy if reaction had won.' On Stalin, 'the actual form in which the distortions of Socialism arose was due to Stalin's personal character', but 'Political power was in the hands of the people' and 'we must also see his great services to the revolution'. 'Revisionism' was defined as the principal problem and danger for the British CP and must be repudiated 'in the first place to achieve the course of development for the British working class put in this report'. The dissidents would never flourish as Marxists outside the party because 'Historical circumstances have created the party organisations of the British working class… There is no such thing as Marxism without the Communist Party.' He called for rejection of the minority report.

It would, however, by dwelling upon the text of the political report, be all too easy to create a misleading impression of personal cynicism on Gollan's part. Entirely lacking Pollitt's platform charisma, he conveyed in public an appearance of nervous intensity that was almost painful, and his near chain smoking undoubtedly sprang from the same source. Coming from the Edinburgh working class, he had joined the party in the late 1920s, impressed by Willie Gallacher, and had received in 1931 a six-month prison sentence for distributing anti-war material among the soldiery. Subsequently National Secretary of the Young Communist League and Scottish Secretary, his energy and organisational ability had made him Pollitt's obvious successor in spite of his nerves. Though not emotionally stirring in the same manner as Pollitt, he came to be regarded with great affection among party members. The political report was of course not his sole responsibility but a collective document discussed exhaustively in advance among the leadership. Its mendacity was not Gollan's but that of the Stalinist reflexes which were the party's inheritance.

Mahon's opening on the split commission reports lacked even as much substance as had been contained in Gollan's. From start to finish it consisted of nothing but rhetorical irrelevancies and denunciation, addressing none of the material points at issue and touching only upon one of any interest. This was a piece of statistical information to the effect that the 401 branches which had nominated candidates for the EC about to be elected had had a total attendance of 3,152 at their nominating meetings – barely a seventh of those entitled to be present and giving an average attendance of eight members at each meeting. He wound up by reminding his audience that: 'The eyes of friends and enemies alike are fixed on this Congress… Our enemies hope that our Party will turn away from the tested principles of Marxism-Leninism, because they want to see it weaken. They will be disappointed', and expressed confidence that 'the joint activity of our members, our Branches and our leading comrades will give the working class a Communist Party capable of leading it to victory'.[32]

Malcolm MacEwen had not been elected as a delegate to the Congress. Christopher Hill spoke on behalf of the minority report, which, in a rather petty piece of censorship, since non-communist reporters were also in attendance, was not reported in the *Daily Worker*. He put his finger on a basic, if not *the* basic, flaw in the CPGB project: 'We have lived in a snug little world of our own invention.' His defeat was of course certain and overwhelming, by a factor of twenty to one. The reaffirmed principles of democratic centralism were applied promptly when the recommended list for the new EC was placed before the delegates, for the one dissident who had emerged on the EC itself, Brian Behan, a building worker, was dropped. Minority viewpoints were explicitly and deliberately excluded: a higher committee was not a representative body in that sense, it had to be a politically united collective.

It is hardly to be doubted that the leadership who steered the Congress and the delegates who cast their votes really believed that they were acting in the only way possible to keep the party unified and effective, and presumably they hoped that when the echoes of 1956 died away the party could go on as before and that, moreover, it could rebuild and extend its strength and influence. Although the losses had been numerically severe, they had not been catastrophic and the leadership were determined to continue with the policy they had begun to develop since 1951 and had been preparing to take to a new stage from the 1956 Congress before the trauma of that year overtook them. In closing, Pollitt urged the party to put the past behind it and to get down to 'mass work', the panacea for difficulties of ideology or policy. The immediate effect of the 25th Congress, however, was to accelerate the pace of resignations, for many who had continued to hold their cards in the desperate hope that the Congress might somehow bring about a change in direction now gave up.

For the party, the numerical size of the loss was not its gravest aspect. Much more serious was the fact that the people who had departed included some of its most energetic and imaginative talents in both the trade union and the intellectual spheres. With Daly's action and subsequent career – he became Secretary first of the Scottish and then the British NUM – its influence among the Scottish miners was severely shaken, although some of this was to be later recovered. The departure of certain ETU leaders was to have even more serious repercussions in due course. The resignation of many of the CP's intellectual luminaries made a greater public impact at the time and the loss was irrecoverable. The emergent New Left movement was not solely the creation of the ex-party members, but they did a great deal to set its direction in its formative phase. The Historians' Group — although it survived and historians of the highest calibre like Dobb, Morton and Hobsbawm remained within the party ranks — was fractured and never again so dynamic as it had been. The degree of loss can be measured by the fact that the ones who left, especially Hill and Thompson, were later to be central influences in reshaping the character of a rather stagnant traditional British historiography.

No less serious was the profound choice that the party had made to reaffirm the essentials of its Stalinist traditions. In terms of the automatic endorsement given to every act of Soviet policy this was the most public outcome. Once again the CP had accorded greater priority to its place in an international movement dominated by the USSR than to a possible independent stance based, not on grounds of national self-sufficiency, but the plain evidence that there was something profoundly wrong with a Soviet regime that had in the past systematically abused the good faith of its foreign comrades, to put it no more strongly, and was continuing to do so. Secondly it had chosen to adhere to internal methods and practices which were part of the same Stalinist evolution, which ensured that the party would remain within a political straitjacket and its internal life be stultified. In doing so it passed by a unique opportunity to become a different sort of political formation and one more in tune with the reality of the social environment in which it had to operate. Both these choices ensured that the CP would remain peripheral to the British political culture.

The possible alternative future, however, for all that many CP members hoped passionately during 1956 that it could be brought to birth, was no more than an abstract possibility. Marx's comment about the dead generations weighing like a nightmare on the brains of the living was all too apposite in this case and to imagine realistically that the party as a whole could have been capable of changing direction at this time is illusory. Unquestioning identification with the workers' state and attachment to the discipline which characterised the communist elect was the bedrock of conviction for too many members. In the unlikely event of a leadership majority having decided to denounce the Soviet action in Hungary and to scrap the principles of democratic centralism, they would have been repudiated by the majority of the rank-and-file, rallied by the traditionalists on the EC. The leaders may have been political despots, but only within the framework which was claimed to make their despotism necessary. As much as Khrushchev himself, the British party leaders were compelled to steer a tight and difficult course, manoeuvring between the impact of new and overwhelming realities which made nonsense of traditional belief, the responses of the disillusioned, and the believers who just did not want to know. Their course kept the ship afloat, but only at the expense of steering it into the doldrums.

It was symptomatic of the choices made that the following year, 1957, Gollan negotiated with the Soviet governmemt (possibly with Khrushchev directly) a secret deal for replacing the funding lost as a result of the resignations. The loss was not only of the standard dues and payments of approximately 10,000 members, but those who left also included people who had donated generously for many years to CP finances. For the next twenty-one years the Soviet Embassy clandestinely handed over large sums, amounting in some cases to £100,000 per year, which were laundered into the appearance of anonymous donations and used to finance the *Daily Worker/Morning Star* and other party activities. Only three individuals, it seems, knew of what was going on – Gollan himself, Reuben Falber, the Assistant Secretary, who handled the money, and David Ainley, the Secretary of the PPPS. The practice ended only in 1979 (though the sums involved were reduced in the 1970s) after the party made a substantial profit on the sale of its King Street premises.[33]

There is no evidence that the subventions affected CPGB policy on other than minor matters, such as blocking an invitation to the Soviet dissident Zhores Medvedev to address a party-organised discussion. They none the less fatally compromised the party's integrity. It was one thing, as had happened during the 1920s, to take money from the Comintern when in principle the CP was a section of a world party and the resources of any part of the International were available to any other part. It was another to accept secret funding from a foreign government at the same time as proclaiming its absolute political sovereignty and intemperately denying any such connection. Had the dishonesty been exposed, as at any time it might have been, it would have inflicted damage worse than that of 1956. It was an unbelievably stupid action as well as a corrupt one.

The traditional strengths of the party, though badly impaired, still remained, however, and could be utilised for regrowth. Just as unforeseen circumstances in the wider universe had struck it in 1956 with the force of a political hurricane, changed circumstances were soon to allow it a new lease of life. All the same, the choices made in 1956-7 were to be ultimately fatal, like a virus slowly multiplying in the organisation's blood-stream. It is not too fanciful to see the remainder of the CP's history as representing the working out of the consequences of its 25th Congress.

5 Regrowth: 1957–1963

No one imagined that the Communist Party was about to die from the external or self-inflicted wounds of 1956–7, but there was a considerable expectation, reflected in the conclusions of Henry Pelling's history published in 1958, that its vitality was irreversibly lost and that it might be expected presently to shrivel into a political sect or a 'holding company' for various Eastern bloc propaganda and publicity services. Though Pelling was not mistaken about the ultimate prospects of decline, nothing like this in fact happened, and indeed so long as the party retained its membership and support in the industrial field it was not likely to; for in day-to-day employment conflicts as well as more high-profile engagements it played a constantly self-recreating role of organised militancy for which it had at that moment no competitors.

In fact, conditions for shop-floor forcefulness were hardly less favourable in the late 1950s and early 1960s than they had been in the first phase of Conservative government, and certain developments improved them even more. In essence the long postwar boom continued, but in Britain from 1956 onwards the road got more rocky, both in the maintenance of a balanced economic expansion and the preservation of the welfare structure erected under Attlee. Balance of payments crises made their return, and the term 'stop-go' entered the political vocabulary in respect of economic policy. The Conservative Prime Minister, Harold Macmillan, having squashed his party's first internal monetarist revolt, easily won the 1959 General Election on the understanding that 'you've never had it so good' and the slogan 'Life's better with the Conservatives: Don't let Labour ruin it!', but by 1961 the Chancellor was trying to impose the first of many attempts at wage control and cutting social service budgets. By the early 1960s, too, a spreading realisation among economic and political commentators of the fact that Britain was losing ground steadily in world markets and industrial performance was generating an acute sense of public unease at the character of its technological underpinning and economic management.

The continuation of full employment, carrying all its natural potential for successful wage bargaining combined with the perception of a significant threat to its existence, represented very nearly ideal conditions for the flourishing of grass roots militancy and an exceptionally favourable environment for the work of the party's industrial branches. On occasion they discussed general politics or even Marxist theory – much depended on the energy and commitment of their leading members.[1] They participated in the party's constitutional processes, submitting resolutions and electing delegates. Their staple fare, however, was the sale of the *Daily Worker* in the workplace, co-ordination of the work of the branch's members and shop stewards in claims and disputes and organising factory-gate meetings for senior party spokespeople. All full-time party employees were expected to conduct such meetings regularly as part of their normal duties; it constituted an important element of 'mass work'.

Most important of all, however, was the mobilisation of support in union elections for favoured candidates, whether or not in the CP. The guidance and advice of District industrial organisers co-ordinated all of those endeavours. In certain industries the party was especially influential and its branches particularly strong. Motor vehicle manufacture and shipbuilding, along with certain coalfields, were the most important of these sectors, while among dockers and transport workers it had considerable rank-and-file influence, although its members were barred from election to office in the TGWU.

The party, too, could still campaign publicly and energetically, at least in its traditional strongholds, on issues of poverty, rents, housing, education and similar matters of social concern, although it was becoming increasingly difficult to translate this work into local election votes. Nevertheless its residential branches maintained a presence, particularly at weekends, by means of street sales of the newspaper on Saturdays, door-to-door canvasses with it,[2] leaflettings on Sundays or, sometimes still in this era, open-air meetings. In the course of 1957 developments on the national left-wing scene strengthened the party's hand.

In the year after his rhetoric had gone a long way towards publicly discrediting the government case over the Suez invasion, Aneurin Bevan made his peace with the Labour Party leadership, not only endorsing a relatively right-wing economic programme but also denouncing at the annual party Conference the very idea of unilateral nuclear disarmament by Britain. With their principal spokesperson switching sides, the Labour left was thrown into great confusion and demoralisation. At the same time there was growing among young educated middle-class opinion an increasingly questioning and less deferential mood, for which the Suez affair appears to have acted as the initial stimulant. Correspondingly, a vacuum was created on the left for the leadership of this potential new constituency, one which the CP might hope to be able to do something to fill.

On its own it could have had no hope of doing so: as an organisation it was far too marginal and discredited and its politics were the reverse of innovative and exciting, the qualities which any project needed if it were to relate successfully to the new climate. It was the first of the major postwar single-issue movements, the Campaign for Nuclear Disarmament (CND), which became the focus for the mass of the newly politicised youth. The ambience of CND was unquestionably left-wing, not least because the Labour Party seemed to constitute the only possible avenue for realising its objectives, but formally it was not party-political and the bulk of its followers did not identify with a more comprehensive left-wing outlook beyond nuclear disarmament. For those who did, the New Left tended to offer the most convincing appeal.

Paradoxically, however, the CP's weakness in these circumstances was capable of becoming its strength, for organisational efficiency was not high on the list of the new movement's priorities, whereas it was the stock in trade of the CP. Communist individuals and branches provided the organisational backbone for many of the new public activities and expressions – for example, the logistics of the anti-nuclear demonstrations – thereby demonstrating their indispensability and finding the opportunity to make a favourable impression upon this new generation of the politically conscious. Wisely, the party had refrained from anathematising those who had left it in 1956–7 – Gollan had stressed that they would be welcomed back – and was able to continue co-operating with most of them (though there were exceptions)[3] in their new roles as independent or Labour Party left-wingers.

Before it was able to exploit those opportunities, however, the Communist Party had to go through one more switch of line, although in this case it did not constitute too agonising a reappraisal. The party had been initially opposed to CND. In the first place it had seen the new movement as a distraction from what was really important, namely disarmament negotiations between the Great Powers, principally the superpowers. 'The most disastrous aspect of the present situation is not that there is no campaign by Labour for unilateral renunciation of the Bomb but that there is no campaign for summit talks.'[4] The second reason for the party's suspicion was that the Campaign was seen as a potential rival to its own front peace organisation, the British Peace Committee, and its youth equivalent, the Youth Peace Committee. As late as the 26th Congress at Easter 1959 the same line was reaffirmed:

Experience has shown that unilateralism only divides the movement, and diverts attention from the real issue, namely, international agreement to ban nuclear weapons. This is the only way to banish the menace of nuclear war and also the issue on which the greatest number of people agree.[5]

In the course of the same year, however, the party leaders came to realise that the CP could not afford to hold aloof, let alone to continue disdaining the movement, without the risk of being sidelined. In any case, since they were not specifically forbidden to do so, members had been getting involved with CND. The party's attitude had been griping rather than denunciatory, it had enough sense not to discredit itself totally by treating CND as an enemy organisation, and its attraction for the party's own members risked weakening their political discipline should they continue to adhere to it with the party remaining unco-operative. Moreover, by late 1959 it was obvious that CND was no passing fad but was evidently going to be very politically important and connection with it could be to the party's benefit, not least as a possible source of recruits. Without any great travail, therefore, the party by 1960 had committed itself to CND's support, was to take part in the Easter Aldermaston march that year and in May formally encouraged its members to join the organisation.

The effects were significant, both for CND and for the party. For the former it meant that the CP's industrial strength was immediately exerted where it had influence in the unions to secure a unilateralist vote in the TUC and Labour Party conferences of that year. Although the crucial development was the adoption of a unilateralist stance by the TGWU where communists had only rank-and-file influence, the outcome would not have been possible without a similar position being taken up by the engineeers, miners and railwaymen, where the CP conversion may have made the vital difference, especially among the miners. For the party it meant that it was brought into close relationship with a growing and dynamic movement. It gained a measure of credit with CND supporters from the fact that the *Daily Worker* was the only national daily to report the movement favourably or give splash coverage to the Easter marches.[6] Very importantly, too, branches of the Young Communist League (and the Youth Peace Committee) were enabled to contact and work in collaboration with the organisations of Youth CND and influence their members towards a definite political line.

There were contradictions of course. Profound suspicion of the Communist Party was second nature to many of the experienced and renowned Labour figures who were CND supporters. They and others did not fail to point out that there was a certain anomaly in support for British nuclear disarmament coming from an organisation which was unwavering in its identification with a nuclear power, the USSR, and many a sneering reference to the 'Workers' Bomb' was to be heard in debates around this subject. CND, however, was mostly made up of people whose political memories did not go back beyond 1957. For them, raking over the past of such a helpful organisation composed of estimable and impressive individuals seemed irrelevant and mean-spirited. The 'double standards' argument was harder to deal with, but the communists could make a convincing case that the Soviet arsenal was a defensive necessity provoked by US aggressiveness – they had offered often enough to negotiate it away, after all. In addition they could point out that CND was advocating unilateral *British* nuclear disarmament, not Soviet or American, so there was in fact no incompatibility.

For the CP the American side of the equation was especially important, since the party viewed the USA as an enemy power and the major threat to world peace in a manner that most CND supporters did not. The party was keen to emphasise the US dimension at every opportunity during the anti-nuclear campaign and during 1960 there was a certain amount of friction over this at grass roots level, with non-communists complaining at finding themselves in the company of placards saying 'Go Home Yank'. There was tension as well at the time of the Eisenhower–Khrushchev summit meeting in the same year when it was disrupted by the American refusal to apologise for the U2 spy aircraft which the Soviets shot down while the summit was in progress. It was readily admitted by CND supporters that it was the Americans who had been flagrantly at fault, but Khrushchev was criticised as well for standing on his *amour propre* and refusing to proceed with such vital negotiations failing an apology.

The following year any such incipient sources of tension between the party and its new audience were overtaken and resolved by the establishment of a US nuclear base in Britain itself,[7] thus coalescing the strands of anti-Americanism and unilateralism. Although unilateralism was currently losing its gains in the labour movement as the result of a successful right-wing campaign in the trade unions to get the 1960 Labour Party conference vote reversed, CND stepped up its demonstrating activities with renewed vigour around the freshly installed US Polaris submarine base in the Holy Loch near Dunoon, not far from

Glasgow, in which civil disobedience taking the form of sit-downs became a regular feature. CP organisations were especially active on those occasions and turned out their members in large numbers, who endured arrest along with the others and were able on the marches or in police cells to give unconstrained expression to their attack upon US foreign policy in the context of a nuclear disarmament campaign. They were, it is true, embarrassed by the manner in which the Soviet government brandished a super bomb around the Berlin crisis in the summer of 1961 – not to speak of the 50-megaton test explosion which accompanied it and the erection of the Berlin Wall itself – but the trend was highly beneficial on the whole. The membership figure, which continued to decline for a couple of years after 1957, stabilised itself and then from 1961 moved sharply upwards.

Nor was the anti-nuclear weapons campaign the only circumstance of these years from which the party benefited. In the 1990s, following the débâcle of the world communist movement and of the USSR itself, it is difficult to recall the manner in which the Soviet Union around this period appeared to be a society of much greater dynamism and hope than the West, overtaking it in technological efficiency and on the way to overcoming its own Stalinist heritage. In September 1957 the USSR scored a technological triumph by launching the first artificial satellite, an achievement to be savoured even more by communists when certain eminent cold warriors at first simply refused to believe in its reality. Less than four years later it was first again by getting a man into orbit,[8] a success reflected in a popular anti-Polaris song:

Why do the Yanks look blue? – Yuri Gagarin!
Why are they number two? – Yuri Gagarin!

The improvement in the Soviet image did not depend only upon technical attainment. At the 22nd Congress of the CPSU in 1961 Khrushchev, having sacked the remaining Stalinist irreconcilables in the leadership, publicly denounced the Stalin regime and created a still greater sensation by undertaking that the USSR would be ahead of the most developed Western states in material consumption by 1980 and entering the society of abundance by the end of the century. The British YCL could publish an edition of its monthly journal, *Challenge*, carrying the main headline 'Communism – Your Future' without appearing absurd.

The Labour Party, in light of the political and cultural ferment going on among the country's younger generations, had felt itself compelled to recreate a youth organisation, which came into existence in 1960 as the Young Socialists, which before long showed itself restive at the leading strings the parent party tried to impose upon it. There was nothing comparable to the events of the 1930s when the communists had effectively captured the Labour League of Youth; the party lacked the ability and possibly the wish to repeat that coup. Instead, it was a pointer to the future that the struggle for the control of this organisation was to be fought out among rival Marxist groupings separate from and indeed hostile to the CP.[9] All the same, at local level during the early days of the Young Socialists the YCL was in touch with its members, trying to influence them and eventually winning over a cetain number.

A third opinion-influencing trend running in favour of the party in the late 1950s and early 1960s was the decolonisation and national liberation movement, or, more accurately, the Soviet relationship to it. Decolonisation and the struggles, tragedies and triumphs which accompanied it caught the imagination of left-wing youth. Three episodes stand out, these being the Algerian war for independence, which finally attained its objective in 1962; the independence of the Belgian Congo in 1960 and the martyrdom of its leftist first prime minister, Patrice Lumumba, in 1961, following undisguised interference from the Western powers; and above all the Cuban revolution and the emergence of a defiant left-wing regime there after defeating US-sponsored invasion forces in 1961.

On all of these occasions the Soviet regime was on the right side and in the Cuban case its material assistance had made the victory possible. It was of course wholly in support of decolonisation in general and on more than friendly terms with the nationalist regime in Egypt led by Nasser, an elder statesman of decolonisation, and the new revolutionary power in Iraq. On the British non-communist left there was at the same time no uncritical embracing of Soviet international perspectives, and on occasions sharp criticism, as over the Berlin Wall. The favoured stance was one of 'positive neutralism', identified with exemplars such as Tito, Nasser, Nkrumah of Ghana, Nehru of India and Sukarno of Indonesia. However, positive neutralism undoubtedly had a left-leaning orientation, it was anti-imperialist and more anti-Western than anti-Soviet – consequently it was regarded with a great deal more indulgence by the USSR than by the West. Even Castro could identify himself with this position. These years were also relatively free, except for the special case of East Germany, of major scandals within the Soviet bloc. The latter's heightened left-wing credibility in international affairs therefore, though it did not lead to a mass accession of members to the CPGB on the scale of the Second World War, was sufficient to sustain a modest stream of recruits.

Once more the CP's international connections were working in its favour rather than to its disadvantage and its relations with the communist movement around the world could be a source of pride rather than embarrassment. At the end of 1960 it was happy to publish the declaration issued by what turned out to be the last united gathering of 81 world communist parties, taking place in Moscow that November, which concluded with the ringing declaration:

> Brothers in countries which have freed themselves from colonialism and in countries which are fighting for their liberation!
> **The final hour of colonialism is striking!**
> We Communists are with you! The mighty camp of socialist countries is with you!...
> THE PEACE FORCES ARE SUPERIOR TO THE FORCES OF WAR!...
> **PEACE WILL TRIUMPH OVER WAR!**

The title which the British CP chose to publish this under was *36 Million Communists Say...*

By the time of its Easter Congress of 1963 the CP, in spite of a major disaster on its trade union side, had cause for moderate satisfaction and, indeed, compared with where it had been in 1957, considerable gratification. At the 27th Congress of 1961 the decision had been taken to launch a Party Building Year and this had been followed by an intensification of publicity, canvassing and public meetings. The result had been a net increase in party membership of 3,405 and in the YCL of 1,187. By the 28th Congress in 1963 membership stood at over 34,000, an increase of nearly 6,000 since 1961.[10]

In the same period the YCL had expanded by more than two thirds to reach 4,666, the highest level it had attained since 1945.[11] A great deal of the credit for the satisfactory progress of the League has to be attributed to the abilities of its National Secretary, Jimmy Reid, formerly an apprentice shipyard worker in the town of Clydebank adjacent to Glasgow and one of the party's lesser strongholds, where he had come to notice through his leadership of an impressive apprentices' strike. The normal YCL age limit was 30, although this could be extended even further in exceptional cases. Its leaders tended to be in the upper age brackets and the organisation was therefore mostly led by mature adults. Reid himself was in his late twenties.

The party was dissatisfied with the numerical relationship between itself and its youth movement, believing that since the YCL was meant to be a 'broader' organisation than the CP proper it ought to have many more members than its parent. Party leaders reiterated constantly that the YCL was not a miniature Communist Party, though in fact that was exactly what it was. What was really important in this relationship, however, was that the YCL was growing at a much faster rate than the party, for that had important implications for the party's future and especially for its leadership cadre. Unless in extraordinary circumstances, not many politically involved people actively change their party allegiance after their early twenties, though of course they are much more likely to drop out. The CP might therefore not hope to retain all, or even the majority, of its YCL recruits, but those that it had represented its future membership base. The faster rate of growth was therefore a very hopeful sign and an indication that the party was successfully renewing itself. It has to be admitted, though, that some of this expansion was secured by means of a frenetic activism and it was not unknown for YCLers to canvass from door to door recruiting any young person willing to sign the aplication form.

The individuals who had for good or ill led the party through the 1956–7 crisis were still mostly in charge. Gollan remained as General Secretary and George Matthews continued to edit the *Daily Worker*. Peter Kerrigan ran the Industrial Department and Palme Dutt still formulated the membership's understanding of national and international trends through his editorials in the *Labour Monthly*. James Klugmann, responsible for the new theoretical and discussion monthly *Marxism Today*, published articles on themes covering the range from Marxist theory and philosophy to considerations of national and international politics.[12] In 1960–61 *Marxism Today* discussed the party's own estranged partial offspring, the New Left, in an article by Arnold Kettle.[13] Kettle, a member of the EC, was an impressive and sensitive literary critic, but his article, while avoiding denunciatory polemics, was insultingly patronising in tone and interpreted the New Left in terms of crude class reductionism.

I mean that the atmosphere of the petty-bourgeois Left has, by and large, the characteristics of the literary intelligentsia, with its special tendencies towards anarchic individualism, love of self-expression (to the point quite often of exhibitionism), ignorance and near-contempt of science and general preference for living in a world of 'ideas' and 'values' rather than practical action...

It is also wrong and dangerous not to recognise that the petty-bourgeois Left *is* petty-bourgeois.

A further contributor to this discussion, noting that Kettle had offered no explanation as to why this supposedly petty-bourgeois anti-Marxist trend had established itself precisely at *this* juncture, also pointed out that the party had initially ignored it in the hope that it would go away.[14]

Nevertheless the style of the party by 1963 was without doubt significantly different from what it had been seven years earlier, for it was no longer embattled, attacked on all sides and threatened with internal disintegration. Having restored a semblance of political unanimity, rebuilt its numbers and preserved its political culture, it was now addressing with fresh determination the project pursued since the early 1950s of entering the mainstream of British politics. Up to 1961 it still envisaged itself as the sole embodiment of the ultimate interests of the British working class and claimed a unique leading role:

It moves together *with*, although it *leads* the working class and the mass of the people...
If...the main decisive sections of the working class could be influenced to accept and follow the leadership of the Communist Party this would profoundly affect the political outlook of the entire working class, and wide sections outside the working class.[15]

The dual aim was continuing accretion of strength in the trade union movement accompanied by an offensive in the electoral arena which would win the party sufficient votes to compel the Labour Party to take it seriously.

A political Party's influence is commonly judged by its electoral support. Building up a substantial Communist vote and the election of Communist MPs and Councillors will enable us to make a greater impact upon the Labour movement and political developments in Britain.[16]

Membership expansion, with a figure of 100,000 as the medium-term horizon, was viewed as the necessary precondition, bringing with it 'a vast network of branches in a large number of towns, cities and villages where there is no organisation today'.[17] Not all residential branches were required immediately to sponsor a local government candidate, but they were expected to set such an undertaking as a target and to participate in electoral contests, local or parliamentary, wherever possible.

Congress declares that increased participation in elections by our local and factory branches will help the struggle for working class unity, for experience has proved that, where electoral activity and local mass work have been conducted, the best and most principled relations with the left have been established.[18]

The party's organisation did not follow electoral boundaries and so, when elections were on, Districts or Areas allocated branches to the constituencies where contests were taking place. Nor had the party abandoned real hope of bringing about a resurgence in its parliamentary vote.[19]

The more systematic our participation in elections, the more we will build up an electoral base and attract people to our Party. In arguing the case for voting Communist, we are opening up the minds of electors to the need for the Communist Party and bringing them nearer the point of joining.[20]

There was therefore an impression of forward movement and satisfaction with the progress that was being made, an atmosphere uncongenial to the striking of sectarian poses or rigid impositions of discipline, especially when memories of the previous episode were still fresh. A further consideration was that many individuals at various levels of the organisation who had publicly expressed concern with the way matters had been conducted in 1956 had nevertheless stayed within the CP ranks, most notably Eric Hobsbawm, one of the signatories to the *New Statesman* letter so rigorously censured by the EC, and subsequent contributor to the *New Reasoner*. Their continuing presence was a reminder that communists were not necessarily all of one mind on important issues, even though dissidents had to be discreet about the fact. As for the recruits newly refilling the CP ranks, they were mostly young people influenced by the consumer society and more relaxed social mores of the 1950s, unwilling to tolerate more than a restricted measure of authoritarianism. John Gollan was fond of boasting at party rallies that, unlike the relations between the Young Socialists and the Labour Party, he had 'never had to discipline the YCL',[21] but although that organisation was certainly more malleable and self-disciplined than its Labour counterpart, it is unlikely that this would have remained true without a degree of concession to the new social climate.

Most important of all was the fact that communism as a world movement had irrecoverably lost its aura of infallibility and undeviating historical correctness. Before 1956 and more especially 1953 individuals and even parties might of course err, but the world movement, whether or not represented by the Comintern, was never wrong and if its line failed to achieve the promised results in any instance that could be only because it had been mishandled and certainly not on account of any intrinsic imperfection. But following the Stalin admissions, however much it might be claimed that the economic, social and even political progress of the USSR had remained basically unaffected by the cult, there was no more disguising that a historical deviation *had* occurred and that important things had been badly wrong for a considerable space of time. Once this precedent had been set the basis of infallibility needed for a cult-style discipline was removed.

It was not that the party had as yet begun to criticise publicly aspects of Soviet policy and behaviour. Even though the CP programme was the *British Road to Socialism,* with the emphasis on 'British Road', the social order of the Eastern bloc was still seen as the appropriate model once the destination was reached. The party adopted in these years as a central educational text a translation of the Soviet *Fundamentals of Marxism–Leninism*, an encyclopaedic work dealing with everything from the history of philosophy to the prospects of extended longevity in socialist society. In spite of that deference, however, in the new conditions a certain distancing from its Soviet mentor was unavoidable compared with the situation in the days of the Comintern and Cominform.

The party's one major setback between 1956 and 1963, on the other hand, although it did not put an end to its growth or its hopes, was devastating and full of portentous consequences. As a result of the 1956 events Les Cannon, an important official of the ETU, had quit the party after urging that it should be dissolved. Cannon was in charge of the union's training college, and in a spiteful reaction by the union leadership he was sacked from this position. The anti-communists in the ETU were able to mobilise around the figure of John Byrne, the Glasgow district secretary, who had with the assistance of Catholic Action maintained an anti-communist stronghold there even during the era of CP dominance. Weakened by the developments, the union leadership was unable to prevent the election of anti-communists, most importantly Frank Chapple, to the union executive.

The campaign moved into higher gear when the press launched a barrage of accusations regarding electoral malpractice within the union and pushed the TUC General Council to call upon the ETU leadership, in the persons of Frank Foulkes, the president, and Frank Haxell, the secretary, to account for itself. The leaders prevaricated until in early

1960 Byrne stood against Haxell for the secretaryship and was defeated. Allegations of ballot-rigging were redoubled, moved from the press to the television screen and culminated in a lawsuit, opening in early 1961, seeking to depose Haxell on the grounds of electoral fraud by the president, secretary and three other officials. In June Mr Justice Winn found against the defendants and judged them to have been guilty of conspiracy to prevent Byrne's election.

The electoral fraud had been accomplished both by disqualifying the votes of branches known to be anti-CP and by stuffing the ballot-boxes in others. Byrne, by order of the court, replaced Haxell in the secretaryship and the TUC demanded that Foulkes submit himself to re-election. When he refused the union was expelled. Shortly thereafter a right-wing majority was secured against the demoralised communists and they were cleared out of the leadership, with their replacements, including Byrne, Cannon and Chapple, gaining readmission to the TUC the following year.[22] The ETU did not thereupon become a haven of industrial democracy, for though the ex-communists in the leadership had changed their political colour, they had not changed their disposition. The apparatus of Stalinism by which it was controlled was maintained and intensified, only now being directed towards opposite purposes. The temptation to any further ballot-rigging was removed by the happy expedient of abolishing most elective offices in the union.

In the run-up to the trial and while it was in progress the CP vehemently defended the accused leaders and denounced the McCarthyist conspiracy said to be directed against them. It did not maintain this stance when the verdict came through, but accepted its validity and promptly 'resigned' Haxell from the party, although in 1959 he had topped the ballot for the EC elected at that year's Congress, coming ahead even of Pollitt.[23] In his report to the 1963 Congress Peter Kerrigan indicated the EC's reaction to the scandal:

> We have declared that the ballot rigging in the Electrical Trade Union was a complete violation of the principles on which Communists have worked for over forty years, and took place without our Party leadership being aware of it. There are unions in which the right-wing are in the saddle and where electoral arrangements provide the opportunity for malpractices. This does not excuse what happened in the ETU...
>
> The conduct of the election at the Head Office of the ETU gravely compromised our Party and all those progressive forces in the trade union movement who, for a number of years, defended the ETU

against attacks of the reactionaries. Our Party has taken steps to ensure that Communist Party members will never again be involved in such an affair....

The question remains as to how far such announcements were no more than a face-saving act of scapegoating, and whether the party leadership was actually complicit in the malpractices carried on within the ETU. Not unnaturally they stressed with all their might that the judge had uncovered no evidence of any such thing. On the presumption that the worst expectation is likely to be true, I have searched for many years for evidence implicating King Street in the affair. I have never found any. The strong balance of probability is that the ETU officials acted independently of the CP leaders, who were not privy to their actions. Nevertheless, these leaders cannot be absolved from all blame. They were as aware as anybody else of the allegations which were circulating, and it is admitted privately that they suspected the stories were true but felt themselves unable to do anything about it. Instead of confronting the situation and publicly advising the ETU to hold its voting under independent supervision, the CP leaders hoped for the best and gave way to the conditioned response of defending a communist attacked from the right, regardless of the merits of the case.

Their dilemma illustrates the reality that, at least since the early 1950s and to an extent since the end of 'class against class', party control over its members who were union leaders had steadily weakened and that in any matter important to their own union affairs they acted autonomously, using the party as a communication, advice and support facility, but not feeling themselves bound to obey it against their own judgement, while the party leaders, unwilling to face a confrontation or be seen interfering in union affairs, endorsed these judgements as a matter of course. It is therefore likely that the party would have been unable to call the ETU to order, supposing it had wanted to, an ironic consideration, for in a sense it did not matter whether Foulkes and Haxell were agents of a communist conspiracy. The point was that it was widely believed that they were and few members of the general public took the party's denials seriously; ballot-rigging appeared an all too likely example of the sort of thing communists would get up to whenever they had the chance – it exactly fitted the popular suspicion.

Taking that into account, it is perhaps surprising that the ETU case did not do the party even more damage than it actually suffered, but certainly, although its position in that union was totally destroyed, other unions did not hasten to get rid of their communist officials, nor was there a general reaction against communist militants and shop stewards at the grass roots of the trade union movement. Things there continued much as before, with the party suffering occasional severe setbacks, such as a lost strike at Ford's in 1962 which sharply reduced its industrial branch there, but in the context of a general trend of making gradual though unspectacular gains.

The ETU débâcle, however, represented in the long run much more than a temporary embarrassment to the party, for it precipitated, if it was not ultimately responsible for, a fundamental shift in its industrial strategy and the final abandonment of the lingering aspiration which had been central to the party's formation, i.e. independently to lead the labour movement and working class of Great Britain. The ETU was by far the most important of the unions actually controlled by communists,[24] and it might be viewed, if rather fancifully, as among the last remnants of the inheritance of the Minority Movement. Henceforth communists resigned themselves to sharing influence in individual unions with other left-wingers and to accepting subordinate positions uncomplainingly for the sake of unity. Although the term did not come into immediate use, the aftermath of the ETU marked the practical initiation of the 'broad left' strategy. A somewhat chastened CP at its 28th Congress did not engage in any far-reaching analysis of what had happened or of its implications for the party, but the lengthy resolution it passed on the future of trade unionism concentrated upon the theme of necessary unity among progressive forces in that sphere, studiously avoiding any pretension to a leading role and referring instead to 'the unity of Communist trade union members with other militants' as the key to advance.

Even as they participated in a Congress which provoked *The Times* to remark that the Communist Party might 'soon become a force to be reckoned with', delegates were faced with a growing awareness that a serious problem was looming from an international direction. It had become public as early as 1961, when Khrushchev at the 22nd Congress of the CPSU had attacked the Albanian CP (the Albanian Party of Labour), accusing it of directing criticism at the Soviet party and of failing to act in accordance with the agreed policies of the 1960 Moscow international conference. The difference was reported in the British CP press:

In particular they disagreed with the decision of the Twentieth Congress to eliminate all the harmful consequences of the cult of the individual, to restore democratic methods in Party and public life, and reinstitute socialist legality. This is because the same methods are being used in their own Party.[25]

It was a disturbing revelation, but Albania was small and peripheral and something much more serious was in the offing. A very alert individual might have spotted as early as 1960 the publication by the Communist Party of China (CPC) of a pamphlet, *Long Live Leninism*, which implicitly attacked some of the central positions of the Soviets, particularly in relation to the limitation of nuclear arms, declaring that if the US dared to launch a nuclear war:

> On the debris of imperialism, the victorious people would create very swiftly a civilisation thousands of times higher than the capitalist system and a truly beautiful future for themselves.[26]

The polemics developed in the course of 1962, but still in a relatively coded fashion, with the Soviets using the Albanian Party, and the Chinese, by contrast, the Yugoslav one, as stalking horses, denouncing respectively 'sectarianism' and 'revisionism'. One did not have to be a member of the British leadership or a veteran of previous schisms in order to read the signs, but protocol was observed and the statement by the Executive in January 1962 aligning the British party with Moscow over the Albanian dispute made no suggestion that wider issues were involved.[27] Following the Cuban missile crisis of 1962 it could no longer be concealed that a rupture was occurring, for the Chinese, further inflamed by the Soviet refusal to support their position in their concurrent border war with India, issued statements implying that the Soviet withdrawal of its missiles amounted to a Munich-style sell-out.

Even so it was January of the following year before the CP formally acknowledged that the two principal communist states were at odds. The EC then issued a statement under the suggestive title *Restore the Unity of the International Communist Movement* which expressed its alarm:

> Any split would be a disastrous set-back to the international working class and the cause of peace. It is unthinkable to any Communist Party worthy of its name. On the contrary, the most urgent duty facing every Communist Party is to do everything in its power to restore the unity of the world Communist movement and resolve its differences in a principled fashion on the basis of Marxism–Leninism.

The statement expressed disagreement with the Chinese castigation of the Russians, although doing so in temperate language. It referred to the notion which the Soviets were floating at this point for a fresh international conference. Rightly fearing a breakdown which would leave the resulting situation worse than it had been earlier, the EC urged a substantial period of earnest preparation, during which public polemics should cease:

> We need as much preparation as is necessary calmly and in a Communist fashion to examine and weigh up honestly held differences, to assess how far, in fact, they exist and what are the possible lines of solution.[28]

The CBGB's 28th Congress discussed the growing rift, but did so at a private session which ended by passing an extremely uninformative resolution endorsing whatever the EC had done or would do. These actions included the dispatch of delegations to both Moscow and Peking, though it is hard to imagine how the leaders felt that a party such as their own could exert any meaningful influence.

During the first six months of 1963 a vestige of restraint between the disputants still persisted, with the CPC directing its main polemical fire at the communist parties of Italy and France, supposedly in the vanguard of theoretical revisionism within the international movement (Yugoslavia being outside), rather than at the CPSU. It was after the signature of the nuclear Test-ban Treaty in July 1963 that the quarrel escalated into vituperation, with Khrushchev being accused of leading the Soviet party into revisionism and the state back to capitalism, of surrender to imperialism and, in signing the Treaty, of committing a 'dirty fraud'. At the end of the month the CPGB's Political Committee issued a statement welcoming the treaty and attacking the Chinese viewpoint.

In September *Marxism Today* carried an article by Palme Dutt ('Problems of the International Communist Movement') and in October another by Klugmann ('Peaceful Coexistence – The Burning Issue of Our Time'). By the standards of previous such controversies both were extremely polite, making frequent acknowledgement of the Chinese communists' heroic and world-shaking achievements, although Dutt could not resist a provocative flash of his magisterial condescension:

> It is possible that a pupil may advance beyond the teacher, though the concrete evidence for that needs to be visible. But a pupil should show some sense of decency before proceeding, as from some lofty height of superiority, to berate the teacher with very foul abuse, especially when that teacher is the vanguard party of the world socialist revolution....

The British CP therefore, like the majority throughout the world, lined up on the Soviet side of the rupture, although it never accepted unreservedly the Soviet position. Apart from continuing professions of respect for the Chinese party (which did not impress the Maoists in the slightest) it declined to support the convening of an international conference which would have had the purpose of formally drumming the Chinese out of the world movement and cancelling their accepted accreditation as a legitimate communist party. However, it made no bones about where its essential loyalties were fixed and Palme Dutt issued a pamphlet to explain the social causes behind the degeneration of the CPC.

It was to be expected that the British party's choice would provoke opposition inside its own ranks, and this was soon forthcoming. The first Maoist breakaway was initiated by Michael McCreery.[29] It did not amount to very much, no more than a couple of branches in London and a few individuals elsewhere. It was supported partly by members who responded on the basis of their admiration for the Chinese regime and by others on their belief that the CP had diluted its revolutionary conviction and that in consequence its organisation and activism were in a state of deterioration. They were prepared to agree that this had occurred under the malign influence of a revisionist Soviet Union and that the deficiency should be remedied by the injection of Maoist principles. Such deficiencies were to prove a recurrent theme advanced from a variety of angles in subsequent decades. In 1963 McCreery formed a Committee to Defeat Revisionism, for Communist Unity, which for a time produced an expensively printed sixteen-page monthly journal in newspaper format under the title *Vanguard*, but neither lasted for very long.[30]

The breakaway itself was of small concern to the CP, but the ground on which it occurred, the international split, was infinitely more important. Although it might not be apparent immediately, the loss of a unified world movement could not fail to do irreparable long-term damage to the morale and world view of communist parties outside the bloc. A major source of strength and confidence to the members, putting into apparent perspective the insignificance and frailty of the party in Britain, had disappeared forever and one more thread was snapped in the logic of justification for the CPGB's existence. More, for an audience wholly unfamiliar with the disputes which had riven the pre-Stalinist Bolshevik party, the fact that accredited Marxist-Leninist parties could fall out raised disturbing questions about the viability of Marxism-Leninism itself. Since both were inspired by the doctrine, how could the two major states in the socialist camp turn into enemies overnight? Evidently it did not represent the unifying revolutionary force which up to that point had been thought to be the case – but what were the implications?

Despite this recent blow British communists in general at the end of 1963 faced the future with a good deal of hope. Hugh Gaitskell's unexpected death had removed a lynchpin of right-wing control in the Labour Party, and if his successor was something of an unknown quantity the new situation at least appeared to offer a lot more scope for the left. In the big trade unions the hard right-wing control of the 1950s was passing; radical leaders were coming to the fore with whom the party had every expectation of being able to co-operate. Best of all, with the Profumo scandal, the Prime Minister's resignation and the messy appointment of his successor against a background of rapidly diminishing economic confidence, the thirteen-year-old Conservative regime and perhaps even the Conservative Party looked as if it might be in terminal crisis.

After a prolonged trauma stretching from the start of the Cold War the party seemed to have achieved a successful adjustment in both its domestic and international dimensions, and if its aims were a good deal more modest than they had been prior to 1947 at least they also looked somewhat more practicable. The party enjoyed the dual advantage of being able to insist on its complete political sovereignty, with only a primacy of honour conceded to the CPSU and emphatically no control over CPGB affairs or policies, while at the same time the latter remained part of a world communist community, albeit one now split down the middle. In the light of its past relationships there could be no doubt about which side of the division the British CP would opt for. So far as its domestic perspectives were concerned it would be unnecessary to labour the point that its programme was rife with contradictions and could only with the greatest indulgence be regarded in any sense as a Marxist document – the realities of its situation left it with very little alternative if it was to find a workable manner of addressing the political universe without losing all touch with the continuity of its history.

The actualities of British social and political life in the early 1960s, notwithstanding the fact that it remained a class society structured to fulfil capitalist objectives, nullified the presumptions upon which the CP had been founded and made nonsense of its original *raison d'être*. That, of course, could not be openly avowed. To justify the continuance of its separate identity it laid great stress upon the superior insight into human affairs derived from its Marxist-Leninist outlook and its recognition of the state as an instrument of class domination and violence, areas in which the Labour left was judged to be woefully deficient. Given the pre-supposition of the need for a communist party and an appreciation of the realities of political consciousness in the working class and among the general public, a patient development of collaboration with the left in the trade unions and the systematic pursuit of an independent electoral presence (while keeping the door open to political collaboration, which at the time did not appear such a forlorn hope) probably constituted the only feasible strategy, however uncertain the outcome.

Such a twin approach was what the party committed itself to at its Congress of 1963. In a sense this was definitive, for one part of it, the electoral strategy, was a perspective to which the leadership was to cling grimly and unswervingly until the body of the party itself was falling to pieces under the strain of trying to squeeze an increasingly weary, alienated and outraged membership into the straitjacket of these postulates. That, however, was for the future. In the immediate term, as the country moved towards the year of a general election promising a Labour victory, the prospects looked bright. In order to realise them and advance in the industrial and electoral fields it was accepted that a mass party was an indispensable requisite. With an immediate target of 50,000 members, the CP now made the attempt to construct one.[31]

6 The 'Mass Party': 1964–1974

The end of thirteen years of Conservative government in 1964 marked such a welcome departure and inspired such far-reaching hopes that the CP's own worse than indifferent electoral performance did not provoke too much discouragement either among the leadership or at the grass roots. The party's disappointing vote was attributed to the conviction of electors that it was essential to vote Labour to ensure the dismissal of the Tories, and communists also blamed the denial to the party of access to the television screen.

The trade union milieu formed the connecting link between the CP's industrial and political strategies, as it not only represented power at the base of industrial society but also disposed of votes at Labour Party conferences and in the selection of parliamentary candidates. The CP identified right-wing dominance in the leadership of the Labour Party as the major obstacle to a rapid radicalisation of the latter's political outlook and purposes. It saw in the replacement of that leaderhip the precondition for creating a united left that would be capable of isolating and defeating the power of monopoly capital and initiating the transition to a socialist Britain. This accorded with the conceptions of the *British Road to Socialism*. In combination with its own independent electoral presence the party anticipated that collaboration with the non-CP left in the trade union field was capable of bringing that about. In addition, confidence in the party's good faith and goodwill would be enhanced among industrial militants once they saw that it sought no position of exclusivity.

In two important unions this strategy soon had practical consequences. Lawrence Daly, having humiliated the party in its home territory, went on to show himself capable of beating any communist candidate for any position in the Scottish NUM he cared to contest, particularly after he had wound up the Fife Socialist League and rejoined the Labour Party in 1962. Soon he defeated a communist rival for the secretaryship of the Scottish miners, but presently he went on to become a candidate for the equivalent position in the British NUM. At this point the party swallowed its pride and backed Daly for the post, for whatever might be the bitterness between them, the CP recognised him as being in the last analysis on the left.

In the Amalgamated Engineering Union the application of the strategy was carried out at some immediate cost. Reg Birch, sitting on the Executive of the AEU, counted among the most important of the CPGB's trade union paladins and the party for its part had shown its confidence in his class resoluteness during the crisis of 1957 when it appointed him to its EC at the 25th Congress. Birch saw himself as a potential president of an increasing left-tending union as the date approached for the retiral of the neanderthal Sir William Carron. The party, however, partly because Birch had started to develop Maoist deviations, partly because it was felt that a non-party left-winger would have more chance in the election, declined to support Birch's campaign and instead threw the weight of its organisation behind the broad left candidate, Hugh Scanlon. Embittered by what he regarded as an unprincipled betrayal in which communists had opted for a social democrat in preference to a revolutionary, Reg Birch quitted the CP and in due course went on to unveil his own groupuscule, the Communist Party of Britain (Marxist-Leninist).[1]

At the shop-floor level no immediate changes were visible; communist stewards and militants continued to function as before. Charges that the party began to smother militancy, accept package deals and productivity bargaining and even sabotage industrial actions so as to make life easier for the trade union hierarchy it now courted may have had some basis but are unprovable. What is certainly true is that the CP was obliged by the logic of its posture and strategy to keep its public statements and analysis of trade union affairs within the bounds of acceptability to its new or potential allies. Fire had to be concentrated against the right, and the left criticised, if at all, only in the mildest and most restrained terms. Being the weaker partner, the party could not avoid having to accept the terms upon which Frank Cousins, Jack Jones, Hugh Scanlon or their counterparts were willing to co-operate. Except where a rogue employer, a witch hunt or a particularly notorious trade union boss of the old school was the target, the CP's industrial commentary on specific fights and episodes, and especially upon internal struggles, began to assume a tone of anodyne blandness and diplomatic evasion, its principal anxiety being to avoid giving offence so far as possible.

The clearly defined resolve to focus upon left unity in the unions was willingly endorsed by the leading CP unionists. The degree to which they participated in the party's internal life was for them a matter of personal preference – some gave considerable attention to it, others did no more than hold a party card. Even the more conscientious, however, found it impossible to maintain regular attendance in the party committees to which they were elected and their basic link with the party therefore normally took the form of ad hoc consultations with the party secretaries or industrial organisers. The CP advisory committees for trades and industries where the party had any significant presence were credited by an alarmist press with being an organisational framework through which a tight stranglehold was maintained upon the country's economic existence; a network through which flowed intelligence and commands enabling the Kremlin via King Street to direct its thrusts at the most sensitive points of the national anatomy. The suspicion was profoundly misplaced. For better or worse the advisories were just that – advice forums – and their co-ordinating function even within the individual area each one covered was rather weak. A common line might emerge from an advisory meeting, but it would emerge out of the opinion exchange and experience of the members as trade unionists rather than in consideration of a party policy or grand strategy.

Expressed most briefly, the Communist Party's essential relationship with trade unionism, more emphatically dominant after 1963, was to mobilise its members at large to support action by workers rather than to instigate workers to industrial action in pursuit of its own policies and aims. In doing so it marked a final break with the traditions of the first fifteen years of the party's existence. Its members would of course continue to argue within their particular unions for the adoption of standpoints which the party favoured, but in the shape of resolutions adopted at union conferences rather than strike action with politically ulterior motives.

The record of Harold Wilson's first administration was an ambiguous one in its handling of the British economy and labour market. Well-publicised commitments to economic planning and a vigorous technological revolution were accompanied by a range of welfare and educational improvements. But the government's response to balance of payments crises and above all its determination to preserve British traditions of capital export and Great Power megalomania had forced it into courses which by late 1965 would have made it apparent to any perceptive observer that no fundamental reconstruction of the British social and economic order was intended to occur. These realities, however, were obscured by the slenderness of Wilson's parliamentary majority, and on the left hope persisted that a Labour government immune to defecting right-wing MPs or procedural ambush could be induced to take on the class enemy and begin making inroads upon the entrenched powers of capital and its ruling class.

If the Labour administration of 1964–6 had disappointed many hopes, the one formed after Wilson's second and definitive victory lurched to the right in every area of economic and foreign affairs more rapidly than even pessimists could have feared.[2] The foreign issues, so far as they relate to the CP, are discussed below. So far as the economic ones are concerned, continued pressure on sterling and the government's resolve to defend it at all costs led to the rapid abandonment of any pretence to expansionism or industrial rejuvenation, and the replacement of those priorities by a drastic squeeze, at first in an unavailing effort to stave off devaluation, and when that failed, to attain a balance of payments surplus.

From 1967 onward plant closures, above all in the peripheral areas of the country, became a consistent feature of the industrial scene. Unemployment mounted, although modestly enough by later standards. The statement above about the abandonment of industrial rejuvenation has to be qualified, for while any rationally planned or coherent scheme was certainly thrown overboard, a substitute continued to be pursued in the shape of takeover and merger, on the presumption that bigger meant better and more efficient. That point may have been debatable, but it undoubtedly meant reduced workforces in the merged enterprises, reinforcing the upward pressure on unemployment. To this was added wage freeze and wage control, both voluntary and compulsory.

In prosecuting the shop-floor struggle in such a climate the CP was in its element. Indeed, there occurred in 1966 an episode quite reminiscent of old times when on the floor of the House of Commons the Prime Minister indicted the CP (quite inaccurately) for fomenting and organising the strike into which exasperated merchant seamen had been driven, accusing King Street of having organised it with the deliberate purpose of inflicting damage on the national economy.[3] It is most unlikely that Wilson himself – who was in a position to know – believed what he was saying. Rather, his vanity being offended by the failure of his personal pleas to return to work, he reached for the most convenient smear to hand.

Critical though this strike was to be in marking the future direction to be taken by the Labour government, for the CP it was only an episode, though important, punctuating the tenor of its endeavours, and these were directed towards forming coalitions inside the unions. That tactic had indeed had a modest measure of success but had unavoidably concentrated the CP's organised attentions upon winning elected positions and securing the adoption of resolutions through the constitutional channels. There is an argument that by this time organisation among the rank-and-file was being discounted and neglected in the pursuit of collaboration with non-party union leaders. While it should not be exaggerated, there is probably a measure of truth in the claim, but a more accurate characterisation might be that the party was trying to direct the pressures of militancy into the official channels of the movement.

There had existed from the early 1960s a 'lobby organising committee' supported by several rank-and-file organisations, principally in London, and with the imposition of a government-prescribed wage freeze following the seamen's strike it attempted to extend its operations to other parts of the country. A meeting of the shop stewards co-ordinating committee on Clydeside decided in September to campaign through mass meetings and deputations. From the junction of these initiatives emerged the Liaison Committee for the Defence of Trade Unions (LCDTU) in February 1967 and this went on to organise a major lobby against the freeze, actions which the party saw as the initial steps in giving grass roots struggle a political dimension.

The maintenance of the integrity of wage and related bargaining against any interference by the state was viewed as central to this purpose. Defining the state as being, in the last analysis, the political instrument of monopoly capital, any measure of wage restraint or interference by it in this particular market must *ipso facto* be disadvantageous to the workforce in the short term and weaken the ability and will of the labour movement to expropriate capitalism in the long term.[4] Although the report of the Donovan Commission which appeared in early 1968 was adamantly hostile to the idea of legal regulation, the CP none the less denounced it fiercely because of its criticism of the practices of shop-floor bargainers and the hint it contained of wanting some manner of voluntary regulation of wages, maybe policed by the TUC.[5]

From 1966 it had become evident that if the Labour government survived, a contest over trade union powers was sooner or later in the offing. Continued industrial unrest during 1968, provoked as much as anything by the official deflationary policies, resulted in the appearance early in the following year of a White Paper proposing wage controls. *In Place of Strife* embodied the conviction which had penetrated the inner circle of Wilson's Cabinet that control of wages through the instrument of trade union regulation and sanctions upon strike action was the only long-run answer to the country's economic problem.[6]

The momentum which the party had succeeded in building up since 1966 in its shop-floor agitation and broad cross-union contacts carried it to a position where it and the LCDTU were able to feature prominently in the opposition to the proposed legislation and even to some degree orchestrate the campaign of demonstrations and industrial action which resulted in Wilson, with his Cabinet ministers defecting all around him, climbing down and withdrawing the intended legislation in June 1969. The CP claimed, of course, especially to its own members, that the victory had been due principally to its efforts, but for once this may have been a pardonable exaggeration, and the role it played represented, all things considered, a fairly substantial achievement.

All the relative success of the industrial policy could not, however, disguise the fact that by the late 1960s the party had a major problem, for its electoral strategy was in tatters. The more energy and resources it put into establishing itself as a force at the polling booths, the more this mirage seemed to retreat over the horizon. The code phrase, endlessly reiterated, was that the electorate must be 'given the opportunity to vote communist', and it was implied that if only this was done persistently and widely enough then the breakthrough must follow. The *almost* complete lack of impact (there was just enough to allow criticism to be parried)[7] was attributed invariably to deficiencies in the election campaigns. The fixation of the CP with conducting election campaigns and its refusal to reconsider what was, by the mid-1970s, a manifestly bankrupt strategy can be rightly viewed as a carry-over into this era of the Comintern principle that a policy could not be wrong – if it did not succeed the application must be at fault.

It is at once apparent that the decision to concentrate on collaboration and agreement in the union field while stepping up the level of communist contests in the electoral one involved an odd reversal. The party was going to seek support and allies, subordinate its own claims, in the area where it was strongest, and fight single-handed, taking on the whole weight of Labour's electoral apparatus, precisely where it was at its most feeble. But there was in fact a logic connecting the two positions. The party's relative strength in the trade unions provided it with a leverage there, gave it something to put on the table when going to negotiate with potential allies. By contrast, in the local government sphere it possessed scarcely anything and in the parliamentary one absolutely nothing. The party leadership therefore intended to mobilise their forces in order to capture an electorate for their candidates comparable in strength to the support they had among trade unionists. What they aimed at above all was to establish an effective bargaining position.

If they were to succeed they had first to halt and then reverse an absolutely consistent trend of decline. Since 1950 CP parliamentary votes had dropped to negligible proportions. The 200-odd local authority seats of 1945 had been reduced twenty years later to 20 or thereabouts, and in not one of these seats had the candidate been elected on the strength of the party's name. They were councillors in spite of the fact that they were communists, not because of it. All of them had secured their seats after years, sometimes decades, of patient work among the grass roots, getting results on the basic issues of welfare benefits, education, road safety, street repair and cleansing, local transport and – especially – housing, and gradually building up a devoted personal following. It was their individual charisma which overbore in South Wales, central Scotland and a few pockets in England – areas mostly though not invariably where the CP had possessed a strong communal base in the 1930s – the culturally conditioned disinclination to vote for communists, even among those who did not view the party with abhorrence.

It should be admitted that the victories were not possible, regardless of the councillor's personal magnetism, without a reasonably strong party organisation to publicise her or his achievements and mobilise the potential vote. Yet unquestionably, and no communist would have denied it, that was a secondary consideration; the primary one was always the candidate's personality and record as a tribune of the streets. In parliamentary contests normal political responses reasserted themselves among the electorate; communists were not viewed as credible outside the limits of their local authority functions and in fact when councillors stood as candidates for Westminster they did not do significantly better than other CP campaigners.

The first major test of the now clearly defined electoral strategy occurred in April 1964 with the initial elections to the newly constituted Greater London Council when the party decided to contest all 32 divisions on a platform demanding that the Council use its existing powers to improve social service provision. An article in *Marxism Today* reminded its readers that 'every elector in the greater London area will have, for the first time, *the opportunity to vote Communist*' (emphasis added)[8]. The GLC electors remained unimpressed with their unprecedented opportunity, but not demoralisingly so, with an overall CP vote of 93,000; thus the party leadership was not abashed and, as noted above, the disappointing statistics of the General Election in the same year were also capable of being explained away.

Convinced that a turning point of great strategic potential now existed, the party leadership mounted the most sustained and ambitious offensive by the CP during its postwar career, to set in motion developments of the kind foreshadowed in its programme as representing initial steps along the British road to socialism. The perspective was one of isolating and discrediting the Labour right-wing, shifting that party measurably to the left and in the process confirming the CP's credentials as the principal and indispensable component of the successful left alliance, regarding itself as:

> the leading political organisation of the working class, its socialist force, the body that can move to the left the organised masses of the labour movement.

This was declared in major guideline articles that appeared in the party press,[9] one of which was headed 'Now the Future Depends on Us and our Campaign', written by Gollan. The position which the CP was trying to assert can be seen in the sort of claim which Gollan made for it *vis-à-vis* the government: 'On behalf of the party I made constructive suggestions for the vital changes in policy needed', and argued that in consequence of these solid proposals being ignored by the Cabinet Labour support had slumped. His conclusion was that '*It is not too much to say that the whole future of the rapidly moving political situation depends on how the Communist party grows and campaigns*' (original emphasis). What is more, these inflated estimates of the party's significance were taken very seriously by its members.

Unfortunately for the party there was not much that it could actually do to bring about the unity it sought, short of the electoral successes which continued to elude it. For all its insistent rhetoric around this theme, the issuance of statements was its major content. As one participant in a *Marxism Today* discussion observed: 'Communist policy statements frequently stress the need for unity, but few positive actions are evident at branch and district level.'[10] Apart from the general disreputability of the party among the political mainstream, its separate electoral pretensions constituted an insuperable barrier to such collaboration, in spite of the fantasies of some communists that left-wing Labour candidates did not mind the CP standing because they liked its policies so much.[11]

Addressing the 1965 National Congress, now shifted to the autumn from the hitherto traditional Easter date, so as not to interfere with local electioneering,[12] Gollan made another public appeal to the non-CP left for joint co-operation and declared that the CP was willing to talk with anybody about anything in order to reach that objective. In the meantime the party's intensification of its electoral campaigning would continue, for:

> The scale of our contests is marginal and our campaign therefore still makes little impact... A party branch that doesn't contest local elections is failing to carry out one of the most essential functions of a political party...give more people the opportunity...

But a very significant admission, surely unintentional, was that electoral concentration in 1964 had been responsible for a membership dip in that year. According to Gollan:

> During most of the year we increasingly concentrated our political work and our resources on our 36 Constituencies. There was no effective national effort to build the party [and] decline in our attention to the factories...[13]

– which constituted an astonishing refutation of an endlessly repeated claim that electoral contests improved political consciousness and activity, enhanced all aspects of party work, including recruiting, and were never detrimental to any of them.

To the appeal for closer co-operation, none of the intended audience paid very much attention. *Tribune* took enough disdainful notice to advise the CP to wind itself up and send its members into the Labour Party, for, after all: 'The programme for the immediate future outlined contains almost nothing to which a Labour left-winger...could take exception.'[14]

These disparagements provoked Palme Dutt to entitle his lead article in the January 1966 *Labour Monthly* 'The Left and Communism', in which he expounded the traditions of the CP as an integral part of the left – even claiming that it had helped to inspire the foundation of *Tribune* – without reference to anything so embarrassing as the 'Third Period' or 1939. In urging the left to co-operate for common immediate objectives, since without communist assistance it had no hope of overcoming its right-wing gaolers, he claimed that: 'As soon as this immediate problem is seen in real terms the question of relative size takes on different proportions.'

Brutal exposure of these illusions occurred with the General Election of 1966. This time the CP presented 57 candidates, sufficient to ensure a five-minute television slot. On this occasion there was no need for potential communist voters to feel compelled to vote Labour to ensure its victory – a large majority was universally and confidently expected. The party therefore entered the contest with high hopes, the culmination of a year and a half of intense campaigning towards the respectable parliamentary vote it needed to be taken seriously on the left following a convincing Labour victory. When the votes were counted the CP had performed markedly less well than it had done at the height of the Cold War in 1950 and 1951. An overall vote of 62,000 measured a 38 per cent drop in the poll of 14 seats contested continuously since 1955. Comparison where possible with 1964 indicated a fall of 16.6 per cent. Among the party rank-and-file the result, bereft of the excuses of 1964, was received as a stunning blow.

The autopsy which followed released a flood of criticism, during which it was pointed out that no real analysis of election performance was ever undertaken, and 'a sloganising and mechanical approach to politics' was indicted by a respected veteran member who complained of the absurdity of the 'attempt to be recognised as the Fourth National party'.[15] The Surrey District Committee voted to reject the report in which the EC made its assessment of the election results.[16] Gollan and the party's National Election Agent, Reuben Falber, however, conceded nothing. Their intransigent defence of the strategy amounted to an exercise in voluntarism, which bitterly contrasted the attitude of the critics with the optimism and positive outlook others had displayed, and attributed the failure to 'serious shortcomings in our public campaign and presentation'.[17]

The CP lacked the mechanisms needed to change gear. The discussion of Gollan's report, where it was not ritualistic, was unfavourable, and so failed to suit the now embedded preconceptions of the Political Committee. Therefore it was ignored. The problem, however, would not go away. The party was in truth the despised 'ginger group' so frequently castigated by its leaders and in no position to be anything else. It lacked any conception of how it might advance to a more convincing political status other than by breaking its fists on the bolted electoral door.

Committing the party therefore to reaffirm and press on with the tactic which had served it so poorly, the leading committees summoned the members to renewed and extended exertions in the local authority contests of 1967. The GLC elections falling due, all the boroughs were contested once more, 'giving every elector the opportunity to vote communist', according to yet another *Marxism Today* article[18] which must have induced in its readers a strong sense of *déjà vu*. For the first and last time every seat in Glasgow was fought. A handful of gains were in fact made in Scotland, all of them in traditional centres of party strength, none in a major city. The GLC results marked a recession on the 1964 election. Local government results in the following two years were no more encouraging. Perhaps these were even more significant than those between 1964 and 1967, for they showed the Communist Party quite unable to profit by the deepening electoral discredit into which the government fell during 1968 and 1969.

Had the party's electoral débâcle represented its only activity outside of the industrial field it is just possible that it might have been more forcefully challenged, but in fact in areas of much greater emotional moment it was playing a substantial part, if no longer the sole or leading one that it had played in former years. This was an immediate product of the stances in foreign affairs adopted by the Labour government out of a mixture of ideological conviction and external pressures. Above all there existed the necessity, springing from the government's determination to guard the position of sterling, of relying upon United States aid in maintaining the exchange rate. In consequence Wilson's Cabinet was forced to accept an American lead on all world issues of substance where United States interests were believed to be at stake.

Labour had actually fought the 1964 election on a commitment to discontinue the intended construction of a British nuclear-armed submarine fleet in addition to the already existing US one in the Holy Loch. Instead a cutback in conventional armaments was initiated to allow this project to continue and in 1969[19] the first British nuclear submarine was launched. Reaction in Britain and in the Labour Party was muted: there was no shortage of political protest going on in the country at the time, but its focus had shifted. Since 1962 CND had been in precipitate decline, its 1965 Easter march being the last such of any size, and what demonstrations as it was able to mount having more the suggestion of quaint traditions. None the less it continued and this was due in no small measure to the CP, whose members interested in this field were among the most devoted in maintaining a skeleton organisation.

Of much greater centrality to the public consciousness was the Vietnam War and the unquestioning adherence of the British government not only to the US war aims but also to its tactics of mass slaughter of the potentially enemy population.

> The general perception was of Wilson unsuccessfully acting as peacemaker...while in practice going along with a highly unpopular US policy of mass bombing of North Vietnam, in return for US financial aid. It was a deeply unpleasant vision of a client relationship.[20]

The CP (and the YCL) directed its chief energies to opposition and protest, both on its own account and as a participant in the ad hoc movements which emerged to prosecute the anti-government and anti-US campaign, although to some extent outflanked by the organisations to its left, which emerged as more aggressive and publicly visible campaigners for the Vietnamese cause. The slogan which the CP preferred was 'Peace in Vietnam', which it saw as likely to unite the widest political support, by contrast with 'Victory to the Vietnamese', favoured by the less cautious and which the party feared to be divisive of anti-war sentiment. After much hesitation the party agreed to co-operate with the Vietnam Solidarity Campaign dominated by its leftist rivals, but this co-operation remained on a very distant basis. The CP in fact largely abandoned the public advocacy of political solidarity to the far left, figures from which, like Tariq Ali, became the most publicly visible spokespeople. The 'broad' solidarity movement having passed outside its control, the CP, though recommending its members to participate, preferred to concentrate upon its own publications and campaigns, such as the YCL's successful medical aid initiative, including tours through Britain with a van specially equipped for this purpose.

Like its CND predecessor, the Vietnam campaign drew most heavily for its mass basis upon the educated youth. The party, too, benefited from the mood of radicalism increasingly prevalent within establishments of higher and further education, manifested by sit-ins and occupations and enhanced enormously by the events of 1968 in France, the USA and elsewhere. Striking advances were recorded in both numbers and organisation. Previously moribund student branches sprang to life and dozens of fresh ones were established in both new and old institutions. During this period the CP employed a full-time National Student Organiser, and a National Student Committee met on a regular basis, as did a yearly student conference. The surge was reflected in the broader field of student politics with the widespread success of communists in student union ballots and in elections to the executive of the National Union of Students, culminating in Digby Jacks's accession to the NUS Presidency in 1971.[21]

Much of the credit for steering these developments was due to the National Student Organiser, Fergus Nicholson, who was also the moving spirit behind the Communist University of London, which started in 1969, as a week-long seminar run by the party, advertised with eye-catching posters and consisting, according to the prospectus, of 'a series of intensive courses in Marxism–Leninism, its impact and use, in the world battle of opposing social systems and ideologies', and which was to become in due course the most publicised aspect of the party's ideological endeavours. With the YCL starting to decline, the student milieu was the principal growth area for the party during the late 1960s and was also the arena of confrontation with groupings which, for the first time in its history, offered a significant challenge to the CP from the left and disputed with the party its possession of revolutionary credentials.

First in the field was the Trotskyist Gerry Healy's Socialist Labour League (SLL), established in the aftermath of 1956 from a small long-term nucleus around Healy and incorporating a number of the party's defectors of that era, such as Cliff Slaughter and Peter Fryer. As these things go it was a significant force even in the early 1960s and showed itself able to capture control of the Young Socialists by 1964 after a conflict inside that organisation with the predecessors of the Socialist Workers' Party (SWP). This latter organisation, then functioning under the title of International Socialism (IS), was still acting as a faction within the Labour Party, while what was to emerge as the Militant Tendency, although also already in existence, was the most obscure of the three – all of them, along with even more obscure grouplets, fragments of the Trotskyist tradition.

As early as the beginning of 1964 the party began to take serious notice of what it always referred to as 'the sectarians' or 'the ultra-left'. A duplicated listing was circulated in March under the title *The Attack upon the Party from the So-Called 'Extreme Left'* and an article appeared in *Marxism Today* written by Betty Reid, who had been given a responsibility for such matters.[22] The stated aim of the circular was to enable party cadres to recognise infiltrators, and its tone is summed up as follows:

> We have to make clear that all these groupings without exception are *out to destroy the party and to weaken and confuse the British Labour Movement* [original emphasis]. We have to explain this, we have to warn against association. Finally we have to make clear that the party is united in its determination to achieve socialism, and will not tolerate association with these people, or failure to fight for our policy when they appear.[23]

What was now occurring was an ongoing and long-term regrouping upon the British left following the failure of the Bevanites or the 1956 New Left to make an impact on the policies or constitutional structures of the Labour Party. Not that the CP at first regarded these organisations with any great degree of seriousness, looking on them as more of a nuisance, a 'dying, rotten organism', than as significant competitors in the area which it considered to be its own fiefdom, and remaining unshakeably convinced that any rival pretenders to Marxism were inevitably splitters and disruptors in the labour movement.

The climate of the student environment, passionately exercised over the national and international issues of the day as well as matters of internal concern, especially civil liberties and accountability within their institutions, proved as favourable to the leftist sects as to the party – all the more so as the traditional Labour left, traumatised by the behaviour of its government, was at that time undergoing a crisis of disintegration and collapse. The Trotskyists throve mightily, and Maoism, after its false start with McCreery's organisation, achieved a second wind in student politics, further stimulated from 1967 by the Cultural Revolution in China with its evocations of revolutionary romanticism.

As with the party's own student complement, Third World issues were the especial focus for the rivals to its left: Southern Africa, the Middle East, but above all, Vietnam. As noted earlier, the CP's ambiguity over the most appropriate means to prosecute the campaign against the US invasion and British government complaisance allowed the leftists to seize the initiative with the formation of the Vietnam Solidarity Campaign, which in the event attained the highest profile and greatest public success, mobilising at least 100,000 people, most of them young, to demonstrate in the centre of London in October 1968.[24] In spite of the strictures of the 1964 circular, party student organisations on the ground found themselves having perforce to co-operate on occasion with these ideological bogeys. They did so as infrequently as possible, however,[25] much preferring co-operation with mainstream Labour or even Liberal students, with whom they formed first the Radical Student Alliance and then the Broad Left to win influence and positions within the structures of the National Union of Students.

With the benefit of twenty-five years' hindsight it is clear that the more successful of the ultra-left organisations, specifically the IS/SWP and Militant (aka the Revolutionary Socialist League), moved in to fill the space created by the CP's implicit evacuation of the Leninist ground on which it had once stood: the relentless promotion of party-led[26] rank-and-file militancy in combination with frenetic revolutionary exhortation. Large or small though it might be depending on circumstances, the audience attracted by that sort of thing never altogether vanished. However, in following this course the leftists rediscovered the same dilemma which dogged the CP until it gave up the strategy. To draw in wider support bodies had to be created officially distinct from the party but in fact controlled by it; their evident lack of autonomy then discredited those 'fronts' and gave the operation a conspiratorial stigma. The alternative, to accept genuine autonomy, violated on the other hand the Leninist prescriptions of leadership.

None the less, in the 1960s the effective monopoly which the party had hitherto enjoyed of organised Marxism and Leninism,[27] publicly recognised, and which it continued to assert, was decisively challenged and broken. This was of great importance, for it meant that anyone developing a Marxist outlook or one in irreconcilable opposition to established society and politics, who would hitherto have found no organisational expression for it other than the Communist Party, had instead a considerable menu to choose from, and that meant in turn a worrying contraction in its potential recruiting base.

In fact the CP's regrowth peaked at just over 34,000 members in early 1964, and from that point decline set in remorselessly with only occasional short pauses. (The YCL's growth continued fractionally longer.) Recruitment, as Gollan was careful to emphasise at the 1965 Congress, was actually quite buoyant during 1964, but had been exceeded by even greater losses. The difficulty revealed here in holding on to members once gained connects with his admission that the consolidation of the organisational structure and the party's communal life had been neglected in the drive for electoral contests. Participation in them was viewed as the most effective means of raising the CP's public profile and also as the highroad to the longed-for goal of a 'mass party' through recruitment of people who had come into contact with it during those campaigns.

As usual, the principal obstacle to the achievement of the goal was thought by the leadership to lie not in the nature of social and political realities but in insufficient conviction on the part of the members that it represented a feasible target. Gollan's reply to the discussion at the 1963 Congress exemplified this attitude:

> When I came into the Congress yesterday, the first man I bumped into was Adam McKay from Thurso...Richard Hitchens is just round the corner from Land's End...So if you fill in the spaces in between we will have the mass party we are all talking about....
>
> Then we have Comrade Welsby. He himself has made twelve new members. It is characteristic of the new members that they have no inhibitions when it comes to recruitment. They feel that if it is good enough for them to join it is good enough for everybody else... Notice

how Comrade Welsby showed that when you build the party you build up the other organisations of the working class.[28]

Indeed, the branches were encouraged to pursue likely recruits as industriously as would Jehovah's Witnesses and 'put the political case for joining' to them. For a branch, Borough or District to finish up with fewer members than at the beginning of reregistration – which lasted from October to the beginning of the new year – was an especially deep disgrace, but to have made only a minimal advance was regarded as scarcely any better.

A profitable source of new members was maintained in the public rallies which the party was accustomed to staging in large cities as a regular, at least annual, event. Not infrequently the General Secretary himself was the star attraction, usually combined with a leading local trade unionist and perhaps a YCL representative or spokesperson for 'women's issues'; the party was not forgetful of these, with Women's Committees at EC and District levels[29] and an official declaration that 'the aim of building a mass party must include the recruitment of many thousands of women into membership'. At some point in the proceedings a member known for special talents in wit and repartee would appear on the platform to conduct the collection, at the end of which anybody who had somehow managed to resist the intensity of persuasion to donate notes would be only too anxious to empty pockets or handbags of small change.

But when the appeal for recruits arrived the rally would take on a nearly evangelistic atmosphere as non-members in the audience were exhorted to commit themselves. Application forms would be handed up to the platform with an announcement of which branch the convert was about to be enrolled in. It was common practice for the forms of applicants who had been recruited shortly beforehand to be retained by their branches and produced at the rally, both in order to get the process going and to inflate the number of recruits which the rally would be recorded as having produced.

From time to time in party discussions questions might be raised as to the probable value of recruits secured in the ways indicated, many of whom would be minimally active or not at all, holding a party card only because they did not know how to say no and could not resist being pestered into joining. The answer to this criticism was that a mass party, as distinct from an activist one, could be constructed only in such a manner and it was implied that to be other than importunate in pressuring likely (or not-so-likely) individuals into joining was equivalent to withholding rights to membership. If people with whom members were in contact were not done the favour of being importuned to join, the members had been negligent in their responsibility towards them.

Targets were set for recruits as they were set for everything else, it was a way of life for the party of the 1960s, and they were handed down from higher to lower committees throughout the hierarchy. 'Political conviction' was supposed to be won, and generally it was. Particular targets were placed within a political context, often enough in a manner which suggested that the future health of the labour movement, colonial liberation and peace depended upon their attainment. In the midst of the feeling generated by this approach private reservations, where they existed, about the feasibility of targets would be felt as guilty self-indulgence and transformed into determination to achieve them, and that, if successful, would result in both personal fulfilment and standing within the party.

> The whole political situation, the growing reaction to Government policies, the disillusionment with Labour, the bitterness of lefts and militants to the latest Government White Paper aimed at degutting the trade unions, the readiness of people to take action, given proper leadership...at least indicates certain new possibilities for building the party.
>
> [C]an you take extra copies of the *Morning Star* at the weekend for sales at stances or on door-to-door canvasses? How many of the new party folder will you handle... are there party contacts, readers of the paper, party voters who might come to a meeting... to hear the case put for our party?
>
> [I]f ever a situation called for people to take their stand with the party of socialism and the working class it is now.[30]

To be sure, activists were sometimes warned in general terms against allowing the party to consume their whole lives, but nobody tried very hard to stop them if they did, and if the expectations imposed upon willing activists were highly exacting, for leading individuals they were stupefying. The branch Secretary was the pivot of the basic unit, had to combine administrative functions with duties of political leadership and was ultimately responsible for whether the branch paid its dues, raised its donations, held its meetings, sold its papers and conducted public agitation and local election contests. A members' manual published in 1962 characterised the paragon of the ideal Secretary who in addition to the above:

keeps well-informed on events, local and national, is familiar with party policy and makes it his or her business to know the leading people in the local labour movement and the principal civic persons...As a result the Secretary is seen as the public representative of the party, speaks at its meetings, on occasion leads the deputations to the various local authorities, writes to the press on behalf of the branch, etc.[31]

Such people seldom had difficulty in making the official viewpoint prevail within commitee meetings, assisted by the mental disposition which the committed activists would bring to a meeting where decisions were to be taken demanding yet more effort and determination, for example to raise *Morning Star* circulation substantially in the face of drooping sales and price increase; a decision requiring more sales pitches maintained over longer periods, more newsagents requested more often to display it on their counters, existing buyers on 'runs' interrogated as to the names of potential new takers and these subsequently followed up. Combined with requirements to raise more cash, sell copies of the latest party pamphlet, mobilise for a demonstration or rally, prepare for a local election, these expectations might well be regarded as likely to numb the imagination and induce a state of demoralised helplessness.

Long service in this style was likely to mould a characteristic approach and attitude combining tenacity, knowledgeability and organisational efficiency with a distinctive narrowness of vision, a studied blindness towards evidence contradicting the mystique which the CP cultivated around its own activities. What may be termed their moral formation was doubly emphatic in the case of the full-time organisers, people who regarded themselves as standing in the tradition of Lenin's professional revolutionaries. For them the burdens were further multiplied. On top of an exhausting working day the majority of their evenings would be spent in meetings or conducting visits with a political intent. Sunday was normally an ordinary working day as important all-day committee meetings tended to be scheduled for that time. Saturdays might normally be a little slacker, but often enough would be taken up with weekend-long meetings, conferences or schools, or perhaps organising and taking responsibility for some measure of social activity. Outside the London centre they were generally responsible for raising their own inadequate wages and there was no pension at the end.

That description is an archetype; individual performances might vary to greater or lesser degree from the ideal, although it is surprising how close to the model the majority of full-timers were able to get. An indolent or incompetent one was, then, virtually impossible to find, and though they might be criticised for unimaginativeness or authoritarianism the relationship between them and the party rank-and-file was normally one of high respect. They did not, however, enjoy the devotion reserved for leading 'industrial comrades', who may be said to have embodied in their persons the CP's aspiration to assume the political leadership of the working class, and whose appearance on party platforms was the signal for enthusiastic acclamation.

In the late 1960s a study was published of the social composition and political culture of the CPGB.[32] It demonstrated, so far as its author was able to acquire the relevant data, that the two major occupational components of the party's membership were engineers and teachers, and – here the author does not quite conceal his own surprise – that its members tended to be socially well-adjusted individuals and its practices not markedly more undemocratic than those of other parties. Although it is impossible to be certain, the probability is that the majority of recruits were made through workplace contacts, though not necessarily or even normally into workplace branches. The party's appeal rested ultimately upon the grass roots behaviour of its members and branches with a daily newspaper to interpret the broader meaning of what they were doing. Probably the absence of the Labour Party as an industrial presence was important here as well. The fact that it was *skilled* workers who were most disposed to join may well be explained by the greater appeal of the party's theoretical concepts to their generally more educated background.[33]

Communist Party members tended to be respectable in a general sort of way, to take their lead in social mores and behaviour, in dress and appearance, from the cultural ethos of the skilled working class which numerically dominated the party. This was deliberately encouraged as the sort of practice most likely to draw support and esteem. Activists were expected to present exemplary models of working-class virtue. The 1960s, unsurprisingly, saw a weakening of constraints and censures in this regard. At their beginning a District Secretary could still compel a prominent YCLer to shave the beard which the Secretary regarded as incompatible with the image he wanted young communists to project; by 1970 such a notion would have appeared laughable.

Simultaneously with the launch of its political offensive from 1963 the party leadership tried to tune up the organisation to cope with more intense demands. In 1965 a Committee on Party Organisation reported in what in many ways was an unusually frank and revealing document, particularly so in its recognition of weaknesses and shortcomings in the standard routines of party life. It was even more interesting in what it hinted at rather than exposed openly regarding malfunctions at the party centre, where it recommended the EC to conduct an examination. In industrial branches only a few carried out a 'high level of *all round political work* with a direct influence in the factory and labour movement and in the fight for Communist representation in local and parliamentary elections' and the document deplored the paucity of contact between factory and local branches.[34]

The conclusion was necessarily an impressionistic one, but most who were in a position to judge would probably have agreed that apart from the fall in numbers the general level of routine party work and activity had declined between 1963 and 1967.[35] The trend is not to be wondered at, for the kind of public activity in which the party engaged and which its electoral aspirations led it even to intensify was made sustainable only by the willing acceptance of an authoritarian leadership style on top of strong political conviction. Conviction might not have diminished – at least before 1968 – but the expanding consumer society and changing social culture of the 1960s was making it more difficult to impose authoritarian norms in a voluntary organisation which maintained any degree of contact with reality.[36]

As might be expected, it was within the Young Communist League that a foretaste of the change, and of a traditionalist reaction to it, first came to light. Membership growth in this instance continued into 1965, when it touched 5,000, and its National Secretary could write, with rather more optimism than judgement, 'The YCL is more and more becoming recognised as a leading force in youth politics'.[37] Trying to increase its numbers and expand its social base, with 'left unity' in mind, the YCL leadership attempted to come to terms, if not entirely identify itself with, the emergent youth culture of the time, and so provoked an indignant outcry. A large photograph of the Beatles on the front of *Challenge* resulted in gratifying sales figures, even if many casual purchasers at street sales were less gratified, not realising at first what they had bought. Trying to follow this up a few months later by a photo of the Swinging Blue Jeans resulted in high sales resistance – not only from the public but also from many YCLers who refused to sell it. More notorious still was a folder entitled *The Trend*. Rather garish in appearance, the title itself was received as a provocation by members convinced that the working-class essence of the YCL was being rejected in the striving to broaden its appeal. Although the crisis blew over and *Challenge* shifted to a format which tried to make it look like *Private Eye*, the organisational capacity of the YCL as well as its numbers were by the late 1960s in visible decline and the lines of subsequent division in the CP clearly apparent.

The first public indication of serious disagreement appeared as early as the open discussion in the party press preceding the 1965 Congress[38] and from a potentially disturbing source. Sid French was the full-time secretary of the Surrey District[39] of the party and the letter he wrote to *Comment*, now the title of the party weekly, combined, in a markedly aggressive if not hostile tone, complaints about deficiency in political motivation with an attack on the British leadership for not supporting as unreservedly as other communist parties had done the CPSU against the CPC.[40] French was not a lone voice but spoke for a section of the party ready to blame internal obstacles and failures for even the most minimal departure from the Soviet model. In the discussion following the disastrous electoral performance of 1966 French returned to the charge, his District having voted to reject Gollan's post-election report, and his demonstration of the secular decline in the party vote was scarcely answered by Reuben Falber's accusation that French was indulging in 'wild assertions'.

Not long afterwards the pursuit of a wider constituency of support continued with the *Daily Worker*'s change of name. The question had not been ventilated at the 1965 Congress but was unveiled in the new year by the EC and the paper's Management Committee. Readers were invited to submit possible new names but hardly any of them thought of the rather clumsy title which the leadership eventually chose, the *Morning Star*. They would have liked to call it the *Star* but that title was owned elsewhere, though not currently in use.

The nature of the decision as well as the manner of its timing convinced the dissidents that the EC was drawing away from the working class and floundering into revisionism. Their fears were not diminished by an EC decision to redraft the *British Road* and a new edition of the programme was got ready for submission to the Congress at the end of 1967. In fact, although the document was rewritten completely, differences were stylistic rather than substantial and were matters of emphasis more than of ostensible content. That did not prevent one critical grouping, the Bexley Borough,[41] from damning it as 'revisionist, non-revolutionary, unrealistic and dreaming of the sweet by-and-by'. Moreover, this political enervation was being connected more explicitly with the party's wretched electoral performances and organisational woes. The columns of the pre-Congress discussion were full of critical voices, now articulated most clearly by French and the Surrey District.

French centred his critique upon the party's failure to lead the growing mass radicalism said to be erupting in Britain, because it was squandering its strength in trying to emerge as the fourth electoral party, and he linked this to its international positions:

> We are seen to be equivocating in our attitude to the world communist movement and concerned to be dissociating ourselves from the Russians to the point of absurdity. Young people are in political ferment on a scale never seen before, yet we seem determined to lower the revolutionary political appeal we have to make. So we produce a youth magazine in the month of the 50th Anniversary which gives 12 column inches to that revolution and 65 to drugs and hippies.

He and Surrey prescribed:

> a greater share of our work directed towards industry and the mass movement, electoral tactics which follow from this, changing the character of the *Morning Star* so that it is a much more polemical, political newspaper, and ending our equivocation about the world communist movement.

Surrey District added that:

> There is a decline in practically every measurable aspect of our work...our electoral policy helps to isolate us from the Labour movement and not only hinders the development of left unity, but our independent work as well...[loss of nerve is exemplified by] the disastrous decision to change the name of the *Daily Worker*.[42]

The party leadership brushed this challenge aside easily enough once the Congress convened, confident that the policies it was following represented 'a major contribution to the development of left unity...to the challenge to right-wing policies in the Labour Party, and the significant progressive advance in policy at the 1967 TUC', but the following year the simmering dissatisfaction was given an explosive focus once again by the party's international relationships. In January 1968 the dismissal of Anton Novotny from the Czech CP leadership was followed by the liberalisation of the 'Prague Spring'. The British party in a statement published in the *Morning Star* of 27 July made no secret of its enthusiasm, compared the events taking place in Czechoslovakia to *The British Road to Socialism* and 'welcomed the positive steps taken to tackle the wrongs of the past and strengthen socialist democracy'.

These sentiments were undoubtedly not shared by members whose conception of socialism was intrinsically an authoritarian one, but so long as relations between the Czech and Soviet parties remained formally correct their scope for expression was limited, although *Labour Monthly* was eloquent in its silence. Nevertheless, a letter appeared in the *Morning Star* of 5 July 1968, from a Surrey address, referring to:

> the drift...to the disruption of the economy, sabotage of the Czech participation in the Warsaw Pact, confusion in the army and an effort to slow down the progress towards socialism.

The British party, the writer opined:

> has come through this affair very badly, repeating parrot-like slogans about sovereign rights and non-intervention while Czechoslovakia appeared ripe for subversion and winning for the policies of the West.

and concluded that the CPGB suffered from:

> Bureaucracy, remoteness from the people, stale out-of-date thinking and resentment of comradely criticism.

It was a foretaste of what was to happen inside the party when the Warsaw Pact invasion eventually occurred on 21 August. This time the British party condemned the Soviet action immediately and categorically, and once more the columns of the party press were filled with embittered controversy. Now, however, the roles were reversed from 1956, with the CP leadership in line with public feeling and the dissidents accusing it of class betrayal. Not that the leadership retrospectively condemned where it had stood on the earlier occasion, excusing the difference on the grounds that in Czechoslovakia the CP had remained in full control of the situation, there were no supposed fascist gangs on the rampage murdering communists and no threat to leave the Warsaw Pact.

In the short term the consequences were a good deal less traumatic than in 1956, though in the long run perhaps even more far-reaching. Over Hungary many members had quit, the party was made the object of vehement public abuse, and its public image, unprepossessing at the best of times, rendered quite abhorrent. Yet the inner leadership, whatever personal qualms some may have had, stayed wholly united, the organisational structure remained relatively undamaged and ideological unity grew more solid. In 1968, by contrast, few losses occurred in the immediate term and there was no campaign of vilification. But on this occasion the rupture extended right into the leadership. Palme

Dutt, unrepentant Stalinist that he was, emerged from retirement to fight against the official line at the 1969 Congress. He was defeated but at least two Districts with their organisational apparatus were in open revolt and in outlook if not in formal terms had seceded from King Street. An internal battle was now joined which grew steadily more all-embracing from congress to congress.

Even outside the bounds of this conflict the party's self-confidence and confidence in the international communist movement were badly lacerated. It had suffered betrayal in an unprecedented fashion in the shape of an attack on a ruling communist party enjoying the evident confidence of its nation and protesting its attachment to the Warsaw Pact and Soviet friendship. Nothing so much as this broke the fetish of the 'workers' fatherland' for the majority of the rank-and-file (or strengthened it for some others) and worked to determine the line of the party's future development.

The party leadership did not by any means renounce their Soviet attachments, and depicted their stance as being one of fraternal criticism. Vietnam continued to be an issue of even greater importance and emotional commitment over which the Soviet role was applauded unreservedly – the great October demonstration occurred in the same year. The course of domestic politics, too, constrained the forces within the party making for disruption and moreover gave it the opportunity to exercise a bigger influence on British history than at any time since its foundation.

The Labour government, having at last achieved a positive balance of payments at the cost of alienating most of its social constituency, and tempted by favourable signals in the opinion polls, went to the country in June 1970 and unexpectedly lost.[43] Edward Heath's administration assumed office with a clear economic strategy in mind. It was defined by three main principles. The first of these was to allow market forces to weed out the hopelessly inefficient sectors of British industry, the notorious 'lame ducks', and to back this up with, secondly, a fresh application for EEC membership. Thirdly, the new government aimed to revive its predecessor's defeated strategy of lowering wage costs by penal legal sanctions upon trade union activity in the shape of an Industrial Relations Bill. In all of these undertakings it ran head on against the resistance of a still undefeated trade union movement in conflicts which both allowed Communist Party members to come to the fore as mass leaders and enabled them to exploit the links with non-communists in the trade union hierarchy which they had been patiently constructing for a decade.

The Liaison Committee for Defence of Trade Unions, fairly moribund since Wilson's capitulation over *In Place of Strife*, was quickly revived and set itself to evoke mass opposition and push the TUC into adopting a militant line. It promoted numerous demonstrations and innumerable resolutions between 1970 and 1972. More pointedly, it succeeded in bringing out over half a million workers in a demonstrative strike in December 1970 and three million in March 1971 when it called for a one-day general strike. This did not prevent the Industrial Relations Bill passing into law, but it succeeded in building up an atmosphere in the union movement which made it inoperable. In July the Industrial Relations Court created by the Act committed to prison five dockers, including two CP members, for being in contempt of its rulings. In the uproar which followed the TUC itself was induced to threaten general strike action and the government quickly climbed down and engineered the dockers' release, its credibility by now hopelessly undermined.

Even as this crisis was approaching its culmination another was emerging which would bring communists still more positively into the public eye. In June the government, in line with its 'lame ducks' intention, announced that it would refuse further assistance to the financially strapped Upper Clyde Shipbuilders' (UCS) publicly owned consortium, and under the shadow of the Liquidator and the leadership of communist shop stewards the occupation of the four shipyards and the work-in began. Its progress and eventual success, together with the party's contribution to saving the yards from closure, were assisted by uniquely favourable circumstances.

The main strategist, inspirational public leader and spokesperson of the work-in was the same Jimmy Reid who had led the YCL in the early 1960s. By the middle of the decade his age was such that he could no longer be decently continued in that office, and so he had been appointed to the position of Scottish Secretary of the Party.[44] That had not proved a success and so Reid had given up full-time party employment and, while remaining within the leadership of the Scottish party, gone back to manual work in John Brown's shipyard, located in Clydebank, his home town, and where he was soon elected as a shop steward. The other three yards of the consortium lay within Glasgow itself. All had been nationalised and combined under the previous government, and, though viable, their financial position was shaky, the pretext for the intended closure.

The political temper of Clydebank can be judged from the fact that it elected two communist councillors and gave substantial votes to others in local elections. In Glasgow the party, though without that electoral base, still had nearly 2,000 members and was strongly represented upon the local trades council. It enjoyed excellent relations with the autonomous Scottish TUC, one of whose leading officials, Jimmy Milne, was a party member. There were other communist stewards in the yards and combined they set the tone of an exceptionally able collective which succeeded in handling the logistics and the publicity of the work-in with the utmost panache, and won it huge popularity throughout Scotland.[45]

The Scottish Committee of the CP, although some of the leading stewards were members of it, did not run the work-in, which was very much the business of the stewards' committee. The Scottish leadership did informally advise Reid and his fellow party stewards, but it was advice and not instruction and the communist stewards did not form a caucus.[46] The Scottish Committee, however, did co-ordinate the work of CP members throughout Scotland in mobilising support for the work-in, especially among trade union organisations, and for the monster demonstrations which accompanied it.

Before the end of the year the government had retreated and discovered a formula to enable all the yards to continue operating and most of their workforce to remain in employment. One commentator[47] regards this capitulation as sparking the beginning of Thatcherite revolt within the Conservative Party. Certainly it greatly strengthened the confidence – and popularity – of the trade union movement and significantly weakened government morale in advance of the next major challenge, from the miners, to its wage restraint policy. The first phase of that culminated again to the government's discredit in the successful strike of January 1972,[48] where once more communist trade unionists were to be found in the forefront. Mick McGahey, more than anyone, had been responsible for putting communist miners back into their leading position in the Scottish NUM after the battering their position had received at the hands of Lawrence Daly. President of the Scottish miners, and though kept out of the British presidency by a right-wing lobby, he was Vice-President and the most forceful left-winger on the NUM Executive. From that position he worked with Daly, now the union Secretary, and such rising militants as Arthur Scargill to organise the strike, being characterised in the press as the hard man of the union in contrast to the more emollient right-wing President, Joe Gormley.[49]

McGahey's role in the strike lifted the party's public profile even higher than it had been as a result of the UCS and the conflicts around the Industrial Relations Act. With all necessary caution allowed for, it is highly likely that if the Communist Party had, as might have been imaginable, disintegrated after 1956, the outcome of the years 1970–3 would have been markedly different. On the other hand, it is equally clear that the gains to the party *per se* were very modest compared to the extent of its public impact in that period. Its numbers did not leap upwards. Jimmy Reid presently secured election as the third communist councillor in Clydebank, but when he stood as a parliamentary candidate in the same constituency in 1974 he polled very disappointingly, presented no danger to the Labour candidate and only just saved his deposit.[50]

During the late 1960s and early 1970s the Communist Party experienced something of an Indian summer. It became briefly a national political force and some of its industrial leaders achieved a real public standing beyond the bounds of their own trade union arena. Its student activists were starting to be elected to leading positions in the National Union of Students, which they effectively dominated through the Broad Left caucus. The Communist University of London became a regular feature of summer vacations, esteemed and successful on the left, attracting interest well beyond the party's own membership and publicising some of the most innovative political and theoretical notions of the day. Furthermore, both the Scottish and Welsh Committees began regular publication of their own journals of theory and political comment.[51]

Yet the overall decline in numbers was not reversed. Hundreds joined, but more departed and slowly but irreversibly the general quality of the party's internal life deteriorated. It was a reality symptomatic of the CP's continuing inability, despite its successes, to situate itself in the British political culture. Although it was still far larger than any of them, the sects to its left dispensing revolutionary intoxication were proportionately growing much faster. To its immediate right, the Labour left, which the party assiduously courted but in vain, was starting to recover its nerve and begin its campaign for ascendancy in the Labour Party, thus emerging as another rival pole of attraction to the CP. As class confrontation mounted and strengthened the party's hand at the industrial but not the political level, as its Soviet links weakened without being broken, as internal tensions simmered, some of its members began to look for a more sophisticated strategy capable of making its policies relevant on the British political stage.

7 New Horizons?: 1974–1984

The rising tempo between 1970 and 1974 of politically associated industrial action, both traditional and novel,[1] acted as a constraint upon the process of internal differentiation within the Communist Party itself. So long as the class enemy was being confronted – on occasion with spectacular success – with the CP in the forefront, there remained enough empathy and sense of political solidarity to hold accumulating tensions and latent hostilities from escalating to crisis point. The fall of the Heath government in February 1974, however, following the débâcle of its economic policy and failure to overcome the miners, faced the CP once more with the question of its basic strategy and the dilemma of the place it occupied within the British labour movement.

The outcome of the 1974 General Elections could, with a certain amount of stretching, be regarded as having partially vindicated the scenario for left advance sketched out in *The British Road to Socialism*. A mass movement led by the working class had, using the electoral process, dismissed a right-wing government. Certainly, its replacement, the new Labour government, could hardly be claimed as left-wing, let alone backed by communist MPs, a vital requirement of the *BRS*'s strategy for transition to socialism: however, the fluidity of the developments then taking place and the elemental mass upsurge, unprecedented in the postwar era, gave every reason to hope that it might be possible to impose a leftward course upon it or else change its personnel in a left direction.

Such at any rate was the perspective to which the CP adhered, seeing its own role as central in the circumstances and judging that a growing Communist Party, able to make a convincing electoral showing, would be absolutely essential.[2] Its view as to what would constitute a left-wing course, beginning to lay siege to the strongholds of state monopoly capitalism, was a wholly classical one. In the field of foreign relations it would have meant nuclear disarmament, withdrawal from the NATO alliance, condemnation of the US war in Vietnam, and friendly relations with the USSR.

161

British foreign policy must cease being subordinated to the United States of America and the interests of British imperialism. The ending of the British Government's support for American aggression in Vietnam is the first essential step in the struggle for world peace...[others are] dissolution of NATO and other imperialist alliances...withdrawal of all British forces from other countries and all foreign troops from Britain.[3]

In social and cultural policy it would entail a dramatic expansion of provision, paid for by taxes on property and large incomes. The heart of the matter, however, was economic and industrial policy.

The left-wing credentials of a Labour government would be judged by its willingness to initiate the extension of public ownership, especially in the sensitive financial sectors, make available state support to traditional industries employing large workforces and impose economic planning and investment policies, carried out in collaboration with labour movement organisations, aimed at satisfying social needs instead of the demands of private profit, 'a radical and undiluted version of the state collectivist mode of economic organisation'.[4] Above all else it would not seek to interfere in the labour market to the disadvantage of the workforce in collective bargaining. It was a fundamental conviction that so long as the economy remained predominantly capitalist wage demands could produce no adverse social effects, and most certainly could not generate inflation.[5] The repeal of the Heath government's industrial relations legislation was a self-evident starting point, to which the entire labour movement was in any case committed and which Wilson quickly implemented, but the party also expressed violent opposition to the voluntary 'social contract' by which the trade union leadership, especially in the person of Jack Jones of the TGWU, undertook to try to secure the abatement of wage pressures in exchange for advances in the 'social wage' and a policy of planned economic growth.

It was the CP's Industrial Organiser, Bert Ramelson, who invented, or at least popularised, the mocking retitlement of 'social contract' as 'social con-trick'. The condemnation was founded upon the proposition that any curb upon wage demands, voluntary no less than compulsory, could be of benefit only to capital and would stymie a programme of socialist advance before it even got started. The CP therefore, far from adopting a position equivalent to its stance during the first two years of the Attlee government, gave aggressive support in both publicity and action to every claim outside the official guidelines.

No less uncompromising was the party's hostility to the continuance of British EEC membership. To a lesser degree, this was based upon the expectation that the requirements of free capital and labour movement across European frontiers would be detrimental to the masses and that EEC trade policies would impose higher food prices without the promised compensation of bigger wage rises. More importantly, the Common Market was viewed in its essence as a conspiracy by European capital to entrench its power more firmly on a continental scale by abolishing national sovereignties which might come into conflict with it. Therefore the central reason for the antagonism towards it of not only the CP but most of the left as well was their conviction that it would be used to block the adoption of socialist economic policies. The implicit political model behind this posture was one of unconstrained and total sovereignty residing in the British House of Commons which, once in the hands of the left (backed, of course, by an extra-parliamentary mass movement), could then be employed to institute an autarkic, collectivist economic programme, a siege economy if necessary.[6]

However, an alternative and opposed conception, still faint and tentative at this stage, was beginning to reveal itself in inner party discussion. It was associated especially with the name of Dave Purdy, an economist at Manchester University. This approach questioned the value of a programme which isolated the labour market from all other aspects of planning, disputed the dismissal of any connection between wage pressure and inflation, and suggested that the left should use acceptance of incomes policy not in a negative but in a proactive fashion to push forward and develop the limited social and planning commitments of the Labour government, describing the Social Contract as 'a radical agreement with a pronounced socialist orientation'.[7] In a special issue of *Marxism Today*, August 1974, the economic problems of the transition to socialism were debated. Purdy wrote on incomes policy, and while not saying anything that would have outraged the mood of the times, wondered whether 'a sound class instinct [alone] can breach the ideological ramparts [of reformism and political subordination]'.

By the time Parliament convened after Labour had secured only a wafer-thin majority in another General Election in October, it had become clear that the qualified promise which the Labour government seemed to offer on its formation was virtually exhausted and that the Cabinet was determined to pursue traditional policies of deflation, retrenchment, wage control, concession to the demands of capital[8] and no less traditional practices in other areas of government. Gollan denounced the government's programme as 'a rehash [of policies] which have failed in the past and will again'.[9] In February 1975 George Matthews, editor of the *Morning Star*, wrote in *Marxism Today* on the Wilson government and its crisis, identifying the essence of its problems as the refusal to be sufficiently left-wing and contrasting its sorry performance with the wonderful economic advance said to be in train in the Soviet bloc. It was an extremely traditionalist analysis, blaming the government for 'failure to make a clean break with bankrupt past policies, an acceptance of capitalist class values, and the operation of capitalist class laws', demanding instead, 'price freeze, slashing of monopoly profits...ending military spending abroad, controlling the export of capital, restricting exports to essentials, and selling private share and bondholding abroad', all accompanied with vigorous domestic reflation. The term 'Alternative Economic Strategy' was used to define the demands.

An attack, indirect but unmistakable, upon the official standpoint defined by Gollan and Matthews appeared in the April number of the journal, written by Mike Prior, a close associate of Purdy. The bitterly attacked object of his polemic was the denial of any connection between wages and inflation,[10] and in developing this he went on to advocate a 'working-class incomes policy' with all its implications.

Purdy and Prior were the most outspoken of a trend within the party increasingly ready to question the traditional political and social verities within which it operated and to point to the inadequacies of its theoretical analysis. The current tended to draw its inspiration from the work of Antonio Gramsci, whose writings had first been published in English in the late 1950s, met with some discussion in the CP during the 1960s and in the 1970s became the hallmark of a newly evolving political and theoretical project. What the new thinkers pointed to was the crudely reductionist nature of the explanations for social behaviour with which communist theory had hitherto been satisfied, its presumption of a direct and simple link between material circumstances and social response,[11] 'economism', as they termed it.[12] Their alternative was to emphasise the notion of 'hegemony' and to take very seriously the importance of cultural traditions, everyday experience and modes of perception which caused subordinated classes to accept the inferior position and exploitative relationships from which they suffered as natural and inevitable. The important conclusion was that the political consciousness of the working class was not 'naturally' radical or progressive, let alone with a ready socialist potential, and that turning it in such a direction might require a very different form of political intervention than the sort which had characterised the left up to that time: instead it should use a 'counter-hegemonic strategy' which actually in the here-and-now would set about the transformation of existing social practice.

The critics of the leadership from the other end of the CP spectrum, those who objected to the line taken on Czechoslovakia and whose disposition was primarily an authoritarian and traditionalist one, saw in the new trend no support for their own critique, but viewed these questionings, which they dismissed as an exotic academic import, with derision and contempt. 'The main reason for the attention given to Gramsci is that he's not Lenin', one of them asserted. The first signs were visible in the National Student Committee even in the late 1960s, where Martin Jacques clashed with Fergus Nicholson over such issues, but only after the stagnation of the 1974 Labour government and the end of the Vietnam War did they begin to make real headway.

If the explicit and thoroughgoing Gramscians represented only a small fraction of the party's membership, the acceptance that political realities could not be explained or analysed purely in terms of class conflict was much more widely accepted. On the one hand the concepts the Gramscians advanced were starting to percolate, most importantly, among the established leadership; on the other the pragmatic orientations of the party compared to the left-wing sects had long given it an instinctive appreciation of the complexities and contrariness of ideological consciousness among the masses. Hence its almost reflex inclination to subsume differences in the labour and progressive movement by promoting the widest measures of working unity against the ultimate enemies, imperialism, Conservatism or monopoly. Its bitter antagonism towards the sects was due more than anything else to their insistence upon the old Leninist principle of dividing the working-class (party) strictly from all other political forces and viewing united action between them as at most a very limited and temporary expedient.

Most probably this disposition is a significant part of the explanation for the receptivity of the party to the movements of women's and gay liberation as they emerged in the 1970s. Many of the most articulate women in the party embraced the movement, and the analysis they advanced of women's particular oppression was accepted virtually without public opposition as the official CP standpoint – though changing ingrained forms of behaviour was a more arduous project. The party, of course, had adhered always to formal principles of sexual equality and – though the conclusion is impressionistic – was perhaps somewhat more likely than most political organisations to appoint women to positions of leading responsibility. Naturally, though, its practice, in conformity with prevailing social norms, had been routinely and unconsciously sexist throughout its history. Party activists, full-timers and leaders were overwhelmingly men, and their ability to perform in such roles depended for the most part upon the availability of a domestic support system provided by women.[13] Although Douglas Hyde's allegations of rampant sexual exploitation inside the party are contradicted by all the other available evidence from that and other periods, instances certainly did occur, sometimes involving leading figures. In the 1960s *Challenge* was notoriously advertised with the slogan 'Are you getting it regularly?' and an issue from early 1969 (not dated) contained not only – with reference to Vietnam – the headline 'How dare they try to end this beauty?' over the photograph of a young woman, but also an advertisment with a photograph of one in a bikini declaring 'I gave my right hand for *Challenge*!'

The gay movement, too, found a welcome, though a rather more formal one, from the CP, and this was a sign of a rapidly shifting outlook as well, for there was little or nothing in the party's past history to suggest that it would be particularly advanced on this issue. It had seldom or never issued public statements upon the question, other than to welcome the partial decriminalisation of consenting male homosexual relations in the 1960s, and the prevailing grass roots reaction would have been that homosexuality was mostly an upper-class perversion of no interest to workers, and politically tainted moreover by association with the Nazi stormtroopers. Again the Gramscian influence is seen in the fact that when awareness did dawn, party discussion treated it as going beyond the question of civil rights into that of sexual politics and the social constructions of gender and sexuality.

Once more, however, distinction has to be drawn between the party's mainstream and its Stalinist or Stalinoid wing. The official lines on women's and gay rights were not openly challenged, but the reactions as expressed informally were often bitter and contemptuous. Issues of that sort were viewed as at best an irrelevance and distraction from the real class struggles in politics and industry. This was particularly so when feminists in the party began to criticise the male orientation of industrial bargaining structures and even to propose that there might be a case for thinking about negotiating structures which favoured women at the *expense* of male workers. Hostility was not diminished in these circles by the explicit attack of feminists upon Leninism for its authoritarian proclivities. Suspicion of the 'new social forces' was increased even more upon this wing of the party by the fact that these forces enjoyed the patronage of those same intellectuals who were accused of being out to dilute its class basis. Finally it must not be overlooked that there was undoubtedly a class division operating here within the party. The majority of its members had been formed by the socio-cultural background of the skilled working class, which tended to inhibit formal discourses on sexuality, whereas the ability to engage in such came much more easily as a rule to people with middle-class antecedents and lengthy educational experience. In any event, while the party did gain a measure of credibility from its prompt and unqualified identification with the aims of the new movements, the divergent reactions of its members to the public argument which had begun around conflicts of gender and sexuality constituted not the least of the tensions pulling it apart.

Comparison of the mid-1970s with an earlier phase of intense social and political conflict is evoked with a consideration of the progressing crisis in Irish affairs. Since the civil rights protests of 1968 had destabilised the Stormont regime in Belfast the conflict had steadily widened and grown bloodier. Amidst internment without trial and escalating violence, paratroopers in 1972 shot dead thirteen unarmed civil rights demonstrators and direct rule from Westminster was imposed. In 1974 Protestant paramilitaries enforced a general lock-out to destroy the attempt at a power-sharing executive in Ulster, and Birmingham pubs were bombed. Among the sectarian left groups the Irish issue became a matter of central concern but mainstream labour organisations in Great Britain, other than on a few rare occasions, maintained a posture of extraordinary detachment and so far as possible treated the terror raging in Ulster as a non-event.

The position which the Communist Party adopted was a 'correct' one in the diplomatic rather than political sense of the term. It did not ignore what was taking place in the province. Through its publications and resolutions it expressed opposition to the anti-democratic Unionist ascendancy and its paramilitary terror, the repressive behaviour of the British security forces and violations of civil liberty such as internment. On the other hand it condemned the terrorist actions of the Provisional IRA[14] and did not involve itself concretely in activities directed towards Irish affairs nor with the nationalist Irish community in Britain. The editions of the *BRS* up to 1968 had declared in favour of Irish reunification but the party did not advance this slogan. Instead it demanded a democratic reconstruction of the Northern Ireland polity – ambiguously, as the central question of the British connection was not addressed – and entrenched guarantees for civil liberties: a Bill of Rights. Overall, it would not be unfair to suggest that, as with the larger sections of the labour movement, the Irish problem was sidelined within the CP's concerns and treated fairly evasively.

With national issues on mainland Britain, where violence and death were not involved, the party had much less difficulty. Although explicitly ultra-centralist in its own practice,[15] it drew in theory a sharp distinction between the standards of a voluntary organisation such as itself, and the constitutional arrangements which affected all citizens. On the basis of the Leninist principle of nationality it had always favoured self-determination for Scotland and Wales, not excluding the right to separation, while making clear that it would argue against the exercise of that right, on grounds of economic integration and labour movement solidarity. At the same time it had been committed for many years to the support of devolutionary assemblies in Scotland and Wales, though it had never treated the question as one of any great priority. The party had been much more vocal, however, in arguing for a voting system of proportional representation both on principle and for the obvious reason that it would, as a minor party, expect to benefit greatly from it. In these respects it was sharply at odds with the Labour Party left, whose attachment to Westminster centralisation and first-past-the-post was no less than that of the right wing.

The Communist Party, therefore, though suspicious of the nationalist parties in both countries and what it saw as their divisive and sometimes potentially reactionary postures, especially in Scotland, was happy enough to tune in with national sentiment and campaign with energy in favour of devolved assemblies, endeavouring as usual to construct broad fronts in the labour movement and outside it in favour of these objectives. On this aspect at least there was an absence of internal division and harmony prevailed inside the party's own ranks. No doubt it was significant that such occurrences were becoming the exception rather than the rule.

During most of the 1970s, between Czechoslovakia and Afghanistan, unity also existed upon the important international issues of the day. At the final defeat of the United States in Vietnam in April 1975 universal rejoicing was evident upon the left, and all trends of opinion within the CP were happy to acknowledge the indispensable character of the assistance which the USSR had provided to the National Liberation Front and the North Vietnamese government. John Gollan wrote a celebratory illustrated pamphlet entitled *Victory in Vietnam*. No less unanimity had been displayed in the opposite direction in September 1973 when an ultra-right military coup overthrew the Popular Unity government of Chile, including communist ministers. The party's response was not merely verbal or expressed in demonstrations; its members put a great deal of effort into organising support for the stream of political refugees arriving in Britain from Chile and in helping to provide them with homes and employment. The Chilean events, however, did cause some to draw comparisons with Britain. There were analogies between the strategy pursued by the Chilean Communist Party and that of the *BRS* – indeed in 1970, following the election of Salvador Allende as the Popular Unity candidate, Gollan had declared that 'The Chilean comrades have stolen *The British Road to Socialism!*'[16] It was therefore not only the ultra-left or those outside the party, like Ralph Miliband,[17] who distrusted the CP's unavowed abandonment of Leninism, who raised questions as to what the events in Santiago implied for the prospects of a peaceful, parliamentary transition to socialism. However, by this time the *BRS* had become so embedded in the party's consciousness that its status as a programmatic blueprint could no longer be seriously questioned – it was merely subjected to different interpretations.

Nearer to home, the collapse of fascist-style regimes in Portugal and Spain, in 1974 and 1975 respectively, and the centrality of the communist movements in both countries, concentrated British party members' thinking on fundamental questions of political power. The two Iberian parties stood at virtually opposite ends of the communist spectrum, for while the Portuguese one was unregenerately Stalinist, the leader of the PCE, Santiago Carrillo, had popularised the term 'Eurocommunism'[18] and led the way in the formal rejection of such terminology as 'Marxism-Leninism' and 'dictatorship of the proletariat'. Nevertheless, however ideologically suspect Alvarho Cunhal of the PCP may have been to British Eurocommunists, all sections of the CPGB applauded the attempt of his party to exercise power in collaboration with the radicalised armed forces and deplored the frustration of that project by the Portuguese socialists in alliance with indigenous capital and European social democracy.[19] Contrariwise, much as Carrillo's writings were distrusted by British traditionalists, no British communist questioned the actual strategy pursued by the PCE following Franco's demise. The activities of foreign CPs in 1973–5 therefore did not become divisive issues in the manner of 1956 or 1968.

In 1976, however, the movement's history came back to haunt the party and dispute around it was to mark the beginning of the run-up to its first major organisational schism. The year before, John Gollan, like his predecessor ill and exhausted from the strains of party leadership, retired. His replacement was Gordon McLennan, who like Gollan was Scottish, originating from the heartland of Scottish communism, Glasgow. McLennan, a draughtsman before he became a party organiser, had been an extremely successful Scottish Secretary, having presided over the regrowth following 1957 and the intense level of activity around the Polaris campaigns. McLennan having been translated to London in the mid-1960s as National Organiser, the choice on Gollan's retirement lay beween him and Jack Woddis, the head of the International Department and author of several books on African politics. McLennan was chosen because he was thought to have the edge in organisational ability, and it was above all as an organiser that he was viewed.

In January 1976 an article by Gollan appeared in *Marxism Today*, written explicitly in connection with the twentieth anniversary of Khrushchev's secret speech,[20] and this was accompanied by a series of meetings around the country at which he discussed the piece and elaborated upon its implications. A controversial flood was released. Gollan was criticised by some for writing at great length without making any real advance in the argument from where it had been in 1956; implicitly accepting the personalisation of the issue; and for complacency in assuming that everything was now lovely in the Soviet garden. Others were outraged that the party should highlight the USSR's discreditable past instead of spending its time and energy fighting for socialism in Britain.

> Anti-socialist opposition must be crushed by the socialist state, because it is illegitimate and has no class basis in a socialist society. It is only kept alive by former members of the ruling classes, their descendants and followers, aided by imperialist intelligence organisations abroad.[21]

The meetings at which Gollan spoke on the subject were well-attended and tumultuous. If what he had said in his article was bad enough, the point that he began to advance in the meetings – namely that not only would a socialist regime in Britain allow a plurality of parties but would step down if defeated electorally – inspired outrage. Given the actual likelihood of such a regime finding itself in office within the foreseeable future, it might be thought that the question was a wholly abstract one and the passions aroused around it entirely synthetic. This, however, would be to misunderstand how close this abstraction was to the centre of communists' identity and how seriously the prospect of exercising power was taken as the justification for the party's existence;

how it abhorred and repudiated any notion that its essential destiny was to remain a pressure or ginger group.

The Gollan 1956 anniversary controversy was the preliminary engagement and the real battle was joined with the preparation for the 35th Congress at the end of 1977. It was decided that an entirely redrafted version of the *British Road* should be prepared, and the commission which was set up for the purpose was composed more or less entirely of supporters of what could be defined as the 'liberal' wing of the party – though within that there were many different shades. By this time the term 'Eurocommunism' was in common currency and taken by its traditionalist opponents to characterise the political drift of the party leaders. Most of those, however, to whom the label was affixed, usually in the contracted form 'Euro', denied its appropriateness, at least in public, and certainly the leadership would have nothing to do with it. An appropriate term to use by supporters of the Executive Committee to designate their traditionalist opponents was not too easy to find. 'Sectarians', 'traditionalists' and 'Stalinists' were all employed, the first being favoured in formal debate, although in private conversation it was usually 'tankie', from the support this faction had given to the Czechoslovak invasion.

Both supporters and opponents of the draft produced by the commission regarded it as a watershed in the party's development. Both made rather extravagant claims; on the one hand that if it were accepted the CP would have ceased to be a communist party and have slumped into revisionism; on the other that adopting it would not only throw off the dead weight of the Stalinist heritage but also could be expected to produce a dramatic turnaround in the party's material fortunes. In their hopes and fears they were both certainly mistaken, for although there was a complete rewriting, the changes proposed from the 1968 edition, as in the previous revision, were more of style and terminology than of real substance; at most it represented a modification of outlook rather than a fundamental alteration.

In the theoretical approach behind the document the Gramscians had achieved their main success in the replacement of the concept of anti-monopoly or 'broad popular alliance' with 'broad democratic alliance'. The distinction is not evident at first glance, but to the initiated was one of great moment. The former notion implied the construction of a popular coalition against the monopolists, who, as rather abstract personifications of capital, were held to be oppressing everybody else in a relatively straightforward and unmistakable fashion. The Gramscians, while not denying the existence of monopoly capitalism, saw oppression as rooted in anti-democratic structures at every level and in every sphere of society – the family and the trade union branch as well as the workplace and the state – and requiring to be countered by a coalition embracing individuals in a multiplicity of roles, for which *democratic* was the metaphor and password. It followed from this that the proponents of the new draft wanted a 'broad' definition of the working class – for it was still common ground that this was the inherently revolutionary social force – and its antagonists a 'narrow' one sticking as closely as possible to traditional male industrial workers.[22]

For those, and they included key individuals in the Political Committee, who recognised Marxist theory as the party's foundation but whose interests were directed towards its political practice and organisation, continuity was the watchword. No radically new directions were proposed for the CP's relations with the labour movement or the Labour Party, nor in the internal CP regime. The vision remained of the party leading or influencing a strengthening left trend within the trade unions and labour politics, making agreements and constructing fronts wherever possible, displaying its goodwill and trustworthiness by seeking no exclusive position of leadership, or any that was not willingly accorded to it. It all needed a bigger Communist Party...able to make a significant electoral impact. The leadership believed that with the adoption of the appealing new programme the party's present internal structures, though possibly needing some modification in detail, were generally adequate for the purpose. Accordingly, it would remain a Marxist-Leninist organisation operating by the norms of democratic centralism.

The Stalinist-inclined opposition thought otherwise. Bitter rancour and intransigent hostility characterised the pre-Congress discussion months of 1977, reflected both in the party press and in branch meetings throughout the country. The doldrums into which the labour movement had fallen after the bright hopes of the early 1970s, the nerveless and stagnant performance of the Wilson/Callaghan governments operating a classic deflationary right-wing policy, the vote for Common Market membership in the 1975 referendum, certainly did not help to improve the mood within the CP, nor did the publicised resignations from the party in the course of 1976 of three of its leading members, Bernard Panter, John Tocher and Jimmy Reid, the last with a degree of vindictive accusation. All three of these had played leading roles of one sort or another within the engineering unions, though that aspect was almost certainly coincidental, though possibly symptomatic.

Sid French and the Surrey District emerged as the focus of the opposition, and anxious calculations were made in loyal offices as to what their potential strength at the Congress might be and whether they could hope even to win a majority for rejection of the draft and the overturn of the existing leadership – indicating an implicit realisation that their viewpoint was indeed a widely shared one among the ranks of the generally silent members. The Frenchites' strongest card was less their theoretical stance on the CP's perspectives for achieving power than the fact that they linked it with the claim to be resisting a creeping anti-Sovietism among the current leaders. The question was whether automatic loyalty to the British leadership would win out over gut sentiment in regard to the USSR.

Consternation was therefore the common reaction when on the eve of the Congress French and his supporters announced their withdrawal from the CPGB and the formation of an ideologically sound New Communist Party (NCP). They had not stayed to conduct the fight in the Congress, claiming in justification that it would be rigged in advance by means of EC manipulation – an exaggerated but not wholly unfounded allegation, as the methods which had served so well twenty years before were still available to the leadership. It has been suggested (I have no firm view one way or the other) that the Political Committee was preparing a case for presentation to Congress asking for French's expulsion on the grounds of factionalism and breach of democratic centralism. This would be followed, it is claimed, by the reorganisation of the Surrey District to destroy his organisational base, and therefore in order to keep it intact he had no choice but to make the break at once. The breakaway involved around 700 members, overwhelmingly in the south of England and concentrated in the Surrey and Sussex Districts, though there were also significant components in Yorkshire and Lancashire.[23]

At all events the defection ensured that the new *BRS* would pass without difficulty once the Congress met, as the remaining opposition was now much too weak to prevent it.[24] The two individuals who with French's disappearance emerged as its most articulate spokespersons were Fergus Nicholson, the ex-Student Organiser, and John Foster, a lecturer at Strathclyde University, Glasgow, and labour historian of considerable repute. The oppositionists felt badly betrayed by the walkout and Nicholson referred to the defectors as 'taking French leave'. If the NCPers had taken part in the proceedings the leadership would almost certainly have won anyway, but the votes might well have been close. Their absence made sure that the draft would be carried overwhelmingly.

Having settled the party's ideological and programmatic future, the Congress had another important matter to address. The daily paper, the *Morning Star*, had since the retiral of George Matthews[25] been edited by Tony Chater, formerly a technical college lecturer, who had first been elected to the EC ten years earlier and had previously run the Press and Publicity department. Sales and readership continued in persistent decline, an intolerable state of affairs, given that the party believed that it had just renewed itself and confidently hoped that it was about to grow and become stronger. The EC therefore moved a resolution calling for a much bigger and better planned sales drive and projecting an increase in the size of the paper. An amendment was moved, supported by some individuals of the retiring EC, which though restrained in its terms clearly implied that higher circulation was impeded by the fact that the paper was unimaginatively edited. It demanded the appointment of a commission to look at all aspects of its functioning and recommend appropriate changes. The amendment, with its critical implications – spelled out in the speeches moving it – was very badly received by Chater and he was supported by the leadership in opposition to it;[26] nevertheless it was passed, a highly remarkable if not unique outcome in a CP Congress and indicative of the degree of grass roots dissatisfaction with the party's daily organ.

The passing of this amendment spun yet another strand in the web of divergences and antagonisms that was increasingly beginning to constitute the fabric of the CP.[27] The commission specified by the Congress was duly appointed, met and reported in the following year. The report was a rather bland and anodyne document which basically did no more than encourage everybody to do better: the editorial team at the paper in improving its quality and presentation and the party at large in promoting its sales. It became clear soon enough that Chater had no intention of taking seriously either the Congress decision or the mildly critical points made by the commission and that the *Morning Star* would continue unchanged in its approach and style. The only alteration of any significance was an increase in the size of the weekend edition from six pages to eight, but this worsened rather than improved its situation, for it did not have the journalistic resources effectively to fill the additional space while at the same time the extra pages represented another financial drain.

The final disintegrative force, and what was to prove in the end the most powerful of all those affecting the party, shattering its industrial core, was also signalled in the course of 1978, from a wholly unexpected and, on the face of it, unlikely direction. In September of that year Eric Hobsbawn in *Marxism Today* published an article – originally the 1978 Marx Memorial Lecture – under the title 'The Forward March of Labour Halted?' In essence it was a warning against complacency and a false confidence that the strength of the left-wing industrial movement was unstoppably in the ascendant. Hobsbawm pointed to important long-term weaknesses – from a trade union viewpoint – in the composition of the workforce, in the organisation of the union movement and in its relations with the political component. He drew attention to the secular decline in Labour voting patterns and stressed most of all the dangers of the labour movement, always uneasily integrated into British social culture, suffering an emphatic rejection by it. His article concluded:

> But if the labour and socialist movement is to recover its soul, its dynamism, and its historical initiative, we...must...recognise the novel situation in which we find ourselves...analyse it realistically and concretely...analyse the reasons historical and otherwise, for the failures as well as the successes of the labour movement...formulate not only what we want to do but what can be done. We should have done this even while we were waiting for British capitalism to enter its period of dramatic crisis. We cannot afford not to do it now that it has.

Hobsbawm at that point was probably inside the party the best known and most respected of its intellectuals. Although in 1956 he had only very unwillingly accepted the line on Hungary and had written in the *New Reasoner,* his position since then had not been a controversial one in inner party disputes. His article now generated intense and highly public argument, with participation from such luminaries as Ken Gill, Kevin Halpin and, outside the party, Stan Newens MP. The dominant reaction of the trade union leaders was categorically to reject any notion that the labour movement was in serious difficulty, to claim that the unions had amply demonstrated their strength over the previous decade, that they were not dangerously compromised by sectional ambitions, that both the Labour Party and the TUC had been won for left-wing positions and that the task now was to secure their implementation. Although not directly contributing to the debate, the party's Industrial Organiser, Mick Costello, made similar points in other contexts. Behind the public terms of the debate, however, could be detected a sense of indignation and resentment that the behaviour of left-wing trade union leaders had been called into question publicly in a party journal and by an academic at that.

It marked the beginning of the presumption that *Marxism Today* and the Gramscian positions which it upheld were anti-trade union, and thus formed the basis for a coalition by the CP trade union leaders offended by the journal's approach to industrial affairs and those party members who disliked it on other grounds,[28] an alliance cemented by commonly held workerist assumptions. It may be judged that this was the likely outcome sooner or later of the party's tacit abandonment of its independent trade union role in the early 1960s and cultivation thereafter of a unified broad left. In doing so it had foregone also an independent critical stance, and had come to be expected to act as a public relations facility for the trade union left. As Sam Aaronovitch put it, referring to an article by Costello: 'There is also a strong impression conveyed...that the CP simply supports whatever it is that trade unions do.'[29] It is therefore perhaps not surprising that when criticism eventually was voiced it was perceived as an astonishing betrayal.

In the meantime yet another source of friction was making its progress through the official channels. The decisions of the 1977 Congress included provision for a fresh look at internal party structures and decision-making processes and resulted in a commission on inner party democracy, intended to report to the Congress in 1979. Once more it finished up with majority and minority reports, although the minority, conscious of precedent and anxious not to isolate themselves, studiedly avoided referring to it as such. Instead the minority, which included Martin Jacques and Dave Cook, the National Organiser, defined their document as 'Alternative Proposals' to the majority ones, which they also signed. Caution was the order of the day. The radical forces, having won, as they thought, a major victory with the 1977 *BRS* draft, were somewhat politically tired and concerned to consolidate their position rather than to provoke their allies in the party bureaucracy. That bureaucracy, however willing to contemplate theoretical or political initiatives, was, as always, wedded to the organisational norms with which it was familiar and by which it was sustained, finding even some of the majority proposals, curtailing the length of full-time officials' service, too strong for its taste.

Consequently even the minority report was a minimalist set of proposals and the majority one, which was eventually accepted with EC amendments diluting its force, no more than cosmetic. The essential character of the party structures was reaffirmed by both, although this did not prevent the supporters of *both* sets of proposals being accused in the preliminary debate of wanting to overthrow democratic centralism, and at the Congress a large vote (102 as against 175) was recorded for making no changes at all. Speaking there for the EC Irene Swan outlined the ideal image of the party they envisaged:

> A Party based on marxism with a developing British tradition – organised for socialist revolution – a democratic party drawing on the initiative and creativity of its membership, a centralised party, a disciplined and united fighting collective for decided policy – a party with an internationalist outlook – respecting the independence and equality of other communist parties with whom we act in solidarity.

Scarcely had the Congress dispersed when the interpretation of what was meant by 'internationalist outlook' erupted again with the introduction in late December of Soviet troops to sustain the pro-Soviet regime in Afghanistan by removing and executing a president who had proved incapable of coping with the anti-communist insurrection. The British CP's Executive (and the *Morning Star*) condemned the intervention, so provoking increased bitterness on the part of traditionalists who found in this action further evidence of a slide into bourgeois liberal values, the search for bourgeois respectability and unwillingness to evince solidarity with the USSR whenever that threatened to make the party unpopular.

The Afghanistan intervention can be reasonably regarded as initiating the 'Second Cold War', which, along with the fall of the Callaghan government and the elevation of Margaret Thatcher to the premiership, formed the main external influences upon the direction of the party's course at the turn of the decade, linked as they were by multiple threads to its internal fractures.

Under the title 'The Great Moving Right Show' *Marxism Today* published an article by Stuart Hall – never a CP member – in January 1979 (hence written in late 1978). It was an extraordinary percipient analysis and forecast, at a point when a Labour government still held office, of the populist appeal and cultural penetration of right-wing radicalism in conditions of a disintegrating social democracy, warning that the left would be extremely foolish to rely upon these values finding no purchase among the working-class and employing the term 'Thatcherism', albeit in quotes. But before the character of Thatcherism had the opportunity fully to reveal itself, the left was more exercised by other consequences of the Labour Party defeat in the May 1979 General Election.

That event unleashed pressures inside the Labour Party which had been building up since the early 1970s and ever more forcefully since the return to office in 1974. The right wing was discredited and demoralised, the left more confident, better organised and with more coherent theory and programmes than ever before in the Labour Party's history. Sweeping constitutional changes were forced through to break the right-wing grip upon the party apparatus, including provision for the compulsory reselection of MPs and the election of the Leader and Deputy Leader by a collegial system which included trade union and constituency votes. The hand of the left was strengthened even more by the defection of many of the irreconcilable right into the Social Democratic Party early in 1981. The policies of the Labour Party, too, swung rapidly leftwards. Unilateral nuclear disarmament became at last officially declared policy while the 1983 General Election saw a manifesto adopted which was the most left-wing in Labour's history. The left added to its strengths by discovering a charismatic leader in Tony Benn and at the end of 1981 an intransigently left-wing trade union militant, namely Arthur Scargill, was elected President of the NUM.[30]

In all of these developments except the last the Communist Party was no more than a spectator and, through the *Morning Star*, a commentator. Completely isolated from contact with the Labour Party in any except the very limited sense of influencing trade union votes, the CP was cut off from any direct influence on the political transformation. Yet now if ever was the reality of what had been envisaged with hope and longing in *The British Road to Socialism* ever since its first edition. The Labour Party was moving left in a dramatic fashion. According to the script which the CP had written for itself this should happen only with the comradely inspiration and guidance of the communists. In fact the CP, regardless of its interminable rhetoric on the theme of unity, was a complete irrelevance, and so far as Marxism was concerned the Marxist sects within the Labour Party, Militant especially, were of far greater significance. Although the CP might feel some gratification that things were moving at last in the Labour universe it could hardly do so without qualms at its own bypassing.[31]

While the Eurocommunist wing of the CP was well aware of the shaky electoral foundations upon which the Labour left was constructing its political edifice, and warned against regarding the chase after the Labour leadership as the answer to all political problems,[32] for the party traditionalists the simplifications of political reality – the assumption that the presentation of a thoroughgoing left-wing manifesto to the electorate would evoke an immediate favourable response – did not fail to exercise an attraction. Such perceptions fitted well with the school of thought that was becoming increasingly alienated by the rigid official insistence on futile electoral contests. Seeing the Labour Party as the only meaningful electoral vehicle for the labour movement, the upholders of this viewpoint urged that the CP should abandon its independent contesting and thus try to make its members eligible for joint Labour Party membership. They argued that such a tactic could be successful since the Labour Party had dropped its list of proscribed organisations. And although the correspondence was far from exact, there was a tendency for this viewpoint to go along with more Stalinist dispositions – centralising, workerist, authoritarian and impatient of subtleties; in the British context all the most negative features of Labourism as an ideology.

Between the congresses in late 1979 and 1981 the several rival tendencies within the party crystallised. Relations across the dividing lines deteriorated to the extent that individuals in the different camps had far more in common politically with elements or parties outside the CP than they had with each other. All kinds of issues came to the fore, suppressed or ignored for many years, reflecting the problematic status of the party in British politics; but the principal mark of division, cutting across all of the others, was that of attitude towards the Soviet bloc – uncritical identification, qualified admiration or severely critical distancing. In that sense, at the start of its terminal crisis, the party was returning to its origins...except that it had never really left them.

By far the largest element in the composition of the party was made up of members who instinctively trusted and were loyal to the leadership. That did not mean that they were passive or unthinking – they would not have been in the CP had that been so but, not themselves aspiring to leading roles, they had confidence in the elected leadership's ability to uphold, and advance as much as possible, the values which had caused them to join the organisation: humane and rational domestic and inter-national policies, a strong and aggrieved sense of social justice, together with support, though not unthinking, for Soviet-type society as the harbinger of a new and better civilisation. It was above all in the old heartlands of British communism, Wales and Scotland, and among the party's working-class members that such sentiments were overwhelm-ingly dominant.

Not unnaturally, the core of the party leadership tended to be drawn from a similar background and reflect the same kind of outlook. It was, however, ageing along with its natural constituency and ceasing to reproduce itself socially. The failure of the YCL from the 1960s onwards to maintain an intake of working-class recruits (whether on account of social trends or because of its own inadequacies) was of major importance in producing this development. The old-style leaders had few or no successors.[33] The consequence was a growing influx into leadership positions of younger individuals with a background in higher education, many of them having been student recruits of the later 1960s. Dave Cook, the National Organiser of the late 1970s, had previously been the National Student Organiser. This did not mean that individuals from a middle-class academic background were necessarily more questioning or iconoclastic about the traditions of the communist movement – many of the sectarian dissidents had comparable social origins – but it did mean that those who had leadership patronage in the early 1970s, when, because of Czechoslovakia and Sid French, ones with a knee-jerk pro-Sovietism were being discouraged, tended to be both academic *and* heterodox because they were the only acceptable people available.

This relationship constitutes the central explanation for the coalition between the Eurocommunists and a traditionalist leadership, anxious not to isolate itself and seeking political openings – which it was certain not to find if it fell back upon pre-1956 verities. Without dismissing a measure of genuine conviction, the Eurocommunists were favoured, pragmatically on the whole, because they promised openings towards what were termed 'the new social forces' of gender politics and maybe youth culture and minority nationalisms. Pragmatic as well, the party's trade union leaders were at first happy to go along with this since their own position did not appear to be affected and with only a few exceptions they preferred to concentrate on their trade union work and see the party continue to do what it had always done.

But whether it should in fact continue along the same lines was exactly what the new thinkers were concerned about. They envisaged what was hardly anything less than a new form of politics and a decisive break with past traditions as well as policies. Keenly aware of the weaknesses of the Labour left's simplicities in confronting a changing social and cultural environment no less than the fact that the Soviet bloc was afflicted with structural defects rather than accidental shortcomings, they were hostile in principle to authoritarianism, centralised structures of control and macho male culture.[34] They tended to regard the modes of organisation employed by the labour movement both industrially and politically as being out of date, and their bolder spokespeople were willing to endorse the principle of incomes polices and to conclude that EEC membership might not have been an unrelieved disaster.

Except for a very general orientation towards social transformation – and there would have been little agreement on what was meant by that – scarcely any common ground existed between these people and the party's hardline traditionalists, for whom its Soviet affiliations were always uppermost. They regarded the CP's behaviour since 1968 if not before as an aberration and ideologically they were much closer to the Frenchites than to the mainstream party. Their quarrel with the NCP was not with its political outlook but its total irrelevance even by the historical standards of British communism and the fact that it could not hope to be recognised by the CPSU as its fraternal British counterpart. Recognising that pro-Sovietism alone was not sufficient basis for an identity and that one was needed also in domestic terms, they came forward as the defenders of the labour movement's cultural and organisational traditions and of the old-style militancy being challenged by the Eurocommunists.

In 1979 there appeared a monthly journal under the title *Straight Left*, which concealed its real character as the public organ of this faction under the guise and pretence of being a broad labour movement publication lacking any specific connection with the CP, declaring itself to be 'strictly non-sectarian' and dedicated to building 'unity of purpose and action'. An editorial advisory board included such trade union and parliamentary luminaries as Ray Buckton, Joan Maynard (who was a regular contributor), Alan Sapper, James Lamont, Bill Keys and others. When CP members wrote for it the byline indicated only their labour movement responsibilities and no discussion of internal party matters was permitted. The journal's real nature, however, was evident in the content whenever it did not confine itself to commentary on industrial disputes and parliamentary affairs. Stalin's centenary was celebrated with a two-page reprint of his conversation with H.G. Wells. Andrew Rothstein wrote in praise of the Soviet action in Afghanistan and the report of another anniversary was headlined 'GDR – A Hard but Glorious 30 Years'. The appointment of Yuri Andropov as General Secretary of the CPSU was reported under the headline 'Railwayman's Son Heads CPSU', with no mention, even in the quotes it reproduced from the commercial press, of his long KGB service.[35]

Fergus Nicholson was thought to have been *Straight Left*'s principal inspiration and resident columnist under the byline 'Harry Steel', an amalgam of the names of Harry Pollitt and Joseph Stalin. The party leadership was perfectly aware of what was involved and in September 1982 the EC issued a statement deploring the diversion of effort by party members into a publication which, while adopting stances in opposition to the party's on various issues, operated a blackout on the name of the CP or *Morning Star*. However, because of the restrictions which *Straight Left* observed and the labour movement figures connected with it, they did not venture to proscribe it or make its handling a disciplinary offence. Less patience was shown towards another factional group and publication entitled *The Leninist*, a splinter from the NCP youth organisation, which, having re-entered the CP, operated secretly inside it as a group of political Don Quixotes to promote notions of ultra-bolshevism and denunciation of *The British Road to Socialism* in all its versions. 'Only we are unambiguously committed to violent revolution, soviets, the dictatorship of the proletariat and uniting genuine communists in a world party.' Being in violation of nearly every item of the party rules, *The Leninist* was promptly banned.[36]

The Young Communist League, as on previous occasions, was showing itself to be the precursor of trends in the party, and within it the factional battle was raging uninhibitedly against a background of numerical collapse. Elements of unregenerate pro-Sovietism had been well represented within it since the beginning of the conflict in 1968, but the Eurocommunists, with the support of the adult party leadership, held the advantage and dominated under the secretaryship of Tom Bell. With the withdrawal of the Frenchites, however, the Eurocommunists secured a complete triumph at the YCL Congress of 1979, elected Nina Temple as National Secretary and introduced a new constitution which rejected both 'Marxism-Leninism' as a defining ideology and 'democratic centralism' as an organisational principle. However, the Eurocommunist majority itself from early 1983 divided between an 'orthodox' and a feminist/anarchist trend, represented respectively by Doug Chalmers, the National Secretary, and Nina Brown, the National Organiser, with the result that internecine warfare continued unabated, while the Straight Leftists who constituted the previous opposition sulked in their tents – the individual branches which they continued to control. The upshot of this conflict was the reimposition of democratic centralism at the 1983 Congress, which simultaneously saw the reappearance of the Straight Left opposition – but by this time the YCL was in such a parlous state that its doings were of little more than academic interest, even to the CP itself, and it contributed nothing to the definitive battle by then underway within its parent organisation.[37]

The last, and as events showed the most significant, of the oppositional groupings, whose appearance prefigured the hopeless disintegration of the Communist Party, did not fully take shape until 1982–3, although its origins went back as far as the 1977 vote on the *Morning Star*, and added a fresh dimension to the arguments hitherto concerning the party's alleged anti-Sovietism and dilution of revolutionary perspectives. Formally, the basis for this last dispute related to interpretations of the party's rules and practices; its substance was the alarm and dismay generated by what was perceived as the abandonment of its basic working-class traditions and culture, with capitulation to trendy academic middle-class fashion.

Relations between the *Morning Star* editor and the party leadership were damaged irreparably at the 1981 Congress[38] when the latter, in an unexpected and sudden reversal, gave its support to a resolution critical of the *Morning Star* after having initially indicated that it would recommend rejection. Tony Chater felt betrayed. Here too more was at stake than technical disagreements over how the paper should be run or even its political line. The critics were urging that the paper must adopt a much more commercial approach and seek to expand its circulation by innovations which raised its appeal to the general public and enabled it to 'sell itself' on the basis of improved presentation and content. Ranged against that there was the attitude which viewed its character as an organ of the labour movement to be the overriding priority and deeply distrusted any surrender to commercial considerations. For this viewpoint, the culture of place-of-work distribution, street sales pitches and door-to-door canvasses – these last had practically died out but were regarded with nostalgia – were the proper way to handle a working-class newspaper, and the mobilisation of the party for harder work in more determined sales drives was seen as the essential answer to the problem of declining circulation. Likewise, so far as content was concerned, the emphasis must be placed on supportive industrial and trade union coverage.

The *Morning Star* followed the EC's condemnation in December 1981 of the Soviet-inspired military takeover in Poland and suppression of Solidarity, to the indignation of the Straight Leftists, who declared that the issue was not one of formal democracy but a question of class power and that the Polish working class required to be disciplined by the Polish and/or Soviet communist parties for having forgotten its class destiny and allowed itself to become corrupted by capitalist and Catholic aspirations. The Annual General Meeting of the PPPS in the following early summer, since time immemorial a formal and perfunctory affair, passed off without incident and the majority of party members remained wholly unaware of the accumulating tensions and approaching crisis. The lines of cleavage ran through both camps, for many of the paper's editorial and administrative staff were Eurocommunist party loyalists, most prominently Chris Myant and Frank Chalmers on the journalistic side; while in the highest reaches of the CP leadership Mick Costello, the Industrial Organiser, had since the mid-1970s been growing more critical of Eurocommunism and increasingly resentful of the downplaying of the party's industrial role. By 1982 he was wholly at odds with his colleagues in the Political Committee and acting in close collaboration with Chater.

The fuse was lit in late August 1982 with the appearance of the September number of *Marxism Today* containing an article by Tony Lane, a sociologist at Liverpool University, on the trade union movement, analysing its growing isolation within British society, in which he made reference to the petty corruption – expense account fiddles – in which lower levels of union officials, including shop stewards, sometimes engaged. On 26 August the *Morning Star* printed on its front page what was ostensibly an interview statement by Costello, in which the Industrial Organiser damned, in the name of the party, the Lane article as an insult to trade unionists, a 'gross slander on the labour movement', and a source of aid and comfort to the class enemy. The latter point was reinforced, in Costello's view, by the fact that the piece had been picked up by the 'anti-left' *Daily Mirror*. In actuality, Costello had used his journalistic contacts to ensure that it would be, just as he and Chater had concerted their action in preparing and printing the statement. Costello, and those who wrote to the paper in his support during the intense correspondence which ensued, did not try to deny the truth in Lane's allegations: the objection was to the exposure of family secrets and the dereliction of solidarity which such behaviour was supposed to represent. As Mick Costello put it:

> The shop stewards' movement, at this critical time for mobilisation of the working class, deserve only the wholesale backing of every progressive, in the spirit of repeated Communist Party Congress resolutions…It is only in the columns of the anti-left *Daily Mirror* and the rest of the capitalist press that one ought to find attacks on the trade union movement.

The party Executive Committee, when it met on 12 September, took a different point of view. Though mildly reproving *Marxism Today* and Martin Jacques for printing the article without fuller consultation, it severely censured Chater, Costello and the *Morning Star*'s Deputy Editor, David Whitfield, all members of the EC, for forming a cabal to attack another party journal and to use the party's name without any reference to the EC. It represented a severe rebuff for the forces which were beginning to coalesce out of the separate issues of dissatisfaction with the CP's progressive dilution of 'class politics' and class rhetoric, and a quarrel over the management and control of the paper. It was perhaps not accidental that shortly after the EC's censure, Chater took an extended trip to Moscow, where Brezhnev was still technically in charge of affairs, and thereafter critical references in the *Morning Star* to the Soviet bloc much diminished, though for the sake of consistency they did not disappear altogether.

From that point onwards the editor and his confederates began to act in a manner quite independent of the party centre, and Chater refused to regard himself as bound by collective decisions of the Political Committee regarding the paper, even though he remained a member of it. The majority of party members, though conscious that there were disagreements, were quite unaware of their depth or the full details of their nature, and were inclined to attribute them less to Chater than to Costello, whose dislike of Eurocommunism was well known. Meanwhile the decline in circulation and in the financial position continued, so that by the end of the year a full-blown crisis and threat to the paper's future was judged to exist.

Relations had not yet broken down so completely as to prevent the initiation of a party campaign in January 1983 to save the *Morning Star* by securing a circulation growth of 3,000 copies per day.[39] A full-time party worker, not, however, generally regarded as the most dynamic of individuals, was delegated to work exclusively on this project. At the same time the alliance between Chater and Costello was confirmed and publicised when in the same month Costello resigned his post as Industrial Organiser (pleading personal difficulties) and seven weeks later was appointed Industrial Correspondent at the *Morning Star*, naturally without consultation with the EC. A further sign of the times came in March, with the commemoration of the centenary of Marx's death, for which the principal feature was a two-page spread written by Tony Chater, whose expertise in the field of Marx studies had previously passed unnoticed. The article itself, flat, banal and boring, would not have looked out of place in the pages of the *Peking People's Daily*.

The circulation campaign was a flop, each side of the dispute blaming the other: the *Morning Star* accusing the party of not trying hard enough; the party leaders complaining unofficially of the dreariness of the paper's content and presentation. Requests by Gordon McLennan for meetings with Chater to resolve the dispute were ignored or evaded. The party leadership was not in a position to dismiss Chater, Costello or Whitfield from their posts, because the PPPS was ostensibly a self-governing co-operative, but decided to strengthen its position and discipline the refractories by introducing party loyalists on to the Management Committee of the paper, Chater's organisational base. The Management Committee consisted of fifteen individuals, six of whom retired yearly on rotation. Consequently nominations for the six places available in 1983 were extraordinarily numerous and the party issued a recommended list on which appeared George Matthews, the former editor, Bert Pearce, the Welsh Secretary, and Dave Priscott, the Yorkshire District Secretary. To preserve the decencies Chater's own name was also included on this list.

On the front page of the *Morning Star* of 1 June, to the startled astonishment of most party readers, there appeared a statement complaining that a 'powerful outside body' was trying to influence the Management Committee elections. The majority who read it did not appreciate at first what was the 'outside body' being referred to.[40] In fact by using this phrase Chater committed a serious tactical error, for it greatly offended the sensibilities of many loyal party members who might have inclined politically towards him, and the party leadership did not let them forget it. In the immediate term, however, it did not prevent the Chaterite candidates, all trade union officials and some non-communists, convincingly defeating the EC nominees in the AGM elections,[41] a humiliating rebuff to the party leadership. Moreover, at the meetings of the AGM sections themselves Chater and the PPPS secretary, Mary Rosser, unveiled a crisis of hitherto unsuspected and unprecedented dimensions. It included a claim that the financial position was so ropey that the co-operative might be in the position of trading illegally. To cope with the approaching catastrophe a survival plan was announced, requiring enormous investment, with the object of extending the PPPS printing operations into the field of trade union journals and commercial operations. The party had not in any way been consulted about the plan but it was made clear that its support and energy were expected to be put behind it.[42]

Two camps now polarised, identified by their attachment to the rival journals. The crisis cemented the alliance of Eurocommunists with the pragmatic traditionalists of the leadership and rank-and-file loyalists who, whatever their politics, resented the 'hi-jack' of the newspaper which had been for decades the party's chief glory and its main channel of communication with the outside world. The new oppositionists for their part endeavoured to appeal to the Straight Leftists on the ground of protecting the party's working-class heritage. They managed to attract a few, such as John Foster and Mary Davis, concerned at Straight Left's increasing trend towards 'liquidation' into the Labour Party and its down-playing of an independent CP political role. The Straight Leftists, however, had not forgotten nor forgiven the *Morning Star*'s stance on Afghanistan and Poland and suspected Chater and Costello as come-lately opportunists aspiring to take over leadership of the opposition. At the AGM Brian Filling, a prominent Straight Leftist, denounced the rival groupings as 'people who've led us to the brink of the abyss', and Straight Left sponsored its own candidates, all heavily defeated.

The Chater/Costello opposition had a great deal more success with their appeal to party trade union officials and to ones outside the party, and its secret was the ability of the Chaterites to stigmatise *Marxism Today*, Eurocommunists and the party leaders under the malign influence of these revisionists as being anti-trade union and anti-working class. The ones who tended to remain loyal to the EC were those, such as the communist leaders of the Scottish NUM, who also had a major involvement in the party leadership; the *Morning Star* supporters tended to be those with a more distant relationship. Of these easily the most significant was Ken Gill, the General Secretary of TASS, who in 1982 at a private gathering of CP members of his union censured the party leadership for an anti-trade union and anti-working-class bias as well as for allowing the party to be torn apart by splits and divisions.

Whatever the arguments over contemporary political realities, however, both sides were essentially appealing to tradition. The ones emphasised by the party leaders were the CP's historic position of central importance in the political consciousness of its members and trust in the self-perpetuating leadership for whatever alignments and compromises they might judge to be necessary in the party's interest. Their opponents counterposed the tradition of the party's working-class and trade union roots, allegedly threatened with being torn up, and the patient, decades-long endeavour to establish close relations with non-CP left-wing trade union leaders now recoiled on the party's head since most of those took the side of the *Morning Star*. After all, it was the aspect of the party's presence with which they were most familiar.

Only a few days prior to the PPPS AGM the 1983 General Election had been held; its outcome and subsequent autopsy further divided the CP contestants, or rather provided another peg on which to hang their disputes. *Marxism Today* now moved to open a full-blown critique of the traditional left-wing policies upon which Labour had fought, to underline the success of Thatcherism in achieving a grip on popular consciousness, and to argue that if it was going to be broken Labour would be compelled to rethink its policies along more popularly acceptable lines and to consider some kind of electoral arrangement with the centre and nationalist parties. From the other camp accusations of class treason therefore became less restrained, while the *Morning Star* in its columns addressed itself to combining the defence of left-wing labourism with intensified admiration for the achievements of the countries in the Soviet bloc.

The very term 'Thatcherism' became itself a focus of attack. Its use, according to critics of Eurocommunism, concentrated on the superficial style of a particular individual and diverted attention from the fact that the components of Tory policy were no more than a classically capitalist response to economic downturn, indicating weakness not strength and providing the opportunity for an effective left-wing counterattack behind the Alternative Economic Strategy, if only the will and resolution were mobilised instead of being dissipated by the politics of pessimism, defeatism and class treason. The *Morning Star* group tried to divide its enemies. While not ceasing to damn *Marxism Today* and all it represented, they simultaneously held out an olive branch to McLennan in the shape of offers to institute regular open and friendly discussions between the opposed leaderships, intended to reach a working arrangement acceptable to both – but only on the understanding that the Management Committee must be treated as an independent and equal partner. Chater's hopes of a satisfactory accommodation were not assisted by his personal style, which infuriated opponents by projecting, consciously or not, an insufferable air of complacent self-righteousness, justifying his refusals to print hostile letters by the argument that too much editorial space would have to be allocated to answering their inaccuracies.

When the dispute broke out the Chaterites had possessed the great advantage that there existed no equivalent channel of communication between the leadership and the bulk of party members since the CP fortnightly, *Comment*, had been discontinued for financial reasons some time earlier, and the advantage was exploited by the paper's editing or refusing to print hostile material emanating from St John Street, the address of the party headquarters since the sale of its King Street premises in 1979. In what was evidently going to turn into a showdown confrontation at the 38th Congress, scheduled for the end of the year, that advantage might prove decisive. The party leadership was reduced to issuing press statements to the commercial media and to the pages of a monthly bulletin, *Communist Focus,* which was set up in place of *Comment*.

The Straight Left faction, seeing the initiative in the inner party dispute falling into the hands of people whom they deeply distrusted, decided to intervene. Selected party members received unsolicited through the post a 34-page pamphlet entitled *The Crisis in Our Communist Party: Cause, Effect and Cure*. It was ostensibly written by Charlie Woods, an 83-year old retired miner from County Durham, but nobody believed that he was the actual author, Fergus Nicholson or Brian Filling being the most frequently suspected culprits. After castigating the leadership for every imaginable political sin and damning their *Morning Star* opponents as opportunists, the pamphlet reached the conclusion that:

This pamphlet sets out here the basic principle around which those wanting serious changes within the Party should be able to unite – the need for an entirely new leadership animated by entirely different principles and priorities to the present occupants of St John St.

Mick Costello's contribution in *Focus* to the pre-Congress discussion said much the same thing in only slightly more temperate language. Party members could no longer fail to be aware that a concerted effort was in train to unseat the existing leadership and replace it with one of a more traditionalist colour. In the course of the autumn savage conflict erupted in the columns of the journal and across the organisation as the contending groups fought to win both the arguments and the delegate elections in the branches. Whether or not the EC had a real majority is uncertain; the result of the PPPS AGM in June is not conclusive evidence either way, for the EC did not have time to mobilise its support, many were confused and the Chaterites were reinforced with non-party shareholders. In any event, the loyalists controlled the central party machinery and a critical proportion of it at the intermediate levels, a vital asset. In the larger party units the oppositionists dominated London but Scotland and Wales, though challenged, were safe. Not a few delegates represented effectively dead branches and had to all intents been selected by District leaderships. The outcome, though in doubt up to the last, was a modest but solid majority for the EC.

The Congress met amid commotion and mutual hatreds unsurpassed at any time in the CP's history and far exceeding those of 1929 or 1957. At the very last moment the two antagonistic opposition factions, perceiving their weakness, endeavoured to combine their forces and produced a clandestine alternative recommended list for the new EC, which was distributed by the Straight Leftists. These also distributed secretly a scurrilous and highly personalised bulletin called *Congress Truth*. Both documents were denounced from the chair and intercepted by the stewards wherever possible. *Congress Truth* offended the Chaterites, who regarded it as excessive and adventurist – apart from the fact that it did not spare them either[43] – and piously disowned as a serious breach of discipline the alternative list they had collaborated in producing, thus destroying all possibility of combining the two oppositions.

The Congress voted to censure Chater and Whitfield; it removed them and most of their supporters from the Executive Committee. As the Congress dispersed it was made clear that party disciplinary procedures, in abeyance for many years, were going to be revived against members who could be demonstrated to have been in breach of rule. The triumph of the leadership and the Eurocommunists, however, was qualified by the fact that the main opposition still had a solid base in the PPPS Management Committee and the party could not evict them from their control over the paper. In addition the CP was now facing a real split, the first in its history discounting the minor breakaway of 1977; its numerical and organisational decline was thereby being accelerated and it was being rendered incapable of doing anything very much apart from operating on its own body.

8   Prostration: 1984–1991

In the course of 1983 the concerns of the Communist Party had come to be dominated as never before by its own internal affairs. In the period which followed that circumstance grew steadily more marked – a situation often enough lamented by articulate members but inescapable in conditions where the logic of each conflicting position revealed itself with growing force and where the defeat and subjugation of the organised labour movement at the hands of the Thatcherite government put into question the strategies espoused by every section of the left inside or outside the CP.

The Congress of 1983 represented only a partial victory for the established leadership. It had saved its own position and excluded its most vociferous opponents from the party's governing body, but they were still in command of the *Morning Star* and farther than ever from being displaced. They had a great deal of strength on the ground throughout the party, above all in London itself, where the District Secretary was a sympathiser and the District Committee under their control.[1] Both sides therefore geared up to prosecute the fight. In January 1984 the EC demanded the resignations of Chater and Whitfield from their editorial offices, which they naturally refused, but then for a time the inner party struggle was overtaken by larger events.

In April the miners' strike began, an industrial conflict putting Thatcherism to the test, exceeding in its virulence and the tenacity with which it was conducted the disputes of the early 1970s; unprecedented indeed since the lockout of 1926. Leading communists were also leading officials of the NUM, both regionally and nationally.[2] Until near the end ten months later they loyally applied, suppressing their doubts, the strategy of mass picketing and physical confrontation formulated by the NUM executive under Scargill's leadership. It was McGahey who had denounced the obsession with 'ballotitis' when some suggested that the executive refusal to conduct a ballot might be a mistaken tactic weakening the presentation of the miners' case.

The strike brought about a remarkable expression of the qualities and abilities of all who were connected with it. It energised the organisations of the NUM, the people of the mining communities and active sympathisers throughout the country. Party members in the coal industry itself were deeply involved in the leadership, logistics and organisation of the strike on the ground in a manner not inferior to that of their predecessors of the 1920s. Others participated in support groups whose main endeavours were centred on collections of money, food and other necessities; sometimes CP branches acted on their own as collecting agencies, especially in cases where the local support group was dominated by the 'ultra left'.

The Communist Party of the 1920s had made considerable if temporary gains from its participation in the lockout of 1926. The same was not to be the case for the mid-1980s. In only one respect did its involvement have any beneficial effect upon its internal disintegration, namely that the opposing elements set aside their differences at the grass roots level sufficient to co-operate in strike support activities. However, the position of the party as such was not spared from becoming a source of recrimination, although its public support for the strike and its objectives never varied. The leaders were accused, despite their public statements, of being lukewarm in their commitment to the strike and disliking Scargill's intransigent class war perspectives and rhetoric. *Marxism Today*, it was claimed, showed minimal interest and gave the strike most inadequate coverage. It was acknowledged that McLennan and his colleagues appeared frequently on strike support platforms but anybody, it was dismissively pointed out, could have done that.

It was less a question of how the Eurocommunists did behave than how their opponents *expected* them to act. When in the wake of defeat criticism of Scargill's tactics and personality did emerge in the statements of party leaders and the party media, this was taken as confirmation of all the suspicions. Implicitly, and in some cases explicitly, the party was being blamed for not leading the strike, which in reality it was in no position to do. It was asserted that the leadership and their supporters were more interested in prosecuting their quarrel with the *Morning Star* than in backing the miners against the class enemy, and even that the inner party dispute was seriously weakening the miners' forces in the titanic industrial struggle and contributing to the government's success.

Certainly, whatever uneasy working relationships the two sides may have established to support the miners, the conflict over the paper did not abate, it intensified dramatically. With the fight out in the open the EC presented a slate of candidates for the PPPS elections, in opposition to the Chater-supported one, and submitted resolutions to the AGM calling for Chater and Whitfield's removal. In the meantime any Straight Leftists (including Charlie Woods) who could be identified as connected with the indiscipline of the 38th Congress and who refused to repudiate their behaviour were expelled. The scenes which accompanied the packed AGMs in June were even more grisly than those of the previous year. In Glasgow the meeting, which was the section for the whole of Scotland, was closed in uproar before any votes had been recorded and outside the hall a steward was assaulted by a participant. When the votes were counted only two of the six places were won by EC candidates: George Bolton, McGahey's vice-president in the Scottish NUM, and Chris Myant. It was overall a victory, though a qualified one, for the Chaterites, and, hopeful that their success could be replicated in a party congress, they called for an emergency one to be convened.

The battle now shifted to the party's basic units and was conducted simultaneously with the ongoing coal strike campaign. While strong challenges were beaten off in Glasgow and in Scotland as a whole, in November the EC suffered a very serious setback when the large North–West District (Merseyside and Lancashire) was captured by the oppositionists. A District Congress vote shredded the recommended list and dismissed both Secretary and Chairperson. But even more alarming dangers were perceived from the London District, with its leadership in the hands of Chaterite opponents, a significant Straight Left presence and a large number of branches, if not the majority, totally disaffected. Accidental events and the tactical errors of the opposition, however, favoured the Executive.

Shortly before the District Congress due in late November, the London Secretary, Bill Dunn, unexpectedly died and the EC moved quickly to appoint as Acting Secretary Ian McKay, the National Organiser, thus giving itself a valuable insertion into the London organisation. Under the aegis of the new Acting Secretary previously ignored allegations of malpractice occurring in Hackney Borough, covering an eighth of the London membership, over the registration of members were at last referred to the EC, which resolved to conduct an investigation. When the District Congress convened at the end of November 1984, chaired by Mike Hicks, Gordon McLennan, on behalf of the EC, forbade it to elect a new District Committee on the grounds that, arising from the Hackney investigations, the credentials of at least ten delegates were questionable. When the oppositionists refused to accept this ruling, McLennan declared the Congress closed and walked out, accompanied by the loyal and the Straight Left delegates – the latter seeing no reason why they should put themselves in an invidious position for the sake of people who had earlier refused to come to their support. The remaining participants then briefly continued the meeting with Hicks in the chair. He was a renowned print union activist and member of the EC; at the 1983 National Congress he had tried to play a conciliating role between the two sides.

By their initial defiance and even more by continuing with the meeting, however briefly, the Chaterites had committed a major blunder, for the leadership now had all the pretext it needed to discipline its leading opponents and break up the organisational network they had created in the London branches. Twenty-two major participants in the 'illicit' meeting were summarily suspended from CP membership. The EC's task was then made all the easier by the fact that the London leaders in their anger compounded their infractions by issuing collective statements and refusing to follow the stipulated procedures for suspended members. Most declined to surrender their party cards and abstain from attendance at party gatherings. The EC was now in a position to sack three London District full-time organisers, co-opt a provisional District Committee of its own choosing and set about reorganising the branches and checking membership returns in the places where it was having trouble. At its January 1985 meeting the EC expelled, along with Chater and Whitfield, the most defiant four of the London twenty-two, Hicks, Tom Durkin, Roger Trask and Ivan Beavis, continued the suspensions on another six and barred the remainder from party office. On the assertion that there had been evidence, albeit unprovable, of factional activity around the North-West Congress, the District Committee there was allowed to meet only under EC supervision. Confident that it now had the initiative, the EC also announced a Special Congress to be held in May. The opposition had been demanding this for months, but inevitably now decried it as gerrymandered.

It would be impossible to deny that in its actions around the London Congress and against the twenty-two dissidents the party leadership had stretched the rules to the limit, to say the least. However, a good deal of the sympathy that the opposition might have hoped to receive was alienated by the practice of even grosser and more blatant forms of manoeuvre and manipulation on their own part. In essence, Chater and his associates employed legalistic devices and evasions to avoid having to face a shareholders' vote on their performance until they judged that they had mobilised enough support to win it; and more damning still was the very principle of using the legal independence of the PPPS to take the *Morning Star* away from party control.

The motion before the 1984 AGM to dismiss Chater and Whitfield was never voted on because it was arbitrarily disallowed by the Management Committee under a claim that appointments were reserved to itself alone. The disruption of the Glasgow meeting was caused by the refusal of the loyalists present to accept that motion's exclusion from the agenda. Had the Scottish section of the AGM voted it is likely that the EC nominees would have won at least five of the six places. Bolton and Myant, who had been elected, were systematically ostracised on the Management Committee. In September the EC collected enough signatures to demand, under the PPPS's constitution, the convoking of a Special General Meeting. Although the procedures for doing so were strictly complied with, Chater refused on trivial pretexts to hold the SGM and ignored the one which the signatories summoned on their own. Had the party resorted to the courts it is likely that it would have won, but apart from the distastefulness of employing those same institutions of the state apparatus as were currently striking down the NUM, it felt unable to risk its resources on the gamble. At any rate, Chater's supporters were scarcely well placed to assume an air of righteous indignation when internal forms of the same practice were turned against themselves.

Once again the party leadership's electoral machinery was employed to the maximum effect in advance of the Special Congress, meeting in May, and this time still more advantageously, as the London situation was now under control. To strengthen its hand, from January *Focus*[3] was turned into a weekly posted free to every party member to keep the official line continuously publicised.[4] Chater did not help himself by indulging in a piece of petty spite by sacking as a part-time correspondent Bill Wainwright, a retired Assistant Editor who supported the EC, nor by his dilatoriness in taking action against an employee who beat up Rob Rolf, the Assistant Circulation Manager, who happened to be an EC supporter.

The atmosphere of the Special Congress was not much less highly charged than that of 1983, though the proceedings were less disorderly. The expulsions were confirmed, the EC positions were carried in every particular and the elections made a clean sweep of the opposition. The break between the CP and its former newspaper was effectively finalised, although there was an epilogue the following month when the party endeavoured on one more occasion to win the PPPS AGM. Attendances at the sectional meetings were again huge, and this time the Chaterites, now sure that they had the upper hand, permitted a resolution *requesting* the *Management Committee* to change the editors –

so that it could be seen to be voted down. Their expectations were well founded and the AGM confirmed the reality, leading to some further expulsions of members, including John Foster, who spoke there against the EC proposals and nominees. Immediately thereafter the EC formally disowned the connection betwen the CP and its daily and absolved members from the party rule which required them to promote the newspaper.

There were certain respects in which the loss of its newspaper need not have been an unmitigated disaster for the CP, for sustaining its falling circulation and trying to overcome sales resistance to it absorbed, more than anything else, the party's energies and resources. Moreover, by the early 1980s, dull, trite and indifferently edited, it was a poor advertisment or public flagship for communist politics. Unfortunately for the party, it was unable to redeploy towards more effective purposes the time, funds and ingenuity thus liberated. Instead, for two principal reasons, the release from this burden and the manner in which it occurred proved highly detrimental.

Firstly, and of overriding importance, it cost the party its base in the trade union movement. The reversal was not absolute to be sure: many trade unionist members took the EC side, and in Scotland and Wales the NUM leaders who were in the party, as well as most communist miners, remained energetically loyal. The STUC, too, while not withdrawing its support from the *Morning Star* as a labour movement newspaper, continued to maintain amicable relations with the Scottish CP leaders. None the less, among communist trade union officials in general and an unknown but certainly large percentage of the rank-and-file membership, the *Morning Star* supporters won the argument. In addition, the paper had served as the party's communication system among its industrial members and the crucial channel between itself and workers outside it. All that was now gone. As an organised force in the trade union movement the party was doomed. The position was symbolised by the fact that among the expellees was Ken Gill, not only the General Secretary of an important trade union but also member of the TUC General Council and chair of the 1984 TUC Conference. Some thought that the action against him represented an admirable attachment to principle irrespective of cost, others that it was merely foolish. Finally, the rupture took away from industrial branches what was, beside involvement in union elections, their principal *raison d'être*, selling the paper.

That last aspect relates also to the second main consideration. For the party branches which still continued to sustain 'public activity' – and by 1985 they were very much a minority – selling the paper was the main ingredient of their effort; their internal life was largely structured around that form of activity and its termination weakened the ligaments of habit binding together their active members. The CP did not simply lose the members – or the branches which went over to the opposition *en bloc* (and there were some) – but what had been since 1930 a fundamental part of its own being.

Independently of the *Morning Star* crisis the central focus of the party's political strategy, its commitment to electoral contests, was by the mid-1980s also visibly coming adrift. The number of communist councillors left in Britain was now down to single figures and its parliamentary votes had shrunk from the negligible to the derisory. Throughout the 1970s the leadership had argued with growing desperation in the face of the inexorable decline that a political party could not hope to be recognised as such unless it contested elections, so that they must continue regardless of the morale-sapping outcomes – together, of course, with the traditional justifications of the opportunities they supplied to make the party publicly visible. Direct challenges at congresses to the policy were always easily defeated, assisted by the fact that the anti-contesting position came to be identified with the Straight Left faction, though opposition to it was to be found across the whole spectrum of party outlook. The nadir was reached at the Bermondsey by-election of 1982, when the CP not only insisted on presenting a candidate against Peter Tatchell, who on the face of it combined in his person various aspects of the new social forces with which the CP was trying to identify, but also ended up with fewer votes than the Official Monster Raving Loony candidate.

Except in one respect the 1980s were for the Communist Party a decade of unrelieved disaster both in the historical development of British life and politics and in its own internal evolution. Paradoxically, as the party was beginning its plunge into decrepitude, the journal *Marxism Today* started to enjoy an exceptional commercial and cultural success. It was widely quoted and respectfully attended to; its circulation moved impressively upwards.

Marxism Today was in every imaginable fashion the diametric opposite of the *Morning Star*, so it is not surprising that the rival political outlooks crystallised around the two journals. Its contributors were academics and upmarket journalists, its approach iconoclastic and consumerist, whereas the *Morning Star* was resolutely class conscious if not workerist. *Marxism Today* was ironic and self-mocking; the *Morning Star* never took itself with anything less than utter seriousness. The magazine constantly experimented with innovations in design and presentation (as did the newspaper, but much less successfully).

From the early 1980s to around the time of the 1987 General Election *Marxism Today* followed a deliberately conceived project of examining and in most cases demolishing cherished traditional myths and totems of the CP and the labour movement. It printed material on foreign communist states and parties that was detached and analytical in tone. It was less than reverential towards trade union institutions and traditions. It drew attention to the secular decline of traditional male industrial employment, and investigated the likely consequences for social structure and political culture. It underlined and constantly reiterated that the forms of political practice and ideology which had sustained the labour movement since 1945 were dead, and if persisted in would lead to disaster and isolation. Consequently it showed itself highly suspicious of traditional forms of militancy and their attempted revival in the form of Bennism. On the eve of the 1987 General Election it advocated an anti-Tory electoral pact and urged tactical voting. It dismissed as fantasy the notion of a socialist Britain cutting its ties with transnational capital, and judged European Community membership to be a *fait accompli* or even meritorious. It probed the inadequacies of the forms of social provision which had characterised the thinking of the left and detected a measure of virtue in the market. The production and marketing of cultural artefacts constantly occupied its attention. Suiting action to theory, it went some way to becoming a vehicle for certain forms of glamorous and sophisticated consumer advertising.

The shock value of such pronouncements emanating from a communist journal was part of its distinctiveness and the reason for the notice which it attracted. The interest was furthered by the interviews it ran with political and cultural celebrities, as often as not vehemently anti-socialist ones. Extracts from its material often appeared as features in the *Guardian* or *Independent*, and its editor was seen from time to time on television. It was commented upon favourably by Neil Kinnock and Roy Hattersley. Nor was its impact confined to the publication itself, even as it extended the range of its commercial outlets. *Marxism Today* also sponsored festivals of political and cultural debate and dialogue, mostly in London but sometimes outside it, to which it did not hesitate to invite as speakers, so long as they might expect to attract an audience, personalities who made their living by denouncing everything the journal and the CP stood for; Sir Alfred Sherman for example.

At a time when every other aspect of its functioning was in desperate difficulty, the publicity success of *Marxism Today* enabled the CP to remain, after a fashion, an actor on the national political scene, indeed, except for the occasions of its greatest industrial influence, more so than ever before. It was a strange paradox. There can be no doubt that it was this success which enabled the Eurocommunist side to win in the inner party conflict, so much against the grain of the party's traditions and the political formation of its chief leaders, and at the cost of its newspaper. It was a powerful, and for many unanswerable, argument that while *Marxism Today* was constantly going forward in terms of circulation and influence its rival was as consistently going backwards. The monthly, for all its increasingly glossy appearance, was a miracle of shoestring production made possible only by the willingness of people who could command large sums for their writing to write for it for nothing.

By the mid-1980s most of its readers were outside the CP; by the time of the first formal readership survey, overwhelmingly so. (So were most of its contributors.) Inside the party the number of unqualified enthusiasts for the journal was not large. Many, probably most, of those who supported it in general terms tended also to have considerable reservations and experience a sense of bewilderment at this phenomenon which appeared to be giving new life to the CP by ideologically flaying it. They would have liked it to continue its achievements while behaving less scandalously and to have acted more like a traditional party publication. There were constant grumbles that it was too trendy and too metropolitan. The sexual explicitness of some of its editorial and advertising material was regarded as offensive by some communists, particularly older ones. Repeated demands were advanced that it should be made more answerable to the EC, publish more party material and use more CP contributors. The editor acknowledged that it had evolved away from being, as its masthead put it, 'The theoretical and discussion journal of the Communist Party' and had become a high-grade commentary on current affairs with a very loose left-wing orientation, but pointed out that to apply the suggested restrictions would alienate its non-CP readership and kill its commercial viability.[5]

Certainly *Marxism Today* was not challenged, either politically or as the party's flagship, by the weekly which was established towards the end of 1985 to take the place of the *Morning Star* as its newspaper. Great hopes were pinned on the new paper, although someone pointed out that the title, *7 Days*, had unhappy precedents, having been used for no less than two failed left-wing journals of the previous fifteen years. As editor the EC appointed Chris Myant, who would have taken over the *Morning Star* had it proved possible to evict Chater. He had an excellent journalistic record and was expected to produce a lively and popular weekly. 7 *Days* never lived up to its promise. It proved unable to find an effective combination of presentation and content. Too many of its articles were weak and uninspired, its graphics were poor and its format unenterprising and stodgy. All too soon it fell into the same spiral of declining circulation and financial crisis as had plagued its predecessor, and expired after five years of struggling existence.

Following the 39th Congress the CP had lost more than its newspaper and the vitals of its industrial constituency; it had in reality also lost its sense of direction and of how it might attain the political role to which it aspired. For all the success of *Marxism Today,* that journal amounted to an autonomous enterprise and owed its unique achievement to that fact: the party as such was falling apart. Not long afterwards the YCL faded out of existence. It is a tribute to the party's tenacity and sense of its own importance to British political life that it did not quietly follow its junior organisation into oblivion nor retreat into sectarian fantasy. Its more conscious and active members continued to be inspired by their image of what the party might be: an ecumenical organisation bringing together the scattered forces of the left and progressive movements in Britain, uniting them on the basis of viable and realistic programmes and strategies which the CP would influence on the basis of its Marxist understanding of social reality and nearly seventy years of experience, errors and successes. It had of course nothing to do with the CP's original purposes, but was none the worse for that and was in many ways an admirable vision. Its critical shortcoming was that the Communist Party, as it was by 1985, had become a wholly unsuitable vehicle to carry it.

This remained true despite occasional flickers of life in its traditional spheres. One of the new faces on the EC following the 39th Congress was John Peck, the most publicly visible and veteran member of the party in Nottingham, a Second World War bomber pilot and holder of the Distinguished Flying Cross. Located in the Bulwell area of the city, he had spent many years repeatedly contesting local and parliamentary elections. He was renowned in the party both as a convinced and articulate Eurocommunist and as its most passionate and consistent proponent of serious electoral contesting as the route to political advance. Gradually and steadily building up his local base of support as a community activist, he finally won Bulwell and a place on the Nottingham city council in the local elections of 1988. It was a great triumph, the more so as there was no tradition of communist councillors in Nottingham. In Govan, Glasgow, the former YCL National

Secretary, Doug Chalmers, now the Scottish Organiser, had also established a practice of consistent campaigning in the local community around
issues of housing and social welfare. Standing on behalf of the CP in
the November 1988 parliamentary by-election which was won by Jim
Sillars for the Scottish National Party he managed to grab media
attention and publicise the communist campaign extraordinarily well,
being referred to as 'Govan's Mr Fixit'. It still resulted in fewer than 500
votes, but was at least an increase on his 1987 General Election score.

The accession in 1985 of Mikhail Gorbachev to the leadership of the
Soviet Union did not produce any immediate implications for the
inner party struggle. Both Straight Left and the Chaterites, having
pinned their flag to the mast of the Soviet regime, had little choice but
to swallow any reservations they might have and applaud *perestroika* and
glasnost as welcome new advances growing naturally from the stem of
Soviet history; while the mainstream could welcome them more
genuinely as innovations and a long-overdue break with the discreditable habits of the past. Only the NCP and the marginal *Leninist* were
bold enough to see in them the repudiation of the fundamental traditions
of Soviet politics and to denounce them on that basis as anti-communist.

The consequent changes in the USSR and the Eastern European states,
the third Thatcher electoral victory in 1987, the remoulding of the
Labour Party under Kinnock's leadership, and not least the heritage of
the Communist Party's internal disputes convinced its leaders that new
perspectives and a new public presentation of the CP were urgently
required. The 40th Congress of 1987, after the pyrotechnics of the
previous two, was a rather tepid and unmemorable affair,[6] apart from
confirming another round of expulsions. Party officials at all levels did
not cease to reassure the rank-and-file that the party had turned the
corner, that the break with the *Morning Star*, however painful and
regrettable, had lanced the abscess and that it could now set about
vigorously overcoming its problems. Nevertheless, apart from *Marxism
Today*, the decline continued in every measurable aspect of its work.

The British Road to Socialism was recognised as embodying concepts
that were increasingly divergent from reality.[7] The last edition had been
published before Thatcher burst upon British politics, its scenario of a
communist/left-Labour majority at Westminster no longer carried any
conviction. Debates were initiated in the party media, Districts and
branches (such as were still functioning). In 1989 a new programme was
drafted in preparation for the Congress that November. Embodying
concepts such as post-fordism – implying the end of the form of indus-
trialism which had characterised the first half of the century and the class

relations which went along with it – explicitly repudiating the barrack socialism of the communist states,[8] addressing as central issues themes such as feminism, gay politics and environmentalism, it hinted at the need for radically remodelling the CP itself and was entitled *Manifesto for New Times*. The conception of 'New Times' was one of which *Marxism Today* had made much and the new manifesto was drafted by a team composed largely of the journal's partisans.

The second principal matter before the 1989 Congress was the succession to the party leadership. Gordon McLennan had been inclined to retire at the 1987 Congress but had yielded to persuasion to remain, in order to neutralise a possibly divisive issue. Two years later he was determined to go and there was in any case a feeling that the new times required a new General Secretary. Contention and a succession struggle were certainly possibilities. Since 1985 the victorious bloc against the Chaterites was showing signs of fracture, though not in any spectacular or uproarious fashion. The inherent tension between the traditional leaders and the new thinkers was always present,[9] and in this the Executive reflected wider strains throughout the surviving active membership. The term 'Eurocommunist' had largely passed into disuse since the politics which it incorporated had died in Western Europe; the trend in British communism which it described was itself fragmenting into two main tendencies. On the one hand there were the *Marxism Today* adherents, pragmatic, orientated towards consumerism and willing within limits to try any political gambit that looked as though it might work.[10] The other grouping was more ill-defined but labelled, by those suspicious of it, as having a politically moralist and puritan inclination. Its prominent representatives were the EC members Nina Temple, former YCL National Secretary and now the CP Press and Publicity Officer, and Dave Green.

All the three main trends had a potential leadership candidate. The traditionalists favoured Ian McKay, the National Organiser, who, while enthusiastically leading the CP in its new paths, embodied all the old party virtues. Universally popular in the party's ranks, admired by everybody for his dedication, sincerity and gracious personality, he would have been the third General Secretary in succession to have come from Scotland. He would doubtless have been acceptable to all the rival trends, although his disadvantage was felt to be a lack of platform and televisual charisma. Those in the *Marxism Today* camp naturally wanted Martin Jacques,[11] and Nina Temple was favoured by the other former Eurocommunist tendency. It was a sign of the times that party organisations throughout the country were invited to discuss the matter and to submit their viewpoint on both these and other leadership positions. In the end the matter was settled without argument, for both McKay and Jacques declined to compete for the position, preferring to continue with their existing responsibilities.

There were significant innovations in the character of the Congress as well. Although the recommended list system of election was maintained, amendments to the *Manifesto* and resolutions were determined by a free vote without advice from the outgoing EC,[12] and the opening political report was given by Martin Jacques rather than by Gordon McLennan. Signs of a conservative reaction against the tempestuous developments of the past seven years were, however, clearly visible.

In spite of a warm farewell to Gordon McLennan, the Congress displayed a rather bad-tempered tone and mood and the substantive decisions evinced a strong inclination to slow down the rate of change. The final acceptance of the new *Manifesto* went through on a fairly narrow vote. An amendment calling for drastic restructuring and overhaul of the party itself was decisively voted down as was a demand for a commission to examine all aspects of its functioning. Two resolutions were passed critical of *Marxism Today* for being insufficiently aligned to the party. The former Treasurer, when asked why she had resigned the office, replied that it was because her financial advice to exercise retrenchment and proper management of funds was constantly ignored. In particular she had wanted to reduce the subsidy to *Marxism Today*. The most symptomatic debate came near the end, when rule changes were proposed. One of these wanted to drop from party rules the term 'Marxism-Leninism'. This time the outgoing EC did intervene to argue against the alteration. The argument advanced by the EC speaker, Bill Innes, did not reject the change in principle, but maintained that it was premature, more time should be allowed for discussion and it should be considered in the context of the 'no holds barred' debate on the party that the incoming EC was committed to instituting. The change was rejected and one of its supporters commented that the EC's attitude reminded him of St Augustine – 'Oh Lord, give me chastity – but not yet!'

Frequent reference was made in the Congress sessions to the events taking place concurrently in Eastern Europe, for it met just at the time when the neo-Stalinist regimes in Czechoslovakia, the GDR and Romania were starting to totter. News of the Czechoslovak development was indeed received enthusiastically by nearly everyone and platform references to Dubček's triumphant return to public life were heartily cheered by the delegates, the majority of whom hoped and expected that some variety of reform socialism was likely to prevail. The Congress, however, formally accepted greetings from the ruling parties in the GDR and Romania, albeit in a rather embarrassed silence.

The delegates left the Congress having resolved to work energetically to restore the party's public presence and to turn its activity away from its internal crisis and towards an outside audience. Within a month it was evident that almost all the decisions of the Congress, and certainly those relating to its campaigning role, were a dead letter. The internal crisis could not simply be commanded to cease, but possessed a momentum of its own and was set to continue until the break-up or transformation of the organisation.

The cataclysms overwhelming the East European regimes brought rapidly to a head the long maturing and fundamental dilemma of the CP's essential purposes and identity as a British political party which was also a section of a world movement. The pages of its journals were quickly filled with anguished comment about what was happening in the USSR and the People's Democracies and the implications for the CPGB. Certainly there were some who affected to treat the developments with insouciance, arguing that since all the party's main objectives related to Britain, its future could not be seriously affected by what was going on in those countries – or even maintaining that the British party could only be strengthened by the spectacular vindication of criticisms it had been advancing for two decades.

Had the collapse of neo-Stalinism been the preliminary to the triumph of the reform communist forces which had either triggered the revolutions or been deeply involved in them, then undoubtedly the British CP would have benefited enormously. Its politics could once again have been presented as following a viable and democratic international model and the morale of its adherents would have been enhanced immeasurably. A rerun of its hopes at the time of the Prague Spring would have been in the making, and without the nuisance of a Stalinist opposition. Instead, the overwhelming rejection of any socialist model whatever was universal and emphatic; it was becoming clear that events in the Soviet Union itself were tending in a similar direction. In Poland, Hungary, Czechoslovakia and the GDR, the democratic left was quickly pushed aside, a breakneck reversion to laissez-faire capitalism was rapidly embarked upon and the recrudescence of xenophobia, anti-semitism and fascism did not wait long to make itself felt. The liquidation of the GDR along with its entire social order was particularly indicative of the direction in which events were moving. Communist

Party members could not escape the awareness that in maintaining fraternal relations with the East European regimes and defending their essence in spite of particular criticisms, they had dramatically put themselves on the wrong side of history.[13]

Closer to home the principal focus of left-wing political campaigning throughout 1990 was the poll tax and the extent of the CP's decline was illustrated by its marginality in an area where even not so very long ago it would have been central. In Scotland, where the tax was instituted a year before the rest of Britain, the party did have a considerable involvement in the official STUC-sponsored campaign, but even in Scotland the running was made in terms of refusing compliance by the Anti-Poll Tax Federation led by the ultra-left groups.[14] Elsewhere during 1990 the party was wholly ouflanked by its leftist rivals and scarcely visible, while Militant and the SWP visually dominated the marches and the billposting.

So it was that when the January meeting of the EC[15] threw open the promised debate, this very rapidly resolved itself into an argument over whether the party should continue to exist or not, a question which the 41st Congress was supposed to have settled. Among the erstwhile Eurocommunists of whatever colour there was little disagreement that its role was played out and that its assets should be inherited by the very different sort of organisation into which the party ought to transform itself, though there were different opinions over the best tactics to use in pursuit of this goal. On the part of their traditionalist colleagues, however, the outlook was a very different one, for to them the party was their identity and whatever else happened they wanted to keep it in being, preferably retaining the name 'Communist' in the title, though usually they were prepared to concede on that point provided the organisation as such with its basic principles and structures stayed in existence.

A further complication was added by the re-emergence in some strength of Straight Left, their attachment to Leninist myth undisturbed by the catastrophe of international communism, and demanding, still more adamantly than the mainstream traditionalists, the retention of the essential CP. Since 1983 they had maintained a low profile, avoided confrontation with the party leadership and worked patiently, by showing willingness to take on responsibilities at a time when few candidates were to be found, to gain whatever positions of influence in the party organisation might be available to them. Their slogan was the furtherance of 'Marxist education' within the party, and whenever they got the opportunity in the branch or District political education programmes which still ran, straight left conceptions became their content. By 1990 they had rebuilt a considerable base in the London District and were thought possibly to command a majority there, as well as having strength in other parts of the country.

While Straight Left saw no necessity for any far-reaching changes in the nature of the CP, and would have preferred a reassertion of its traditional values and organisation, the options which exercised the rest of the party members divided between 'transformation' – rejected at the 1989 Congress but now seen as the traditionalists' last hope – and the dissolution of the party followed by its re-creation as an 'association' or 'network' which would keep its members together (and hopefully increase them) while ending their political isolation by allowing them to join other parties. Nina Temple endeavoured to reconcile the two positions and avoid total collapse by proposing what she called a 'twin track' solution: to do both by bringing into being a transformed political party while simultaneously launching a project to set up a left-wing political association linked to the party but capable of attracting a wider audience. When it was pointed out that this seemed a somewhat impracticable venture given the state of the CP's resources, both human and material, she argued that while continuance in the old forms was unquestionably a dead end, a Congress majority could never be found for dissolving the party, in view of the known prevailing sentiments at its grass roots, and therefore the simple 'association' option, however logical or attractive, was also impracticable. The other most substantial argument against turning the CP into such an association was that, functioning without the organisational backbone and specific objectives of a political party, such bodies were inherently difficult to perpetuate and tended to be short-lived. The precedent of the New Left clubs was recalled.

Through the course of the year the debate intensified, but, though not without bitterness, it never reached the levels of vituperation that had been characteristic of the previous conflicts. The proponents of the 'association' project were told by the traditionalists and the Straight Leftists that since they had despaired of the party they ought in honesty to depart and leave it to those who still had confidence in it. It was said that Martin Jacques, having used the party to make himself a celebrated public figure, was now getting ready to throw it over now he no longer had need of it. The 'associationists' who stayed in the party and fought their corner were alleged to be doing so only so that they could capture its fixed assets – which were considerable, amounting to around £3 million – for the use of the intended new formation. As for the journal Jacques edited, in the course of the year it became evident that the subsidy with which the party sustained it, amounting to around £50,000 per year, would have to be discontinued. Two options were presented: either a more modest journal which the party could afford to keep, or for *Marxism Today* to seek outside finance – and inevitably control – and cease to be a CP publication. Each had its supporters, but the EC finally decided to let the journal go from its control in order to sustain and develop its public character, rather than return it to the ghetto of left-wing publishing.

In the meantime, membership continued to slump so that the quoted figure by the end of the year was down to 6000, back to where the party had been over fifty years earlier and with a painful comparison in activism and commitment between that time and its present. Those quitting the party included some of its most loyal activists and eminent personalities. Among them were Douglas Bain, who had been the Glasgow Secretary during some of the tensest internal conflict, Jane McKay, Secretary of the Glasgow Trades Council, and Hywel Francis, the leading historian of the Welsh miners. The most sensational of these resignations occurred in September when John Peck, at the meeting of the EC itself, announced that he was leaving to join the Green Party. That same meeting saw a proposal to dissolve the party gain the largest single block of votes and the proposition failed to become the official recommendation to the forthcoming Congress only because the supporters of Nina Temple's 'twin track' and the party preservationists combined against it, but it won 13 votes against 19.

The Special Congress had in April been fixed for the spring of 1991, but so swift was the process of disintegration and the virtual cessation of all activity apart from the internal debate that it was brought forward to December. The key to its outcome and whether or not the Secretary[16] could carry her proposals was held in Scotland. The loyalty of the Scottish delegation, the largest single component of the party and traditionally the leadership's praetorian guard, had been critical in ensuring the passage of the *Manifesto* in 1989. It was obvious from various gatherings in the course of the year that the members there were overwhelmingly attached to the preservation of the party, reluctantly accepting its 'transformation'; that support for the 'association' proposal was virtually zero and its few proponents had to assume a 'twin track' face just to get a hearing. Scottish members, including leading ones, declared that if the British EC went off the rails the Scottish members should continue with their own separate Communist Party.[17] Doug Chalmers, by that time the Scottish Secretary, worked to achieve a compromise, persuading the

Scottish Committee to accept a watered-down version of the 'twin track' which made its 'association' element much vaguer and fainter, and then inducing the EC to alter its proposals so as to accommodate the Scottish position. It was understood that the restructured party would be a federal organisation with virtually complete autonomy for its Scottish and Welsh components.

The Congress convened at the beginning of December in the TUC premises in Great Russell Street. It was well ordered and free from disruptions or even a great deal of passion, surprising in view of its momentous character, but perhaps all sides had reached a degree of exhaustion by that point. Outside, a group of *Leninist* supporters chanted that as the party was now liquidating itself *they* were the party. Ironically the Scottish delegation had to leave prematurely and abruptly because of transport disruptions arising from the blizzard which struck the country that weekend, but not before their votes and the advocacy of one of their most effective speakers in the traditionalist mould, John Kay, had secured the acceptance of the EC propositions. A decision was taken in principle to change the nature of the CP in both politics and structure. The recommendation on *Marxism Today* was endorsed. A constitutional Congress for late 1991 was agreed to effect the necessary changes. Marxism-Leninism was finally rejected. So was the recommended list system, leaving the vote on the new EC to the individual judgement of the delegates, although there were unofficial rival lists circulating, no one being much perturbed about the fact. A handful of Straight Leftists managed to get elected, but the outcome was a safe majority of moderate traditionalists and former Eurocommunists willing to accept the compromise. Martin Jacques did not stand.

The aftermath brought further resignations of leading advocates of the 'association' project unwilling to be reconciled to the line adopted. They included Brenda Kirsch, the former Assistant Editor of 7 *Days*, Simon Barrow, the editor of its more modest replacement, *Changes*, Paula Lanning, Vicky Seddon, prominent in the women's miners' support groups, and Dave Green, the London Secretary. Some had been members of the previous EC. The changed character of the party was reflected in the fact that it was done without much fuss on either side and those who departed continued to work amicably with their co-thinkers who chose to remain inside, trying together independently to create the sort of political association they had envisaged.

In March 1991 the EC circulated its proposals for a 'transformed party'. In substance they amounted to something very little different from the rejected propositions of the previous year. Although the term 'party' was used in the draft rules, it was not proposed that it appear in the title of the new organisation. Precisely what this should be was left for further discussion leading up to the final Congress, but the preferred alternative was 'Democratic Left'. After many a premature and exaggerated obituary this time it really was the end.

Conclusion

It was indeed the end, but not before still another encore had been played in the drama of split and mutual anathema that had characterised the previous fifteen years. The decision taken by the EC in March 1991 was perceived, quite accurately, as one to stop continuing the pretence to be a political party and opt instead for the role of an organisation trying to exercise a more indirect political and cultural influence – no different in essence from the proposal which had been rejected in November.

The realities of the party's situation had convinced members of the Executive who had opposed this departure during the previous year, including the key figures in the Scottish leadership, but they did not convince many of the members who had gone along only reluctantly with the 'twin track' option in the expectation that what was being buried was the 'association' proposal rather than the party.

Their indignation assumed, in Scotland, an organised form, with the promotion of meetings and the publication of a bulletin entitled *Alert Scotland*, declaring in one issue that 'a Communist Party which rejects the depressive politics of the Democratic Left can make a major contribution towards unifying the Left in British politics' – a triumph of hope over experience. The Straight Leftists, there and elsewhere, renewed their factional energies and formed a working arrangement with the new Scottish dissidents.

It might be supposed that the attempted coup in the USSR during August and the débâcle and then suppression of the CPSU following its collapse would have demoralised the continuing adherents of Leninism inside the British CP. Certainly it strengthened the conviction of those who wanted to distance the party yet further from the Soviet experience, but for others this was not the case. Dissidents who accepted the EC's condemnation of the putsch still objected to the leadership drawing comparisons between the attitudes of the plotters and Stalinist tendencies surviving inside the CPGB. For Straight Leftists, who had anyway approved of the venture as they had approved of those in Czechoslovakia and Poland, the closing of ranks syndrome came into operation. The adversaries squared up for one last round at the 43rd Congress.

The end of the international communist movement and consequently of the global competition between the two rival social systems may have detonated the terminal crisis of the CPGB, but it did so only by overlaying a profound internal crisis that was chronic and cumulatively destructive. That, too, was intimately linked with, though not wholly derived from, the international and specifically Soviet dimensions of the party's identity. As always throughout its career the interconnection of domestic and international threads was a tight one, and both have to be appreciated if there is to be any understanding of what the party represented and the nature of its development. In 1989–91 it was not a question of some scandalous act by the USSR which the British party had to lacerate itself by endorsing or rejecting. Rather it was that all Marxist perspectives appeared to have come to naught and history to have delivered a verdict against socialism in virtually any shape whatever.

Was the terminal splintering of the organisation of great significance to anybody beyond its own ageing and rapidly shrinking membership? The question is perhaps best approached by asking why anyone should wish to join the CP in the first place. The general answer would, of course, have varied very greatly depending on the time when the question was posed. In the early days it would have related to the party's claim to be the revolutionary vanguard in Britain of the international proletariat about to consign capitalist rule to the historical dustbin. Later on it would have related to the prominence of the CP and the USSR in the combat against fascism and/or as the precursors of a new and better world order. In the 1970s and afterwards the reason might have been that the party still remained the political entity which best combined theoretical boldness with contemporary relevance. At all times the exemplary behaviour of individual communists, their selfless energy in small matters and large, their ability to exact concessions from bosses and local or state authorities, was an important factor.

But beyond any particular attraction which the Communist Party might exercise, drawing them all together and a cardinal element of its appeal was the universalising perspective and outlook for which it stood. In marked contrast to the mainstream of the Labour Party it went far beyond immediate or medium-term concerns of economic relations or social justice; like the Catholic Church the party thought in centuries without losing sight of the significance of the here-and-now. All communist parties were informed by a historical theory which in its broad dimensions did not change from first to last, whatever doubts or disputes there might be about the role or destiny of particular social forces within it, especially the proletariat. The communist parties have constituted the first (and to date only) world movement which has treated with deadly seriousness the project of transforming social relations on a planetary scale for the benefit of the world's masses – as well as appearing to achieve stunning successes in terms of that objective. Communist activists shared a historical conviction which could and often did turn into a quasi-religious one.

According to Marx, 'What the bourgeoisie produces is above all its own grave-diggers', and Lenin had declared that the definition of a Marxist was a person who recognised the inevitability of the dictatorship of the proletariat. The working class, the proletariat created by modern industry, was the vehicle by which the history of class society would be transcended and the gateway opened to the classless millennium of equality and abundance. Such a process could not be other than an integrally international one, and the world party of the Comintern was its logical political counterpart. Conceiving themselves as guardians of the revolutionary consciousness of that part of the historical vanguard class which happened to be located in Britain – a position formally maintained at least up to the late 1970s – communists could not be other than simultaneously part of an international and a British labour movement. The problem of reconciling the two aspects would have been a severe one – for they were bound to conflict on occasion – even if the international movement had not come to acquire so morally dubious a character; as it was, the nature of Stalinism compounded the dilemma intolerably. The solutions arrived at by the leaders of the British party were not in principle the happiest ones but, as Eric Hobsbawm has pointed out, if they wanted to remain part of the international movement they had no choice.

People who joined the British CP, moreover, were, so long as they adhered to that decision, cutting themselves off from access to conventional sources of authority and influence or routes to high office, in short the political power which the party claimed to be its goal. In the early days, of course, it did not matter, indeed the party was only too anxious to do exactly that, for it expected shortly to dispose of rival contenders and to lead the government of a soviet Britain – an outlook resurrected during the 'class against class' era, although with a much greater measure of desperation.

Apart from these exceptional phases the CP was conscious that it could not achieve the revolution, or even much more limited objectives, single-handed, and that progress necessitated the search for 'unity' on a variety of bases. Until its last decade, however, the CP never ceased to regard itself either as the only or at least the most historically legitimate representative of the British working class.[1] The attitude gave rise to major problems, for it took the CP a very long time to overcome its instinctive disposition to exercise control over any organisation with which it collaborated or of which it was a part, and to treat them as adjuncts of the party. In the early days such domination was naked and unashamed, in principle as well as practice, being justified on the best Leninist theory. The control of the party fraction within its own creations, such as the Minority Movement, was almost written into their constitutions, and within independent organisations such as trade union branches the fraction strove to capture unqualified leadership.[2]

The approach, it must be stressed, had been designed for what was expected to be a short-term necessity leading towards the revolution and was not sustainable in the long run because of the conflicts created and the suspicions generated. The existence of this practice was the main weapon used by the Labour Party leadership to exclude the communists from affiliation or membership. It took until the 1960s, however, following the different experiences of 1956, CND and the ETU scandal, for the party to treat its subsidiaries as autonomous, its partners as equals and eschew any suggestion of manipulative relationships.

More than one commentator has specified the central contradiction in the CP's existence to be the fact that it was a revolutionary organisation placed in non-revolutionary circumstances.[3] The British political culture, with its revolution three centuries in the past and the product since then of a glacial process of compromise, negotiation and accommodation, was even in times of social or political crisis enormously resistant to the CP's project, regardless of what form it took. The party never fitted in with the indigenous political climate and there was no equivalent of the opportunity which the continental CPs had to establish their national credentials in the context of occupation and resistance. As an explanation for its long-term deficiencies and failure to achieve an effective insertion into the British political mainstream, however, this explanation is too facile. There was no *intrinsic* characteristic of the Communist Party which prevented it from adapting to the historical realities and carving out for itself a modest but significant place on the British left, with a parliamentary presence and a strong role in local government, perhaps becoming the longed-for socialist alternative on the left of the Labour Party, exerting a steady pull in more radical directions.[4]

The fact that it did not do so was the outcome of particular actions rather than any original historical sin. The CP's birth as a combination of revolutionary sects rather than as a left-wing split from the mainstream socialist movement, and therefore lacking a solid base in the latter, was admittedly a disadvantage, but other communist parties had equally unpromising beginnings and were not crippled by them. In any case, by the late 1920s the party had gone a long way towards repairing the deficiency by its construction of the Minority and National Left-Wing Movements, as well as the NUWM. Of several decisive turning points in the party's career, the 'Third Period' probably therefore counted for most, for it represented the self-liquidation of the CP base in the unions and the Labour Party, as well as erecting insurmountable barriers of distrust. The trade union base could be rebuilt, though never again on such effective foundations, but the Labour Party one was lost for ever. By the time the party did try seriously to take stock and adapt to the realities of British politics it was too late.

Claims were frequently voiced after 1956 and the resurgence of the British left that the CP, by its existence and the trade union influence it continued to exercise, was blocking the emergence of a healthier alternative uncontaminated with the party's discreditable past. That certainly was the conviction of some trends descending from the New Left, such as the *Socialist Register*, and of the ultra-left groups and parties, each of which saw itself as the potential successor. Whether, had they had the field to themselves, they could have done better than the CP is questionable. Even making the very considerable assumption that their analysis and theory were superior, correctness in those areas provides no guarantee of a workable strategy or effective political style.

The party had two great advantages over its rivals among the sects. The first of these was the thing which so often in other circumstances proved a liability, its international links. While the Trotskyist tradition and the memory of 1917 furnished a shadow alternative for a world movement and the hope of what might yet be, it was a poor substitute for one which was actually holding power in the name of a third of the globe's inhabitants and, in spite of setbacks and wrong turnings, advancing and developing towards better things. The second was the disenchanted outlook with which the CP approached its tasks of mobilisation and struggle in industry or elsewhere. In spite of officially propounded optimism, the real instincts which it cultivated in its activists were ones of ingrained caution and unwillingness to get euphoric about limited successes – and in British circumstances people led by communists were generally well served by attitudes of that sort.

That sobriety, induced by a long record of defensiveness and damage limitation, combined with the proficiency of communist militants in conduct of struggles, generally compared well with the heated revolutionism of the sects, who threw accusations of treachery right and left.

Once the party had been overtaken by the international communist failure, however, it was clear that it did not have the internal resources to sustain the blow in anything resembling its existing form. All the options available for the foundation of its project – international communism, the British labour movement, the peace movement, the new social forces – had been progressively exhausted so far as the CP was concerned. From its foundation and in spite of all its transformations the party had never abandoned its ambition to provide the political leadership for the most advanced and progressive elements in the British social structure, but equally certainly it had never, except occasionally and ephemerally, succeeded. Far-reaching changes in its mode of operation that might have allowed it to exploit developing opportunities were never made in time. The Communist Party was a very conservative organisation. The conservatism was ingrained in the core of its membership, attached to the perception of a heroic and sacrificial past and to the alternative cultural universe which shaped their identities and justified their life histories.

The leadership largely shared that outlook, but in so far as it did not and was conscious of the need to adapt – increasingly true in the later years – it had a problem. Its relations with its rank-and-file were such that so long as the leaders stayed within the shared traditional assumptions they could do largely what they liked, but trying to step outside them was sure to provoke a hostile reaction. Two decades of such reaction, from the changed name of the *Daily Worker* to sponsorship of *Marxism Today*, in combination with the erosion of communist and labour movements, could not fail in the end to wither the vitality of the organisation.

As the Congress of November 1991 approached, only two possibilities remained open to an organisation which still possessed several thousand members – on paper – a great deal of property and still some individuals trying to infuse it with new energies. Estimates made in the early autumn showed a roughly equal balance as being the likely outcome of delegate elections and therefore a conceivable if narrow majority for a traditionalist reaction which could overturn the EC's proposals and reassert in their place the venerable style and structures of the past. Were that to happen the name of the CPGB would continue[5] but attached to an irrelevant sect on the lines of the NCP without any effectual insertion either into the labour movement or a wider constituency.

By the time the congress was convened, however, it was evident that the traditionalist challenge had faltered and the renovators had a safe majority, even in Scotland. It was clear therefore that a new formation would emerge, although even so it would be bound to lose a good deal of the remnant still holding on to their cards. Democratic Left, or whatever title came to be adopted, would also have to struggle to establish a meaningful niche for itself in the spectrum of British politics and might well not be up to the undertaking. It would not have a labour movement base nor *Marxism Today*[6] either, and on top of that would be haunted by the embarrassing scandal of the Moscow gold revelations, which caused Martin Jacques and others promptly to resign their membership. Yet with all those disadvantages the new body would have to reverse the stagnation in which the dying party was trapped and start reproducing itself as an organisation.

There is a further consideration. As the world approaches the third millennium of the Christian Era environmental catastrophe looms, ideologies and institutions of revolutionary hope dissolve and collapse, and among the economically advanced and comfortable nations postmodernist culture advances. The very notions of progress and universalism, the absolute centrepoint of the Marxist tradition, are increasingly at a discount. All of these things weigh very heavily against the prospect of Marxist or socialist revival on a world scale, quite aside from the particular circumstances applying to a British fragment. At the same time, as an increasingly sinister new world order emerges, built upon the twin pillars of unconstrained military savagery and capitalist rapacity,[7] it is hard to envisage anything other than global solutions being possible to global problems. Some of the qualities and traditions which have enabled the CP to survive through almost constantly adverse circumstances and to exert an influence, however limited, on the course of British history could be a valuable component of the social and political enterprise which confronts the monumental problems of the future, but there is no certainty that a continuing organisation will exist to embody them.

Afterword

As expected, the 43rd Congress, held in late November 1991, proved to be the last. In the event, the voting was even more decisive than had been predicted, with regular 2–1 majorities in the votes dismantling the existing structures, replacing them with others of a loosely articulated federal sort and changing the name of the organisation.

The Congress proceedings, as might have been expected, generated a degree of bitterness as the minority, having lost the decisive first vote on adopting the proposed new constitution as the basis for discussion fought tenaciously throughout to save whatever could be retained of the rejected traditions. Around thirty or so (out of around 220 delegates) were prepared to applaud the principle of receiving secret money from the CPSU.

The renovators nevertheless, in spite of their numerical losses following the 1990 Congress, emerged triumphant, winning not only all the important votes but also every place on the Federal Executive, as the new directing committee was to be titled, as well as achieving their favoured name of Democratic Left. It was the more surprising perhaps in that the Congress was not a particularly youthful one, the biggest single age-band being the over-forties.[8]

Some at least of the defeated traditionalists vowed, in one manner or another, to continue the sacred traditions and the communist name. The formation of yet another splinter communist party was thus in prospect, though common sense suggested an attempt, in spite of deep antagonisms, to link up with the CPB and the NCP. Democratic Left, however, as a result of the Congress votes, had both the legitimacy of descent and the physical resources of the former CPGB.

Appendix: Communist Party Membership, 1920–1991

Year		Members	Year		Members
1920		4000	1947		38579
1921		2500	1948		43000
1922		5116	1950		38853
1924		4000	1952		35124
1925		5000	1954		33963
1926	(Apr.)	6000	1956	(Feb.)	33095
	(Oct.)	10730	1957		26742
1927		7377	1959		25313
1929		3200	1961		27541
1930		2555	1963		33008
1931	(June)	2724	1964		34281
	(Nov.)	6279	1965		33734
1932	(Jan.)	9000	1967		32916
	(Nov.)	5600	1969		30607
1934		5800	1971		28803
1935		7700	1973		29943
1936		11500	1975		28519
1937		12250	1977		25293
1938		15570	1979		20599
1939		17756	1981		18458
1941	(Dec.)	22738	1983		15691
1942		56000	1985		12711
1943		55138	1987		10350
1945		45435	1989		7615
1946		42123	1991	(July)	4742

Notes and References

INTRODUCTION

The place of publication in notes to this volume is London unless specified otherwise.

1. The minute Socialist Party of Great Britain, founded in 1904, has existed for even longer, but it has made a virtue out of its character as an irrelevant propagandist sect of no interest to anyone outside its own membership. This organisation is not to be confused with the British Socialist Party, the successor to the SDF.
2. For example, the *Independent*, 25 November 1990, and the *Guardian*, 10 December 1990.
3. At the 1943 Congress the name was altered to British Communist Party. According to Malcolm MacEwen, *The Greening of a Red*, Pluto, 1991, p. 98, the change was made on his initiative. Following the 1957 Congress the original name was restored.
4. The Social Democratic Party of Germany (SPD) was a good example of a professedly revolutionary socialist party which had in reality adopted a constitutionalist orientation, while the British Labour Party adhered to constitutionalism as a central principle.
5. An interesting sidelight on syndicalist influence on Britain is its effect upon labour movement iconography. At the beginning of the twentieth century this tended to favour a bucolic imagery in conjunction with representations of female figures (the Walter Crane style for example). Syndicalism emphasised the muscular male industrial worker as a more appropriate symbol.
6. Lenin's attitude to these same individuals before 1914, while often critical, was far from derogatory. See, for example, *Lenin on Britain*, Moscow Foreign Languages Publishing House, Moscow, n.d..
7. Although this assessment represents the overwhelming consensus of historical opinion, it has been challenged recently by Piero Melograni in *Lenin and the Myth of World Revolution: Ideology and Reasons of State 1917–1920*, Humanities Press, New Jersey, 1990, who contends that Lenin 'conceived the idea of "Socialism in one Country" from the moment he took power'. Though energetically pressed, the argument is unconvincing and proceeds by ignoring awkward counter-evidence. Even Melograni acknowledges that all Lenin's colleagues had international revolution principally in mind.

8. E.H. Carr, *The Russian Revolution from Lenin to Stalin*, Macmillan, 1979.

9. See Fernando Claudin, *The Communist Movement from Comintern to Cominform*, Penguin, Harmondsworth, 1975, p. 55, for a discussion of the weaknesses which were ignored at the establishment of the Third International.

10. E.J. Hobsbawm, *Revolutionaries*, Weidenfeld & Nicolson, 1973, p. 13.

11. Ibid., p. 4.

12. M. Woodhouse and B. Pearce, *Essays on the History of Communism in Britain*, New Park, 1975, p. 20.

13. The CPGB was not part of the Communist Information Bureau (Cominform), membership of which was confined to parties of the Soviet bloc (less Albania) plus the two biggest Western parties, the PCI and the PCF. Liaison with the British was maintained through the French party.

14. The last significant occasion was the construction of the Berlin Wall in 1961; the first publicly voiced criticism came over the manner of Khrushchev's removal in 1964.

15. In the *Bulletin of the Society for the Study of Labour History* No. 44, Spring 1982.

16. T. Bell, *The British Communist Party: A Short History*, Lawrence & Wishart, 1937. The book was subjected to savage strictures by Allen Hutt in the June 1937 number of *Labour Monthly*, then functioning as the CP theoretical journal. It was attacked not only for its political short-comings, but also for its meandering style and numerous factual errors (which was justified). The following month the journal apologised for the tone while upholding the substance of the review.

17. Hobsbawm, *Revolutionaries*, pp. 3–10.

18. See also the three articles dealing with the 1956 crisis in the CPGB in the *Socialist Register* for 1976.

19. Striking examples are D. Hyde, *I Believed: The Autobiography of a Former British Communist*, Heinemann, 1951; C.H. (Bob) Darke, *The Communist Technique in Britain*, Penguin, Harmondsworth, 1952; and N. Wood, *Communism and the British Intellectuals*, Gollancz, 1959.

20. In this regard, and as it well exemplifies the spirit in which I am writing, I am unable to resist quoting from the Preface of Norman Hampson's *St Just*, Basil Blackwell, Oxford, 1991, p. [ii]:

   I am not so naive as to be unaware how quaint this approach must appear to anyone brought up on a modern diet of symbolism and semiotics. To suggest that, on the whole, the revolutionary orators said what they meant and that their audiences generally understood what they said in the sense in which they meant it, is to confess oneself a very dull dog indeed. I remain impenitent.

CHAPTER 1

1. For European socio-politcal development in the early twentieth century see E. Hobsbawm, *The Age of Empire 1875–1914*, Weidenfeld & Nicolson, 1987.

2. See M. Langan and B. Schwartz, eds, *Crisis in the British State 1880–1930*, Hutchinson, 1985.

3. For German society and German Social Democracy prior to 1914 see H.-U. Wehler, *The German Empire*, Berg, Leamington Spa, 1985; W.L. Guttsman, *The German Social Democratic Party 1875–1933*, Allen & Unwin, 1981.

4. See, for example, J. Foster, *Class Struggle and the Industrial Revolution*, Methuen, 1977, Chapter 7; J. Saville, *1848: The British State and the Chartist Movement*, Cambridge University Press, Cambridge, 1987; and, for a contrary or at least divergent interpretation, G.S. Jones, *Languages of Class: Studies in English Working-Class History 1832–1982*, Cambridge University Press, Cambridge, 1983.

5. R. Gray, *The Aristocracy of Labour in Nineteenth-Century Britain c. 1850–1914*, Macmillan, 1981.

6. It is perhaps of some significance that the English word 'skill' is not precisely translatable into any other language.

7. W. Kendall, *The Revolutionary Movement in Britain 1900–1921*, Weidenfeld & Nicolson, 1969, Chapter 1.

8. It may be remarked that 'inevitable' was one of the favourite terms in Lenin's polemic: 'the Marxian doctrine...proves the inevitable...replacement of the present system by a new order'. V.I. Lenin, 'Marxism and Revisionism', *Collected Works*, Vol. 15, Foreign Languages Publishing House, Moscow/Lawrence & Wishart, 1963, p. 31.

9. Kendall, *Revolutionary Movement*, p. 11. He quotes Engels:

The Social Democratic Federation here shares with your German-American Socialists the distinction of being the only parties which have contrived to reduce the Marxist theory of development to a rigid orthodoxy. The theory is to be forced down the throats of the workers at once and without development as articles of faith instead of making the workers raise themselves to its level by dint of their own class instinct.

10. For France see T. Zeldin, *France 1848–1945: Ambition and Love*, Oxford University Press, Oxford, 1979, pp. 231–43; T. Judt, *Socialism in Provence 1871–1914*, Cambridge University Press, Cambridge, 1979, pp. 93–7; F. Ridley, *Revolutionary Syndicalism in France*, Cambridge University Press, Cambridge, 1970.

11. For the SLP see R. Challinor, *The Origins of British Bolshevism*, Croom Helm, 1977.

12. For Ireland and the British left see D. Greaves, *The Life and Times of James Connolly*, Lawrence & Wishart, 1961; M. Milotte, *Communism in Modern Ireland: The Pursuit of the Workers' Republic since 1916*, Gill & Macmillan, Dublin, 1984.

13. Victor Grayson, aged twenty-five, achieved a sensational by-election victory at Colne Valley in 1907. Although an ILP member, he stood as a 'clean Socialist' opposed to the whole trend of Labour parliamentary co-operation with the Liberals. In constant conflict with the Labour MPs and attracting huge audiences on speaking tours, he advanced the notion of establishing a mass socialist party. For Grayson see Kendall, *Revolutionary Movement*, pp. 35–41.

14. Ibid., pp. 23–45.

15. Ibid., pp. 84–104.

16. Under the Treasury Agreements, named after their place of signature in 1915, the trade union leaders for the sake of the war effort undertook to accept arbitration in disputes, skill dilution and industrial peace in general.

17. For Maclean see Kendall, *Revolutionary Movement*, pp. 105–41; N.M. Maclean, *John Maclean*, Pluto, 1973; W. Gallacher, *Revolt on the Clyde*, Lawrence & Wishart, 1978 (reissue); H. McShane, *No Mean Fighter*, Pluto, 1978.

18. Kendall, *Revolutionary Movement*, pp. 187–95.

19. During his imprisonment he was, however, subjected to a regime which permanently damaged his health.

20. Though a left-wing ILP candidate, Neil MacLean, standing in Govan, did take the seat and was the only successful Labour candidate in Glasgow.

21. Kendall, *Revolutionary Movement*, pp. 187–291.

22. V.I. Lenin, *Collected Works*, Vol. 31, Progress Publishers, Moscow/Lawrence & Wishart, 1966, pp. 83–4.

23. R. Miliband, *Marxism and Politics*, Oxford University Press, Oxford, 1977, p. 169.

24. Kendall, *Revolutionary Movement*, pp. 199–200; G. Brown, *Maxton*, Mainstream, Edinburgh, 1986, pp. 104–9; J. Klugmann, *History of the Communist Party of Great Britain. Vol. 1: Formation and Early Years, 1919–1924*, Lawrence & Wishart, 1966, pp. 27–30.

25. Kendall, *Revolutionary Movement*, pp. 212–19; L.J. Macfarlane, *The British Communist Party: Its Origins and Development until 1929*, MacGibbon & Kee, 1966, pp. 55–9; Klugmann, *History*, pp. 38–50; Challinor, *Origins*, Chapters 10 and 11, in which it is argued that if Lenin had understood the British situation better he would have looked with greater favour upon the anti-Labour Party affiliation standpoint of the SLP majority.

26. Kendall, *Revolutionary Movement*, pp. 289–90.

27. B. Schwartz and M. Durham, 'A Safe and Sane Labourism: Socialism and the State 1910–1924', in Langan and Schwartz, *Crisis*, pp. 126–50.

28. Macfarlane, *British Communist Party*, pp. 102–9; Klugmann, *History*, pp. 166–81; N. Branson and B. Moore, *Labour–Communist Relations 1920–1951. Part I: 1920–1935*, Our History Pamphlet No. 82, July 1990, pp. 1–39.

29. Official electoral discrimination against women ended in 1928. The general election of 1929 was the first to be fought on a gender-blind suffrage. The early CP showed some sensitivity to gender issues beyond those encountered in the workplace. *The Communist* for 11 March 1922 carried a double-page spread under the title 'Communism for Women: Women for Communism' and referred to the 'obsolescent debris of a patriarchal family system'.

30. C.L. Mowat, *Britain between the Wars*, Methuen, 1955; N. Branson, *Britain in the Twenties*, Weidenfeld & Nicolson, 1975.

31. E.J. Hobsbawm, *Revolutionaries*, Weidenfeld & Nicolson, 1973, p. 9.

32. In 1925 the CP expected to receive £1,000 from its members and £16,000 from the Comintern. Macfarlane, *British Communist Party*, p. 149.

33. Macfarlane, *British Communist Party*, p. 59. See also S. Macintyre, *A Proletarian Science: Marxism in Britain 1917–1933*, Cambridge University Press, Cambridge, 1980, p. 29, for an identical comment.

34. There is no satisfactory biography of Pollitt, for that by J. Mahon, *Harry Pollitt: A Biography*, Lawrence & Wishart, 1976, is much too uncritical and reverential and dodges difficult issues. There is no biography at all of Palme Dutt, which is regrettable, as apart from his importance to the history of the CPGB he was a very representative communist intellectual functionary. But see J. Callaghan, 'The Heart of Darkness: Rajani Palme Dutt and the British Empire – A Profile', *Contemporary Record* Vol. 5, No. 2, Autumn 1991, and 'Reminiscences of Palme Dutt' (anon.), *Our History Journal* No. 11, January 1987.

35. Macfarlane, *British Communist Party*, p. 77. (Callaghan, 'Heart of Darkness', considers it probable that Comintern influence was also exercised.)

36. Ibid., pp. 80–3; Klugmann, *History*, pp. 200–13. For the Bolsheviks see M. Liebmann, *Leninism under Lenin*, Merlin, 1980.

37. Klugmann, *History*, pp. 257–62; Macfarlane, *British Communist Party*, pp. 189–91.

38. Macfarlane, *British Communist Party*, p. 111–12, 143–62; Klugmann, *History*, pp. 278–84. For full-scale studies see J. Hinton and R. Hyman, *Trade Unions and Revolution: The Industrial Policy of the Early British Communist Party*, Pluto, 1975; R. Martin, *Communism and the British Trade Unions 1924–1933: A Study of the National Minority Movement*, Clarendon Press, Oxford, 1969. Attitudes at the beginning of the party's career are well expressed in the resolution, quoted by Martin

(p. 19), of the National Administrative Committee of the Shop Stewards' and Workers' Committee Movement in January 1921:

... the need for a national unofficial industrial movement is urgent and ... every effort should be made to secure that the control of this movement should be in the hands of members of the Communist Party of Gt. B...
   It is the business of the Communist Party to secure that all key positions are held by Communists...

39. W. Hannington, *Unemployed Struggles, 1919–1936*, Lawrence & Wishart, 1979 (reissue); R. Croucher, *We Refuse to Starve in Silence: The History of the National Unemployed Workers' Movement*, Lawrence & Wishart, 1987.

40. Another Little Moscow was Chopwell in County Durham. This, however, was dominated by the Labour Party left, not the CP.

41. J. Melling, 'Locating the Little Moscows', *Our History Journal* No. 7, Winter 1982–3.

42. S. Macintyre, *Little Moscows: Communism and Working-Class Militancy in Inter-war Britain*, Croom Helm, 1980, provides an exhaustive account.

43. J. Callaghan, *The Far Left in British Politics*, Basil Blackwell, Oxford, 1987, pp. 34–5, 52–3.

44. Macfarlane, *British Communist Party*, pp. 162–6.

45. For example, M. Woodhouse and B. Pearce, *Essays on the History of Communism in Britain*, New Park, 1975, pp. 66–103, 149–52.

46. H. Laski, *Communism*, 1927, quoted in ibid., p. 151.

47. Macfarlane, *British Communist Party*, p. 173.

48. J.T. Murphy, 'Forty Years Hard – For What?', *New Reasoner*, No. 7, Winter 1958–9.

CHAPTER 2

1. Although it comes from a later decade, the following quote suggests the flavour of the attitudes to their personal commitment cultivated by CP activists:

Meanwhile I had become engaged to a girl who was not at all interested in the Party. The engagement was later broken off but in the meantime I began to spend more time dancing and taking her to the pictures than was consistent with efficient and practical Party work... To make matters worse I frequented the Empire Club, a real sink of iniquity... spending my time gambling and playing cards, when I was needed by the Party in a critical period.

   E. Trory, *Between the Wars: Recollections of a Communist Organiser*, Crabtree Press, Brighton, 1974, p. 67 (written in 1940).

2. N. Branson and B. Moore, *Labour–Communist Relations 1920–1951. Part I: 1920–1935*, Our History Pamphlet No. 82, July 1990.
3. For a detailed account of the end of the Minority Movement see R. Martin, *Communism and the British Trade Unions 1924–1933: A Study of the National Minority Movement*, Clarendon Press, Oxford, 1969, Chapter 7.
4. L.J. Macfarlane, *The British Communist Party: Its Origins and Development until 1929*, MacGibbon & Kee, 1966, pp. 189–91; N. Branson, *History of the Communist Party of Great Britain 1927–1941*, Lawrence & Wishart, 1985, Chapter 1.
5. It is important to emphasise the substantial *internal* support there was within the British CP for a much more confrontational policy than that pursued up to 1928, even if not for the extremism of the line actually adopted. The most recent account to underline this is Mike Squires, *Saklatvala: A Political Biography*, Lawrence & Wishart, 1990.
6. The CPGB endorsed without demur the increasingly vehement condemnations issuing from the Soviet Politburo of Trotsky and his political line. Reviewing, in the *Labour Monthly* for June 1925, Trotsky's reminiscences of Lenin, W.N. Ewer castigated him, speculated that his thinking was affected by illness and wrote that 'Either Trotsky must, at any cost, be disciplined; or he might, by reason of his very greatness, destroy the Revolution.' (Ewer himself left the CP in 1930, judging that the 'class against class' line was out of touch with reality, and was thereupon abused and insulted by Palme Dutt.) In 1925 the CP published *The Errors of Trotskyism*, a selection of condemnatory articles by Zinoviev, Kamenev, Stalin and others. However, in the introduction, by J.T. Murphy, Trotsky himself was still referred to in respectful terms and his own 'Lessons of October' was also included in the collection. At the time of Trotsky's expulsion from the Executive Committee of the Comintern Murphy was the British representative on the ECCI, and actually moved the motion of expulsion, occasioning Deutscher's caustic description of him as 'an insignificant envoy of one of the most insignificant foreign Communist parties'. I. Deutscher, *The Prophet Unarmed*, Oxford University Press, Oxford, 1970, p. 359.
7. The most accessible account is to be found in A. Nove, *An Economic History of the USSR*, Penguin, Harmondsworth, Chapter 5; E.H. Carr, *The Russian Revolution from Lenin to Stalin 1917–1929*, Macmillan 1979, p. 78.
8. Nove, *Economic History*, Chapters 6–7; S. Cohen, *Bukharin and the Bolshevik Revolution*, Oxford University Press, Oxford, 1980, Chapter 6.
9. Branson, *History*, Chapter 3. See particularly the 'Closed Letter' from the ECCI to the Central Committee of the CPGB, reprinted as an appendix in Macfarlane, *British Communist Party*.

10. A historical analysis of the Young Communist League is currently being prepared by Mike Waite, to whom I am grateful for pertinent observations.

11. Branson, *History*, pp. 45–51. 'The denial of the wildest assertions of the critics on the left was taken as the strongest proof of their correctness.' Macfarlane, *British Communist Party*, p. 235.

12. Macfarlane, *British Communist Party*, p. 264; Branson, *History*, pp. 85–88; J Fyrth, 'Arthur Horner and the Third Period', *Our History Journal* No. 12, January 1988.

13. Macfarlane, *British Communist Party*, p. 241.

14. Branson, *History*, pp. 31, 35–8; G. Brown, *Maxton*, Mainstream, Edinburgh, 1986, p. 201. 'Down with the Social-Fascist props Maxton, Cook and Co.' declared the Resolutions of the party's 11th Congress.

15. Branson, *History*, p.35; Macfarlane, *British Communist Party*, pp. 223–9.

16. Macfarlane, *British Communist Party*, p. 202; Branson, *History*, pp. 34–5, 38–43.

17. Branson, *History*, pp. 41–2, 182–3; Macfarlane, *British Communist Party*, pp. 265–74; R. Page Arnot, *A History of the Scottish Miners*, Allen & Unwin 1955, pp. 213–22; Martin, *Communism and the British Trade Unions*, pp. 92–3, 127–9.

18. Martin, *Communism and the British Trade Unions*, pp. 136–42; Macfarlane, *British Communist Party*, pp. 255–60; Branson, *History*, p. 42.

19. S. Macintyre, *Little Moscows: Communism and Working-Class Militancy in Inter-war Britain*, Croom Helm, 1980.

20. W. Hannington, *Unemployed Struggles 1919–1936*, Lawrence & Wishart, 1979, Chapter 11 ff. Hannington makes no reference to 'class against class' and very little to the Communist Party.

21. Macfarlane, *British Communist Party*, p. 240; Branson, *History*, Chapter 4. Bill Rust's own *Story of the Daily Worker*, PPPS, 1949, provides, not unexpectedly, a highly sanitised version of the paper's origins.

22. See N. Wood, *Communism and the British Intellectuals*, Gollancz, 1959, for an informative but very tendentiously hostile account.

23. For Cornford, see P. Stansky and W. Abrahams, *Journey to the Frontier*, Constable, 1966.

24. Wood, *Communism*, Chapter 5. Maurice Goldsmith's biography of Bernal, *Sage*, Hutchinson, 1980, is of little merit.

25. Branson, *History*, p. 217.

26. Especially the voluminous effusions of Chapman Pincher. The story is repeated (without substantiation) in Denis Healey's autobiography, *The Time of My Life*, Penguin, Harmondsworth,1990, p. 38, where Klugmann's name is misspelt.

27. Unpublished reminiscences of Bill Cowe, Scottish Organiser and Central Committee member.

28. See K. Morgan, *Against Fascism and War: Ruptures and Continuities in British Communist Politics 1935–1941*, Manchester University Press, Manchester, 1989, for a sympathetic and detailed examination of this phase in the party's development.

29. The fullest account of these events is in Alan Merson, *Communist Resistance in Nazi Germany*, Lawrence & Wishart, 1985.

30. *Seventh Congress of the Communist International.* Abridged stenographic report of proceedings, Moscow 1939, p. 565.

31. Ibid., pp. 565–6.

32. See J. Fyrth, ed., *Britain, Fascism and the Popular Front*, Lawrence & Wishart, 1985.

33. R. Thurlow, *Fascism in Britain*, Basil Blackwell, Oxford 1987; N. Branson and M. Heinemann, *Britain in the Nineteen Thirties*, Weidenfeld & Nicolson, 1971, Chapter 19; Branson, *History*, Chapter 12.

34. Branson, *History*, Chapter 16; B. Alexander, *British Volunteers for Liberty: Spain 1936–1939*, Lawrence & Wishart, 1982; H. Francis, *Miners against Fascism*, Lawrence & Wishart, 1984.

35. J. Saville, 'Valentine Cunningham and the Poetry of the Spanish Civil war', *Socialist Register*, 1981 ; V. Cunningham, 'Saville's Row with *The Penguin Book of Spanish Civil War Verse*', *Socialist Register*, 1982.

36. H. Pelling, *The British Communist Party: A Historical Profile*, A. & C. Black, 1958, p. 94.

37. Branson, *History*, pp. 213–16; J. Lewis, *The Left Book Club: An Historical Record*, Gollancz, 1970; B. Pimlott, *Labour and the Left in the 1930s*, Cambridge University Press, Cambridge, 1977, Chapter 16; B. Reid, 'The Left Book Club in the Thirties', in J. Clark et al., eds, *Culture and Crisis in Britain in the 1930s*, Lawrence & Wishart, 1979; Morgan, *Against Fascism*, pp. 254–76.

38. Branson, *History*, pp. 155-7; Pimlott, *Labour and the Left*.

39. Such evidence as exists suggests that their assessment was mistaken, for 'People's Front' candidates won the Bridgewater by-election in 1938 (Vernon Bartlett) and polled remarkably well at another in Oxford (A.D. Lindsay). See Pimlott, *Labour and the Left*, pp. 167–8.

40. Branson *History*, p. 114; Pelling, *British Communist Party*, p. 97.

41. Interview with Bob Horne, member of the League of Youth committee.

42. For the growth of tripartite corporatism between the TUC, employers and government, see K. Middlemas, *Politics in Industrial Society*, André Deutsch, 1979.

43. Branson, *History*, pp. 182–3.

44. For the Welsh miners and Horner see H. Francis and D. Smith, *The Fed: A History of the South Wales Miners in the Twentieth Century*, Lawrence & Wishart, 1980; A. Horner, *Incorrigible Rebel*, MacGibbon & Kee, 1960.

45. An extensive literature exists upon the purges, although little on their impact in Western countries. See R. Conquest, *The Great Terror*, Penguin, Harmondsworth, 1971; R. Medvedev, *Let History Judge*, Spokesman, 1976; J. Arch Getty, *Origins of the Great Purges*, Cambridge University Press, Cambridge, 1987, presents an impressively documented and argued but rather contentious case that the purges were more of a structural phenomenon than a deliberately planned exercise.

46. *Daily Worker*, 5 February 1937.

47. Ibid., 17 March 1938.

48. P. Sloan in *Russia Today*, July 1937.

49. *Daily Worker*, 4 September 1836.

50. D.N. Pritt, Introduction to D. Collard, *Soviet Justice and the Trial of Radek and Others*, Left Book Club, 1937.

51. Ibid., p. 84.

52. Ibid., p. 79.

53. J.R. Campbell, *Soviet Policy and its Critics*, Left Book Club, 1939, p. 6. It is worth recollecting that individuals accused of terrorism in Britain in the 1970s were receiving life sentences on evidence no stronger than that adduced in the Moscow Trials.

54. Anon., 'Reminiscences of Palme Dutt', *Our History Journal* No. 11, January 1987.

55. Branson, *History*, Chapter 17; Pelling, *British Communist Party*, p. 100.

56. W. Thompson and S. Hobbs, 'Scottish Communists and the War', *Oral History* Vol. 16 No. 2, Autumn 1988; B. Moore, 'Why Did We Believe?', *Our History Journal* No. 12, January 1988.

57. 'Worker's Councils will break up the capitalist machinery of government and take the place of it.' *For Soviet Britain*, CPGB, 1935.

CHAPTER 3

1. *Labour Monthly*, April 1972.

2. G. Matthews, review of K. Morgan, *Against Fascism and War* in *Our History Journal* No. 17, May 1991.

3. Ibid.

4. That there was an element of continuity between the 'people's front' and 'imperialist war' standpoints is brought out well by Kevin Morgan, *Against Fascism and War: Ruptures and Continuities in British Communist Politics 1935–1941*, Manchester University Press, Manchester, 1989, in pointing out that for the CP the main source of fascism in Britain was to be found in the National Government itself: 'the danger of fascism in Britain came not exclusively from Hitler and certainly not from Mosley's Blackshirts, but from the frock-coated National Government', p. 22.

5. W. Thompson and S. Hobbs, 'Scottish Communists on the War', *Oral History* Vol. 16, No. 2, Autumn 1988.

6. Ibid.; F. King and G. Matthews, eds, *About Turn: The Communist Party and the Outbreak of the Second World War*, Lawrence & Wishart, 1990; J. Attfield and S. Williams, eds, *1939: The Communist Party and the War*, Lawrence & Wishart, 1984.

7. See the testimonies quoted in Thompson and Hobbs, 'Scottish Communists', and others reproduced verbatim in Attfield and Williams, *1939*, as well as E. Trory, *Imperialist War*, Crabtree Press, Brighton, 1977; N. Branson, *History of the Communist Party of Great Britain 1927–1941*, Lawrence & Wishart, 1985, pp. 271–4.

8. The prohibition on sabotage was stressed specifically at the critical Central Committee meeting. See King and Matthews, *About Turn*, p. 55. See also Branson, *History*, p. 319. 'Inasmuch as it opposed the war at all, the Communist Party's politics were characterised by economism... and pacifism...', Morgan, *Against Fascism*, p. 109.

9. For remembered responses to this development see Thompson and Hobbs, 'Scottish Communists'.

10. Branson, *History*, pp. 307–8; interview with Bob Horne.

11. E.J. Hobsbawm, *Revolutionaries*, Weidenfeld & Nicolson, 1973, p. 6.

12. H. Pelling, *The British Communist Party: A Historical Profile*, A. & C. Black, 1958, p. 115.

13. Branson, *History*, pp. 303–4.

14. 'Instead, when the various points in its propaganda were assembled together the Party put forward a convincing case for a popular government to lead a popular war effort.' Morgan, *Against Fascism*, p. 179.

15. Branson, *History*, pp. 308–10. For the People's Convention see Morgan, *Against Fascism*, pp. 201–12; A. Calder, *The People's War*, Cape, 1969, pp. 243–7. See Attfield and Williams, *1939*, pp. 185–8 for the full text of the resolutions. However, Home Secretary Anderson noted that the party refrained from industrial disruption directed against the war and even generally from direct anti-war propaganda. Morgan, *Against Fascism*, p. 237.

16. Branson, *History*, pp. 292–301.

17. *The Week*, the investigative news-sheet edited by Claud Cockburn, was also banned. The Communist Party of Ireland *Workers' Weekly* was banned in the Six Counties as early as April 1940; its successor, *Red Hand*, in October of the same year. See M. Milotte, *Communism in Modern Ireland: The Pursuit of the Workers' Republic since 1916*, Gill & Macmillan, Dublin, 1984, pp. 184–5. Willie Gallacher in 1941 wrote a pamphlet denouncing the British government's wish to encroach on Eire's neutrality: *Ireland: Can It Remain Neutral?*.

18. Branson, *History*, pp. 316–22.

19. D. Hyde, 'Preparations for Illegality', *Our History Journal* No. 14, October 1989.

20. Thompson and Hobbs, 'Scottish Communists'; Branson, *History*, pp. 329–35. There was, however, some initial nervousness among party members that the German attack on the USSR might become the basis of an Anglo-German reconciliation rather than an Anglo-Soviet alliance.

21. For the CP's industrial activity after June 1941 see Calder, *People's War*, pp. 395–6; R. Croucher, *Engineers at War*, Merlin, 1982; J. Hinton, 'Coventry Communism: A Study of Factory Politics in the Second World War', *History Workshop* No. 10, Autumn 1980. For the attempt to affiliate to the Labour Party see N. Branson and B. Moore, *Labour–Communist Relations, 1920–1951: Part II: 1935–1945*, Our History Pamphlet No. 83, March 1991, pp. 39–40.

22. F. Claudin, *The Communist Movement from Comintern to Cominform*, Penguin, Harmondsworth, 1975, Chapter 5.

23. Pelling, *British Communist Party*, p. 131.

24. *Report of the Executive Committee to the 18th Party Congress*, 1945.

25. Ibid.

26. Ibid.

27. An extensive literature now exists on the 1945–51 Labour governments' great power aspirations. For a recent summation see K.O. Morgan, *The People's Peace: British History 1945–1989*, Oxford University Press, Oxford, 1990. For a critique see J. Saville, 'Ernest Bevin and the Cold War', *Socialist Register*, 1984, and 'Labour and Foreign Policy 1945–1947: A Condemnation', *Our History Journal* No. 17, May 1991.

28. Claudin, *Communist Movement*, Chapter 8.

29. For an able discussion of the origins of the Cold War see D. Yergin, *Shattered Peace*, Penguin, Harmondsworth, 1980.

30. Morgan, *People's Peace*, pp. 53–60. See also M. Dockrill and J.W Young, eds, *British Foreign Policy 1945–1956*, Macmillan, 1989; J. Zametica, ed., *British Officials and British Foreign Policy*, Leicester University Press, Leicester, 1990; and A. Deighton, *The Impossible Peace: Britain and the Division of Germany and the Origins of the Cold War*, Clarendon Press, Oxford, 1990.

31. Morgan, *People's Peace*, p. 79.

32. N. Branson, ed., *London Squatters 1946*, Our History Pamphlet No. 80, August 1989.

33. *EC Report to 18th Congress*.

34. See Croucher, *Engineers*.

35. Pelling, *British Communist Party*, p. 137.

36. The pamphlet was published in August 1947. The inauguration of the 'two camps' position and the definitive consignment of social democratic

governments to the outer darkness occurred with the establishment of the Cominform in October.

37. *Looking Ahead,* CPGB, 1947, p. 24. It must be acknowledged that while the hopes Pollitt expressed in the pamphlet were confounded, his fears of the direction in which the international scene was moving proved acute and perceptive.

38. M. Mitchell, 'Looking Ahead' (review), *Communist Review,* October 1947.

39. *Communist Review,* August 1948.

40. See, for example, Morgan, *People's Peace,* pp. 98–9; Pelling, *British Communist Party,* pp. 153–9.

41. See Claudin, *Communist Movement,* pp. 376–9.

42. State Prosecutor's Office, *Laszlo Rajk and His Accomplices before the People's Court,* Budapest, 1949; D. Kartun, *Tito's Plot against Europe,* Lawrence & Wishart, 1949; J. Klugmann, *From Trotsky to Tito,* Lawrence & Wishart, 1951.

43. D. Hyde, *I Believed: the Autobiography of a Former British Communist,* Heinemann, 1951; C.H. (Bob) Darke, *The Communist Technique in Britain,* Penguin, Harmondsworth, 1952.

44. Pelling, *British Communist Party,* pp. 136–7.

45. J. Davies-Smith, 'The Attlee Government and the BBC', Institute of Contemporary British History seminar, 1990.

46. Hints of this are to be noted in Ernie Trory's *War of Liberation,* People's Publications, Brighton, 1988.

47. P. 149. I have been unable to confirm a rumour that the content was ghosted by Bill Wainwright, a prominent *Daily Worker* (and *Morning Star*) journalist.

48. R. Samuel, 'The Lost World of British Communism', *New Left Review* No. 154, November–December 1985; 'Staying Power – The Lost World of British Communism' pt 2, *New Left Review* No. 156, March–April 1986.

49. A left-wing, CP-influenced journal with the same title existed briefly from 1938–9. The postwar *Modern Quarterly* was effectively but not formally a CP publication.

50. A fictionalised account of Lawrence & Wishart in the early 1950s appears in Doris Lessing's *The Golden Notebook,* Michael Joseph, 1962.

51. Samuel, 'Lost World'.

52. See M. MacEwen, *The Greening of a Red,* Pluto, 1991, pp. 170–3, for a moving account of the persecution visited upon Winnington in reprisal by the British and US governments.

53. Claudin, *Communist Movement,* Chapter 9.

54. G. Matthews, 'Stalin's British Road?', *Changes,* 14–27 September 1991. See R. Black, *Stalinism in Britain,* New Park, 1970, for an accusation.

55. J. Callaghan, *The Far Left in British Politics*, Basil Blackwell, Oxford, 1987, p. 164. George Matthews's article underlines the point.
56. Pelling, *British Communist Party*, p. 163.

CHAPTER 4

1. Under the organisational forms adopted in 1922, factory nuclei – later groups – were combined with residential (and functional) groups in party Locals, later Branches. The distinction between residential and workplace branches was consolidated in the 1950s. Compare Dutt's opinion in 1922:

    The Commission is strongly of the opinion that the term 'branch' should be completely abolished along with the form of organisation it represents… A member should not think of himself as a member of XYZ Branch or Local (with the suggestion of local separatism thus given): he is a member of the Communist Party working in such and such a group or nucleus.

    1922 Report on Organisation, p. 23.

2. *Report of the Commission on Inner-Party Democracy*, December 1956, pp. 18–19.
3. Ibid.
4. George Bernard Shaw, 'The Great Lysenko Muddle', *Labour Monthly*, January 1949.
5. H. Pelling, *The British Communist Party: A Historical Profile*, A. & C. Black, 1958, pp. 164–7; N. Wood, *Communism and the British Intellectuals*, Gollancz, 1959, pp. 189–93.
6. There were considerable other connections between Czech communists and British CP members. See for example R. Kavan, *Love and Freedom*, Grafton Books, 1989.
7. *Communist Review*, March 1953. Having discussed with Klugmann his writings on these themes, which he acknowledged in 1968 to be 'nonsense', I have no doubt that he was perfectly sincere at the time he wrote them.
8. Palme Dutt in *Labour Monthly*, April 1953.
9. James Klugmann, 'Does Labour Deserve Gaitskell?', *Labour Monthly*, March 1956.
10. The hesitation came in 1952 when the 'Robot' scheme for floating sterling was advanced in the knowledge that it would involve higher food prices and the abandonment of the commitment to full employment. It was vetoed by Churchill. See K.O. Morgan, *The People's Peace: British History 1945–1989*, Oxford University Press, Oxford, 1990, pp. 119–22.

11. The existence or otherwise of a postwar consensus has been heatedly debated among historians of Britain's contemporary epoch. The most effective statement of the case against has come from B. Pimlott, 'Is Postwar Consensus a Myth?', *Contemporary Record*, Summer 1989, but ultimately his argument appears unconvincing. See R. Lowe, 'Consensus and the Foundation of the Welfare State', *20th Century British History* Vol. 1, No. 2, 1990, for a recent discussion of the issue.

12. For example by W. Gallacher, 'Against Wage Freeze and War', *Labour Monthly*, February 1950.

13. *Labour Monthly*, May 1954.

14. *Labour Monthly*, March 1955.

15. *Labour Monthly*, November 1955.

16. *Labour Monthly*, May 1956.

17. Ibid.

18. Ibid.

19. J. Saville, 'The XXth Congress and the British Communist Party', *Socialist Register*, 1976.

20. For an account see W. Thompson, 'The New Left in Scotland', in I. MacDougall, ed., *Essays in Scottish Labour History*, John Donald, Edinburgh, 1978.

21. Saville, 'XXth Congress'.

22. This of course begged the question of the status of *Labour Monthly*, which was not a party publication or a formal co-operative like the *Daily Worker* but Dutt's own property, yet nevertheless as influential in party affairs as any strictly CP journal.

23. Resolution of the Communist Party EC, 'Lessons of the 20th Congress of the CPSU', *Marxist Quarterly*, July 1956.

24. Saville, 'XXth Congress'.

25. M. Heinemann, '1956 and the Communist Party', *Socialist Register*, 1976.

26. M. MacEwen, 'The Day the Party Had to Stop', *Socialist Register*, 1976.

27. MacEwen, ibid., and *The Greening of a Red*, Pluto, 1991, pp. 179–99. For James Friel, the cartoonist 'Gabriel', see P. Mellini, 'Gabriel's Message', *History Today* Vol. 40, February 1990.

28. Saville, 'XXth Congress'.

29. Heinemann, '1956'.

30. Published accounts of how the commission functioned have come from authors of the minority report. It is only fair to state that members who were on the other side have held to a different recollection of events and attributed the acknowledged deficiencies of the proceedings to material problems of time and travel. Three women sat on the commission out of fifteen members.

31. MacEwen, 'The Day'.

32. *Communist Party 25th Congress Report*, 1957.

33. The scandal came to light in November 1991 as a result of KGB documents released in Moscow which were picked up by *The Sunday Times*. Forewarned of what was about to happen, the party itself rushed an emergency number of its journal *Changes* (15 November) into print with an article by Falber (unrepentantly) confessing everything, including the fact that he had concealed the information from Nina Temple when she became Secretary. The Political Committee issued a statement deploring the secret funding. On 17 November *The Sunday Times*, exhibiting an incorrigible police mentality, ran a vintage Cold War article suggesting that these thousands of Soviet pounds had altered the course of British postwar history by funding communist industrial subversion. (See also, pp. 216–7.)

CHAPTER 5

1. M. Hunter, 'On the 26th Congress of the Communist Party of Great Britain', *Marxism Today*, May 1959. (At this Congress the name Communist Party of Great Britain was used again, having been shortened to 'Communist Party' in 1943 at the suggestion of Malcolm MacEwen.)
2. On Sundays the Saturday, or as sellers preferred to say, 'weekend', edition of the paper was sold.
3. Among the exceptions were Lawrence Daly of the NUM, who, although becoming very hostile to the CP, remained on the left, and the ETU leaders Cannon and Chapple, who moved over to the extreme right wing of the TUC and Labour Party.
4. *World News*, 15 March 1958.
5. M. Hunter, 'On the 26th Congress'. Palme Dutt in the *Labour Monthly* of January 1958 had been even more dismissive: 'the no doubt well meant, but very confused proposal…is so hopelessly inadequate and irrelevant'.
6. This was noted even in such remote quarters as the Aberdeen University student newspaper.
7. The anouncement that the base would be installed was made in November 1960.
8. And also the first woman, Valentina Tereshkova, who orbited in 1963.
9. At the open-air May Day rally in Glasgow in 1962 the star speaker, Gaitskell, was severely barracked. His response of 'peanuts!' to his tormentors gave the incident its name. It was generally assumed in the newspaper reports that the people responsible had been YCL members, but in fact this was not the case. The hecklers were drawn mostly from the Woodside branch of the Young Socialists, dominated by members of the International Socialism group, the Socialist Workers' Party's predecessor. The Glasgow YCL, taking a 'responsible' stance, had actually tried to prevent the disruption.

10. *Report of the Executive Committee to the 28th National Congress*, 1963.
11. The figures for the CP and the YCL cannot be added to each other to give a figure for card-carrying British communists. Double counting would occur as the majority of YCLers over 18 were also party members.
12. Gramsci's name appears in an early number of *Marxism Today*. George Thomson, 'The First Italian Marxist', November 1957.
    The review by Andrew Rothstein, in *Marxism Today*, November 1958, of Pelling's history of the CP is worth reading for its distilled venom if not for its historical and political honesty. Dutt, though scathing enough, was marginally less bitter in the May 1959 *Labour Monthly*.
13. A. Kettle, 'How New is the "New Left"?', *Marxism Today*, October 1960.
14. R. Russell, 'On How New is the "New Left"?', *Marxism Today*, January 1961.
15. W. Lauchlan, 'The Communist Party and the Daily Worker', *Marxism Today*, June 1959.
16. *27th Communist Party Congress Report*, 1961.
17. One town mentioned specifically as lacking a branch where there ought to be one was...Grantham. Lauchlan, 'The Communist Party and the *Daily Worker*'.
18. *27th Communist Party Congress Report*, 1961.
19. Genuine conviction existed at this point that sufficient determination and exertion in electoral work must necessarily produce results. The argument that endless experience of negligible votes was more likely to produce apathy and inactivism cut no ice.
20. B. Matthews, 'Party Building Prospects', *Marxism Today*, October 1963.
21. YCLers themselves, however, in spite of their discipline, felt the remark to be patronising.
22. The fullest account of the affair is contained in C.H. Rolph, *All Those in Favour?*, André Deutsch, 1962. See also R. Bean, 'Militancy, Policy Formation and Membership Opposition in the Electrical Trades Union 1945–1961', *Political Quarterly* Vol. 36, 1965.
23. There were some among the CP rank-and-file who argued that the party should have disregarded the truth or otherwise of the accusations and continued to fight on behalf of the ETU leaders as victims of ruling-class justice.
24. The party's influence among the Scottish and Welsh miners, though more deep-rooted, was ultimately less significant in that these were not sovereign unions but parts of a larger non-communist one.
25. N. Jeffery, 'The 22nd Congress of the CPSU', *Marxism Today*, December 1961.

26. *Long Live Leninism*, Communist Party of China, Peking, 1960, p. 22. Soviet technicians had been withdrawn from China, occasioning severe economic disruption, in July 1962.
27. *Daily Worker*, 19 January 1962.
28. *Restore the Unity of the International Communist Movement*, January 1963.
29. McCreery by origin was a New Zealander. The New Zealand CP was later one of the few 'Western' parties in which the Maoists won control.
30. Subsequently it became clear that *Vanguard* was disproportionately lavish for the size of the organisation which produced it and had been financed by McCreery's personal wealth.
31. *28th Communist Party Congress Report*, 1963.

CHAPTER 6

1. The only detailed account of what happened is printed in an extremely obscure Maoist publication, the *Marxist Leninist Quarterly*, Winter 1972-3, which also describes the origins of the McCreery organisation (see also p.131).
2. This administration did, to be sure, pass invaluable legislation towards the abolition of capital punishment and the decriminalisation of male homosexuality, but in these respects it did only what a self-respecting Liberal government might have done.
3. It is now generally recognised that the notion of the party having instigated or even co-ordinated the strike was either an overheated fantasy or a cynical manoeuvre. Bert Ramelson, the Industrial Organiser, had given advice when it was requested but was most certainly not running the action.
4. The position which was forcefully argued was that in the perspective of officialdom and the employers it was *only* wages which were envisaged as being strictly planned.
5. The Donovan Report was stigmatised by the party in a pamphlet titled *Donovan Exposed*. At the time a pop singer of that name was high in the charts and the title caused some amusement to members of the public to whom the pamphlet was hawked.
6. For a discussion of the episode see K.O. Morgan, *The People's Peace: British History 1945–1989*, Oxford University Press, Oxford, pp. 300–5; C. Ponting, *Breach of Promise: Labour in Power 1964–1970*, Penguin, Harmondsworth, 1990, pp. 350–71; for insiders' accounts see the diaries of Richard Crossman (*Diaries of a Cabinet Minister*, ed. Janet Morgan, Hamish Hamilton/Jonathan Cape, 3 vols, 1975, 1976, 1977) and Barbara Castle (*The Castle Diaries: 1964–70*, Weidenfeld & Nicholson, 1984).

7. In *Comment*, 23 May 1963, Henry Suss describes how he eventually won a local government election in Lancashire after 10 contests in 13 years. His first vote was 49 and he eventually won with 256, a majority of 30. He comments: 'Only the independent policy of the Party, presented boldly and clearly, can unify the people in action', and asserts that if he can do it so can others.

8. J. Mahon, 'The Greater London Elections', *Marxism Today*, April 1964.

9. *Comment*, 6 February 1965.

10. T. Webb, 'Labour, What Next?', *Marxism Today*, July 1965.

11. T. Durkin, 'Labour, What Next?', *Marxism Today*, September 1965.

12. The speech was reprinted as a pamphlet under the title *Turn Left for Progress*.

13. Ibid.

14. *Tribune* editorial, 3 December 1965.

15. C. Sweet, *Comment*, 9 July 1966.

16. *Comment*, 16 July 1966.

17. *Comment*, 16 April 1966 and 23 July 1966.

18. J. Mahon, 'The Greater London Council', *Marxism Today*, April 1967.

19. The initially intended date of the launching was 6 August, Hiroshima Day. Wilson's attention being drawn to this by a former CND back-bencher, he changed the date and promoted the backbencher.

20. Morgan, *People's Peace*, p. 269.

21. The autonomous Scottish area of the NUS also elected a communist president not long afterwards.

22. The circular, unlike the *Marxism Today* article, dealt also with Maoist groupings. In neither publication is there mention of the Revolutionary Socialist League, the predecessor of the Militant organisation.

23. B. Reid, 'Trotskyism in Britain Today', *Marxism Today*, September 1964.

24. A Maoist leaflet distributed on the demonstrations and entitled 'YCL Revisionist Leaders Unmasked as Police Agents and Stooges of US Imperialism' characterised the YCL as the 'Young Cops League'.

25. With manifest lack of enthusiasm the CP National Student Committee agreed to allow its branches to participate in the Revolutionary Socialist Students' Federation, a body dominated by the far left groupings. The communist participation was never more than nominal.

26. The distinction which has to be drawn here is militancy led by party members acting as trade unionists, about which the party was enthu-siastic, and industrial action led by the party as an organisation, which it had long abandoned. The far left regarded CP practice, when not actually engaged in betrayal as, at best, 'tailing' the labour movement.

27. There were, of course, notable individual Marxists outside the CP – Isaac Deutscher, for example – but the Trotskyist organisations did not

become serious competitors in any sense until the Socialist Labour League began to make an impact inside the Young Socialists, established in 1960. For the development of the Trotskyist groups between 1945 and 1980 see J. Callaghan, *British Trotskyism: Theory and Practice*, Basil Blackwell, Oxford, 1984, and his *Far Left in British Politics*, Basil Blackwell, Oxford, 1987, which also covers the CPGB but not the Maoists.

28. *28th Communist Party Congress Report*, 1963.

29. It should be noted, however, that in the climate of the times special committees or groupings for women were felt by some members to be invidious and discriminatory.

30. Scottish Committee *Circular to Branches*, February 1969.

31. *A Handbook for Members of the Communist Party*, pp. 20–1.

32. K. Newton, *The Sociology of British Communism*, Allen Lane, 1969.

33. See also R. Samuel, 'Class Politics: The Lost World of British Communism', pt. 3 *New Left Review* No. 165, September–October 1987.

34. *Report of the Committee on Party Organisation*, 1965.

35. The practice of open-air street corner platforms, once a mainstay of the party's propagandising, died out around this time.

36. The Socialist Labour League, which *did* maintain an ultra-authoritarian internal regime, did so on the basis of continuously stoking among its members apocalyptic expectations of a revolutionary or counter-revolutionary overturn. See, for example, Callaghan, *Far Left*, pp. 55–83.

37. B. Davis, 'British Youth: Progressive, Reactionary or Indifferent?', *Marxism Today*, March 1966.

38. In the months preceding a congress party members were entitled to state points of view as critically as they wished in the party press.

39. The Surrey District membership was of course drawn from south London rather than the stockbroker belt.

40. *Comment*, 13 November 1965.

41. There were fourteen in attendance at this meeting.

42. *Comment*, 2 September 1967.

43. The party candidates suffered the usual decline in votes.

44. The appointment was decided at King Street and made over the intense reluctance of the Scottish leadership who favoured the Scottish Organiser, Alec Murray, and who had to be individually pressurised to obtain their agreement. No official intimation of this dispute was made to the Scottish membership.

45. The Scottish media, for instance, were almost universally behind the work-in. For a detailed account of the event see J. Foster and C. Woolfson, *The UCS Work-In*, Lawrence & Wishart, 1986.

46. There was in fact very considerable enmity between some of the party shop stewards, one of whom even canvassed the expulsion of

another from the CP. The Scottish Committee mediated between the antagonists and preserved public appearances.

47. Callaghan, *Far Left*, p. 176.
48. Morgan, *People's Peace*, p. 327.
49. The presentation was a caricature. McGahey was in fact distinguished among trade union leaders in his avoidance of macho postures and sometimes referred to himself with conviction as 'an innocent abroad'.
50. Jimmy Reid, however, was elected by the students of Glasgow University as Rector (the formal Chair of the University Court), an office of medieval origin existing only in the ancient Scottish Universities.
51. Respectively *Scottish Marxist* and *Cyffro*.

CHAPTER 7

1. The most frequently employed novel form of industrial action was the work-in, the UCS example being widely copied, with different degrees of success, for a number of years.
2. By the mid-1970s, however, the consistent decline in electoral performance was beginning to evoke restlessness among the party membership. This dissent was strongly expressed though easily defeated at the 1975 Congress.
3. *The British Road to Socialism*, 1968 edition, pp. 36–7.
4. D. Purdy, 'The Left's Alternative Economic Strategy', *Politics and Power* No. 1, 1980.
5. R. Bellamy, 'More on Inflation', *Marxism Today*, November 1974.
6. D. Priscott, 'The Communist Party and the Labour Party', *Marxism Today*, January 1974.
7. Purdy, 'Left's Alternative'.
8. For an analysis and condemnation of this government's approach, see D. Coates, *Labour in Power?*, Longman, 1980.
9. *Morning Star*, 30 November 1974.
10. Bellamy, 'More on Inflation'.
11. At least in formal pronouncements. British communist writers and historians were less simplistic, for instance Maurice Cornforth, Eric Hobsbawm and A.L. Morton, to mention only three significant examples.
12. The term as originally coined in the disputes of Russian Marxists at the turn of the century had meant something altogether different: not a theory of social consciousness but the contention that Marxists should concentrate their attention on the economic interests of the working class rather than on political issues.

13. This is true as a generalisation, but there were of course significant exceptions.

14. The communist parties in both Britain and Ireland had had a lengthy, complex and tortured relationship with the republican movement. In the 1960s their influence upon the leaders of the IRA had been very significant and at that time the IRA's most considerable political theorist, Roy Johnson, was a communist and a former branch secretary in London. See M. Milotte, *Communism in Modern Ireland: The Pursuit of the Workers' Republic since 1916*, Gill & Macmillan, Dublin, 1984, for a well documented though hostile account. In the early 1970s communist spokespersons were still prepared to refer in public to their common positions with the Official IRA.

15. Until the 1970s the Scottish and Welsh collectives of the party continued to be designated as 'Districts'. Afterwards they were termed 'Nations', though their constitutional status did not change in any manner.

16. The claim was made at the North-West District Congress held in Manchester in 1970.

17. See R. Miliband, 'Moving On', *Socialist Register*, 1976.

18. Though he always put it in quotes.

19. At the time the Portuguese CP's conduct was frequently cited by British communists as a model of how a communist party should behave in a revolutionary situation.

20. J. Gollan, 'Socialist Democracy – Some Problems: The 20th Congress of the CPSU in Retrospect', *Marxism Today*, January 1976.

21. A.J. Papard, discussion contribution in *Marxism Today* Supplement on Socialist Democracy, November 1976.

22. Under the 'broad' definition the traditionally understood sections of the working class, employees in factory industry and equivalent occupations, were designated as the 'core' working class.

23. The NCP also had scattered members elsewhere in England, but was virtually absent from Scotland and Wales.

24. This Congress was extensively covered on TV; a special three-part programme in the 'Decision' series, during which the TV cameras were admitted to an EC meeting, being made about it.

25. Matthews himself participated very actively in the 1977 discussion, frequently as the opening speaker in branch and District meetings.

26. Formally, the advice to reject the amendment came from the Congress Arrangements Committee, supposedly elected by the Congress and independent of the retiring EC, but in fact dominated by its nominees. The amendment's acceptance therefore constituted a deliberate rebuff to the leadership.

27. The CPGB was far from being the only Western communist party beginning to fragment at this time, more or less around the same sorts

of issue. As well as a number of minor examples, the PCE was about to enter a state of rapid disintegration.

28. The appointment of Martin Jacques as editor of *Marxism Today* in 1977 provoked a certain amount of opposition among activists on the grounds that his publicly expressed views deviated from Marxism, but at that point the leadership remained united.

29. S. Aaronovitch, 'The Working Class and the Broad Democratic Alliance', *Marxism Today*, September 1979.

30. However, at the same time the right wing was establishing firm control over the engineers' union.

31. See, for example, D. Priscott, 'Can Labour Succeed?', *Marxism Today*, October 1981.

32. S. Aaronovitch, 'Recipe for Defeat', *Marxism Today*, April 1982.

33. One exception was Pete Carter, the party's Industrial Organiser in the 1980s and a former building worker.

34. Sarah Benton, the editor of the party fortnightly, *Comment*, resigned in 1980 (and left the party soon afterwards), arguing that her position had become impossible because of sexism and bureaucratic interference on the part of the leadership. See also S. Benton, 'Century of Destruction', *Marxism Today*, October 1991.

35. Current issues of *Straight Left* make it clear that little has changed in its approach during the intervening years.

36. The group who founded *The Leninist*, at first as an infrequent publication in magazine format, later as a fortnightly newspaper, were strongly influenced by one of the factions disputing ownership of the name of the exiled Turkish CP.

37. Publicly available accounts of these developments are rare. This one is based on oral recollections and on a critical reading of *The Leninist*.

38. The division really dated, however, from the 1977 Congress. Although Chater had been supported over the critical amendment by the other leaders, he nevertheless blamed them for not doing so with sufficient energy.

39. Circulation at the time stood at around 30,000, a fair proportion of it represented by sales to the Soviet bloc.

40. The author of this book was in the same position.

41. In order to allow the maximum number of shareholders to participate *Morning Star* AGMs were held over several days in different locations. When they were over the votes were counted together.

42. S. Benton, 'Comrades Divided', *New Statesman*, 11 November 1983.

43. The Straight Leftists reminded the delegates that in the past it had been agreed that 'no political differences' separated Chater and the leadership.

CHAPTER 8

1. The EC elected at the 1983 Congress also contained supporters of both tendencies, though the anti-Chaterites had a safe majority.
2. Joe Gormley, the right-wing President of the NUM during the 1970s, deliberately held on to his office until Mick McGahey had become ineligible through age to stand as his successor. The result was the regroupment of the left behind Scargill's candidature.
3. The detailed record of the conflict can best be followed in the pages of *Focus* and the *Morning Star*.
4. This move was indignantly denounced by *Morning Star* supporters on the grounds that it would enable the Special Branch, working through the Post Office, to compile an up-to-date membership list of the party.
5. The commercial viability of *Marxism Today* did not, however, extend so far as actual profitability and its continuance required a constant subsidy out of party funds.
6. As was openly declared in the pages of 7 *Days*, 5 December 1987, by Mark Perryman, a key figure on the *Marxism Today* editorial team.
7. The party eventually formed by the *Morning Star* dissidents in 1988, the Communist Party of Britain (CPB), claimed to be the re-established Communist Party and in direct line of descent from that of 1920; accusing their opponents of having betrayed the conceptions of *The British Road to Socialism,* they continued to use that title for their own newly formulated programme of 1989.
8. The Tiananmen massacre occurred at the time the document was being drafted. Some leading individuals in the CPB publicly voiced their reluctance to condemn the Chinese government for its actions.
9. Two individuals who had up to that point been in the forefront of the changes to the party's character, Dave Priscott and Monty Johnstone, now found themselves out of sympathy with the direction in which matters were developing. Dave Priscott resigned in consequence from the *Marxism Today* editorial board.
10. In response to criticisms of its provocative style, spokespeople for the journal declared that the only limits to what it would publish were racist or sexist materials.
11. The author was one of those pressing him to stand for the post in spite of his cogently argued reluctance to do so.
12. Although, because of the number of resolutions submitted, selection over those to be debated was exercised by Congress committees.
13. A newly recruited member, attending one such debate in Glasgow, opined that he got the feeling of intruding on a private grief.
14. The Scottish National Party also promoted a non-payment campaign, but this, too, made far less impact than that of the Federation.

15. One of the innovations introduced by the new EC was an open election to renew the Political Committee halfway through the year. When it was held a number of the sitting PC were dismissed and the resulting gender balance was even more uneven than it had initially been. The outcome was quoted by traditionalists as illustrating the merits of the recommended list.
16. The title of 'General Secretary' had now been changed to 'Secretary'.
17. The claim was widely made among the Scottish communists that the party there was in a much healthier state both politically and organisationally than in England. There was no great factual basis for this claim. The point is argued in W. Thompson, 'The Scottish CP', *Radical Scotland*, April/May 1990.

CONCLUSION

1. See, for example, the letter by Hyman Levy in 1957, even as he was leaving the party, quoted in H. Pelling, *The British Communist Party: A Historical Profile*, A. & C. Black, 1958, p. 181.
2. See, for example, the CP documents reproduced as appendices in L.J. Macfarlane, *The British Communist Party: Its Origins and Development until 1929*, MacGibbon & Kee, 1966.
3. The point was stressed in Pelling, *British Communist Party*, and has been often repeated. Kevin Morgan, *Against Fascism and War: Ruptures and Continuities in British Communist Politics 1935–1941*, Manchester University Press, Manchester, 1989, notes that while he disagrees with virtually every aspect of Pelling's book, he is constrained to acknowledge the strength of this assessment.
4. Left-wing commentators outside the Communist Party would sometimes discuss its suitability for such a role, but always ended by rejecting the CP as too historically compromised. See for example R. Miliband, 'Moving On', *Socialist Register*, 1977.
5. The *Leninist* group have in fact taken to referring to themselves on posters and stickers as the CPGB Provisional Committee.
6. It had been decided in the spring of 1991 that *Marxism Today* would cease publication at the end of the year and it was intended that it should be succeeded in 1992 by a larger publication in which the party or its successor would have a shareholding but no overall control. Accordingly, the December 1991 issue was the final number of the journal. At the time of writing it is unclear whether the new publication will actually appear.
7. Exposed most effectively in the writings of Noam Chomsky, especially *Deterring Democracy*, Verso, 1991.

8. There were very few industrial workers among the delegates and the biggest single category of answers to the question 'which trade union?' was 'none'. Given the age composition, however, there were undoubtedly a fair number of retired industrial workers and former trade unionists. The largest single occupational group of employed delegates consisted of teachers and lecturers.

Select Bibliography

Unpublished Sources
See Acknowledgements.

CP or Closely Aligned Journals
Challenge (YCL)
Changes
Cogito (YCL)
Comment
The Communist (weekly, to 1922)
The Communist (monthly journal, 1927–9)
Communist Focus/Focus
Communist International (Comintern)
Communist Review (1921–5)
Communist Review (1946–53)
Daily Worker (from 1966 *Morning Star*, CP connection ended in 1985)
Eurored
For a Lasting Peace, for a People's Democracy! (Cominform)
Industrial and General Information
International Press Correspondence (Inprecorr) (English edition of Comintern
    publication)
Labour Monthly
Labour Research
Left Review
Mainstream (CP students)
Marxism Today
Modern Quarterly
New Propellor
News and Views (internal discussion journal 1986–90)
Our History (pamphlet series)
Our History Journal
Party Life
Red Letters
Red Rag
Russia Today
7 Days
Socialist Europe

Sunday Worker
The Week
Workers' Weekly (latterly *Workers' Life*)
World News and Views (replaced *Inprecorr* 1938; latterly *World News*)

Non-CP Journals
Communist (Straight Left publication)
History Workshop Journal
International Socialism (Socialist Workers' Party)
Keep Left (Socialist Labour League, later Workers' Revolutionary Party
    Young Socialists)
The Leninist
Living Marxism (Revolutionary Communist Party)
Marxist (SLL/WRP)
The Marxist (Maoist)
Marxist-Leninist Quarterly (Maoist)
Marxist Review (CPB)
Militant
New Left Review
New Worker (NCP)
Newsletter (SLL)
Newsline (WRP)
Politics and Power
Red Mole (Trotskyist)
Socialist Challenge (Trotskyist)
Socialist Register
Socialist Worker (SWP)
Straight Left
Tribune
Vanguard (Maoist)
The Week (Trotskyist, 1960s)
Workers' Press (WRP)

Books and Pamphlets
Published by CP or closely associated publishers. Place of publication London
unless otherwise stated.

Attfield, J., and Williams, S., *1939: The Communist Party and the War*
    (Lawrence & Wishart, 1984).
Bell, T., *The British Communist Party: A Short History* (Lawrence & Wishart,
    1937).
Bishop, R., *Soviet Millionaires* (Russia Today Society, 1943).

Branson, N., *History of the Communist Party of Great Britain 1927–1941* (Lawrence & Wishart, 1985).

Campbell, J.R.,. *Soviet Policy and its Critics* (Left Book Club, 1939).

Clark, J. et. al. (eds), *Culture and Crisis in Britain in the Thirties* (Lawrence & Wishart, 1979).

Collard, D., *Soviet Justice and the Trial of Radek and Others* (Left Book Club, 1937).

CPGB, ed., *The Errors of Trotskyism* (CPGB, 1925).

CPGB, *Report of the Commission on Inner Party Democracy* (CPGB, 1956).

——, *Handbook for Members of the Communist Party* (CPGB, 1962).

——, *Report of the Commission on Party Organisation* (CPGB, 1965).

——, *The Role of Communist Party Branches* (CPGB, 1974).

Dutt, R.P., *India Today* (Left Book Club, 1940).

——, *The Crisis of Britain and the British Empire* (Lawrence & Wishart, 1953).

Foster, J., and Woolfson, C., *The UCS Work-In* (Lawrence & Wishart, 1986).

Francis, H., and Smith, D., *The Fed: A History of the South Wales Miners in the Twentieth Century* (Lawrence & Wishart, 1990).

Gallacher, W., *Revolt on the Clyde* (Lawrence & Wishart, 1978, reissue).

——, *Ireland: Can It Remain Neutral?* (CPGB, 1941).

Hannington, W., *Unemployed Struggles 1919–1935* (Lawrence & Wishart, 1979, reissue).

King, F., and Matthews, G., eds, *About Turn: The Communist Party and the Outbreak of the Second World War* (Lawrence & Wishart, 1990).

Klugmann, J., *History of the Communist Party of Great Britain. Vol. 1: Formation and Early Years, 1919–1924* (Lawrence & Wishart, 1966).

——, *History of the Communist Party of Great Britain. Vol. 2: The General Strike, 1925–1926* (Lawrence & Wishart, 1969).

Mahon, J., *Harry Pollitt: A Biography* (Lawrence & Wishart, 1976).

Morton, A.L., *A People's History of England* (Left Book Club, 1938 [in print, Lawrence & Wishart]).

Piratin, P., *Our Flag Stays Red* (Lawrence & Wishart, 1978).

Pollitt, H., *How to Win the War* (CBGB, 1939).

——, *Looking Ahead* (CPGB, 1947).

Robinson, P., *The Environmental Crisis* (CPGB, 1973).

Rust, W., *The Story of the Daily Worker* (PPPS, 1949).

Small, R., *Women: The Road to Equality and Socialism* (CPGB, 1972).

Squires, M., *Saklatvala: A Political Biography* (Lawrence & Wishart, 1990).

Other Books and Articles

Anderson, P., 'Communist Party History', in R. Samuel, ed., *People's History and Socialist Theory* (Routledge & Kegan Paul, 1991).

Black, R., *Stalinism in Britain* (New Park, 1970).

Callaghan, J., *British Trotskyism: Theory and Practice* (Oxford: Basil Blackwell, 1984).

——, *The Far Left in British Politics* (Oxford: Basil Blackwell, 1987).

——, 'The Heart of Darkness: Rajani Palme Dutt and the British Empire – a Profile', *Contemporary Record* vol. 5, No. 2, Autumn 1991.

Challinor, R., *The Origins of British Bolshevism* (Croom Helm, 1977).

Claudin, F., *The Communist Movement from Comintern to Cominform* (Harmondsworth: Penguin, 1975).

Croucher, R., *Engineers at War* (Merlin, 1982).

Darke, C.H. (Bob), *The Communist Technique in Britain* (Harmondsworth: Penguin, 1952).

Gallacher, W., *The Case for Communism* (Harmondsworth: Penguin, 1949).

Heinemann, M., '1956 and the Communist Party', *Socialist Register*, 1976.

Hinton, J., *The First Shop Stewards' Movement* (Allen & Unwin, 1973).

——, 'Coventry Communism: A Study of Factory Politics in the Second World War', *History Workshop* No. 10, Autumn 1980.

Hobsbawm, E.J., *Revolutionaries* (Weidenfeld & Nicolson, 1973).

Horner, A., *Incorrigible Rebel* (MacGibbon & Kee, 1960).

Hyde, D., *I Believed: The Autobiography of a Former British Communist* (Heinemann, 1951).

Johnstone, M., Review of John Mahon, *Harry Pollitt*, in *Bulletin of the Society for the Study of Labour History*, No. 33, Autumn 1976.

——, 'Harry Pollitt' (letter), *Bulletin of the Society for the Study of Labour History* No. 35, Autumn 1977.

——, 'Communist Party History' (letter) *Bulletin of the Society for the Study of Labour History* No. 37, Autumn 1978.

Kendall, W., *The Revolutionary Movement in Britain 1900–1921: The Origins of British Communism* (Weidenfeld & Nicolson, 1969).

MacEwen, M., 'The Day the Party Had to Stop', *Socialist Register*, 1976.

——, *The Greening of a Red* (Pluto, 1991).

Macfarlane, L.J., *The British Communist Party: Its Origins and Development until 1929* (MacGibbon & Kee, 1966).

Macintyre, S., *Little Moscows: Communism and Working-Class Militancy in Inter-war Britain* (Croom Helm, 1980).

——, *A Proletarian Science: Marxism in Britain 1917–1933* (Cambridge: Cambridge University Press, 1980).

Maclean, N.M., *John Maclean* (Pluto, 1973).

McShane, H., *No Mean Fighter* (Pluto, 1978).

Martin, R., *Communism and the British Trade Unions 1924–1933: A Study of the National Minority Movement* (Oxford: Clarendon Press, 1969).

Mellini, P., 'Gabriel's Message', *History Today*, February 1990.

Miliband, R., *Marxism and Politics* (Oxford: Oxford University Press, 1977).

Milotte, M., *Communism in Modern Ireland: The Pursuit of the Workers' Republic since 1916* (Dublin: Gill & Macmillan, 1984).

Mitchell, A., *Behind the Crisis in British Stalinism* (New Park, 1984).

Morgan, K., *Against Fascism and War: Ruptures and Continuities in British Communist Politics 1935–1941* (Manchester: Manchester University Press, 1989).

Newton, K., *The Sociology of British Communism* (Allen Lane, 1969).

Pelling, H., *The British Communist Party: A Historical Profile* (A. & C. Black, 1958).

Pimlott, B., *Labour and the Left in the 1930s* (Cambridge: Cambridge University Press, 1977).

Rolph, C.H., *All Those in Favour?* (André Deutsch, 1962).

Rothstein, A., 'Harry Pollitt' (letter), *Bulletin of the Society for the Study of Labour History* No. 34, Spring 1977.

——, 'Communist Party History' (letter), *Bulletin of the Society for the Study of Labour History* No. 36, Spring 1978.

Samuel, R., 'The Lost World of British Communism', *New Left Review* No. 154, November–December 1985.

——, 'Staying Power: The Lost World of British Communism' pt 2, *New Left Review* No. 156, March–April 1986.

——, 'Class Politics: The Lost World of British Communism' pt 3, *New Left Review* No. 165, September–October 1987.

Saville, J., 'The XXth Congress and the British Communist Party', *Socialist Register*, 1976.

——, 'The Communist Experience: A Personal Appraisal', *Socialist Register*, 1991.

Spriano, P., *Stalin and the European Communists* (Verso, 1985).

Thompson, W., and Hobbs, S., 'Scottish Communists on the War', *Oral History* Vol. 16, No. 2, Autumn 1988.

Thompson, W., 'The New Left in Scotland', in I. MacDougall, ed., *Essays in Scottish Labour History* (Edinburgh: John Donald, 1978).

Trory, E., *Between the Wars: Recollections of a Communist Organiser* (Brighton: Crabtree Press, 1974).

——, *Imperialist War* (Brighton: Crabtree Press, 1977).

——, *War of Liberation* (People's Publications, 1987).

Wood, N., *Communism and the British Intellectuals* (Gollancz, 1959).

Woodhouse, M., and Pearce, B., *Essays on the History of Communism in Britain* (New Park, 1975).

Index